Microsoft® XNA™ Game Studio 2.0: Learn Programming Now!

Rob Miles

PUBLISHED BY
Microsoft Press
A Division of Microsoft Corporation
One Microsoft Way
Redmond, Washington 98052-6399

Library of Congress Control Number: 2007942086

Printed and bound in the United States of America.

1 2 3 4 5 6 7 8 9   QWT   3 2 1 0 9 8

Distributed in Canada by H.B. Fenn and Company Ltd.

A CIP catalogue record for this book is available from the British Library.

Microsoft Press books are available through booksellers and distributors worldwide. For further information about international editions, contact your local Microsoft Corporation office or contact Microsoft Press International directly at fax (425) 936-7329. Visit our Web site at www.microsoft.com/mspress. Send comments to mspinput@microsoft.com.

Acquisitions Editor: Ben Ryan
Developmental Editor: Devon Musgrave
Project Editor: Victoria Thulman
Editorial Production: S4Carlisle Publishing Services
Technical Reviewer: Kurt Meyer
Cover: Tom Draper Design

Body Part No. X14-40147

To Mary, David, and Jenny.

Contents at a Glance

Table of Contents

What do you think of this book? We want to hear from you!

Microsoft is interested in hearing your feedback so we can continually improve our books and learning resources for you. To participate in a brief online survey, please visit:

www.microsoft.com/learning/booksurvey/

Part III **Games and Programming**

10 **Using C# Methods to Solve Problems 163**

11 **A Game as a C# Program 189**

What do you think of this book? We want to hear from you!

Microsoft is interested in hearing your feedback so we can continually improve our books and learning resources for you. To participate in a brief online survey, please visit:

www.microsoft.com/learning/booksurvey/

Acknowledgments

Thanks to everyone at Microsoft Press, especially Ben Ryan and Devon Musgrave, for getting the show on the road, and Victoria Thulman for making sure that it was always headed in the right direction. I'd also like to thank Kurt Meyer for his thoughtful and constructive criticism of the material. And, of course, the folks on the XNA team for making such an inspiring product.

Introduction

With XNA Game Studio 2.0, Microsoft is doing something really special. They are providing an accessible means for people to create programs for the Xbox 360. Now pretty much anyone can take their game ideas and run them on a genuine console.

This book will show you how to make game programs and run them on an Xbox 360 or Windows PC. It will also give you an insight into how software is created and what being a programmer is really like.

Please note that the full product name is XNA Game Studio, but in this book I refer to it as XNA. In the world outside this book, XNA refers to the larger group of game developer technologies from Microsoft.

Who This Book Is For

If you have always fancied writing software but have no idea how to start, then this book is for you. If you have ever played a computer game and thought, "I wonder how they do that?" or, better yet, "I want to make something like that," this book will get you started with some very silly games that you and all your friends can have a go at playing and modifying. Along the way, you will also get a decent understanding of C#, which is a massively popular programming language used by many thousands of software developers all over the world.

The book is structured into 14 chapters, starting with the simplest possible XNA program and moving on to show you how to use the Xbox gamepad, the keyboard, sound, and graphics in your games. In the course of learning how to use C# and XNA, you will create some very silly games, including Color Nerve, Mind Reader, Gamepad Racer, Bread and Cheese, Button Bash, and Pell Mell Pellmanism. You can even download the full versions of these games from my Web site *http://www.verysillygames.com* and use them at your next party.

With this book, I will show you that programming is a fun, creative activity that lets you bring your ideas to life in a way that nothing else can.

System Requirements

You'll need the following hardware and software to build and run the code samples for this book. Chapter 1, "Computers, Xboxes, C#, XNA, and You," explains how to set up your environment and gives more details on Windows PC hardware requirements.

- Windows PC with 3D graphics acceleration, if you want to run your XNA games on your PC.
- Microsoft Windows XP with Service Pack 2 or Windows Vista.

- Microsoft Visual Studio 2005 C# Express Edition or Microsoft Visual Studio 2005 Standard Edition or Microsoft Visual Studio 2005 Professional Edition or Microsoft Visual Studio 2005 Team Suite.

- Microsoft XNA Game Studio 2.0.

- To test your games on a console, you will need an Xbox 360 fitted with a hard disk. Your Xbox 360 must be connected to Xbox Live and you will need to join the XNA Creators Club.

Code Samples

All the code samples discussed in this book can be downloaded from the book's companion content page at the following address:

http://www.microsoft.com/mspress/companion/9780735625228/default.aspx

There are also code samples and games at *http://www.verysillygames.com.*

Support for This Book

Microsoft Press provides support for books and companion content at the following Web site:

http://www.microsoft.com/learning/support/books

Find Additional Content Online

As new or updated material becomes available that complements your book, it will be posted online on the Microsoft Press Online Developer Tools Web site. The type of material you might find includes updates to book content, articles, links to companion content, errata, sample chapters, and more. This Web site will be available soon at *http://www.microsoft.com/learning/books/online/developer*, and will be updated periodically.

Questions and Comments

If you have comments, questions, or ideas regarding the book or the companion content or questions that are not answered by visiting the previously mentioned sites, please send them to Microsoft Press via e-mail to *mspinput@microsoft.com.*

Or via postal mail to

Microsoft Press
Attn: Microsoft® XNA™ Game Studio 2.0: Learn Programming Now!
One Microsoft Way
Redmond, WA 98052-6399

Please note that Microsoft software product support is not offered through these addresses.

Part I
Getting Started

In this part:

Chapter 1
Computers, Xboxes, C#, XNA, and You

- Discover what makes a good programmer and what makes a great one.
- See what computers are all about.
- Find out why C# is a language you can love and XNA is a framework you can adore.
- Get your system set up so that you can write code.
- Run your first-ever XNA program.

Introduction

Welcome to the Wonderful World of Rob Miles. This is a world of bad jokes, puns, and programming. In this book, I'm going to give you an introduction to the C# programming language and show you how to use C# to create XNA games. If you have programmed before, I'd be grateful if you'd still read all the text. It's worth it just for the jokes, and you may actually learn something while laughing.

Learning to Program

If you haven't programmed before, don't worry. Programming is not rocket science. It is, well, programming, and there are many more people in the world who have learned programming than rocket science. The bad news about learning to program is that you have lots of different things to learn when you start, and this can be confusing. But the keys to learning programming are simple:

- **Practice**   Do a lot of programming and force yourself to think about things from a problem-solving point of view.

3

- **Study**   Look at programs written by other people. You can learn a lot from studying code that others have created. Figuring out how somebody else did the job is a great starting point for your solution. And remember that in many cases there is no best solution, just solutions that are better in a particular context. (In other words, sometimes you need an approach that is the fastest or the smallest or the easiest to use, and so on.)

- **Persistence**   Writing programs is hard work. And you have to work hard at it. The main reason most folks don't make it as programmers is that they give up. Not because they are stupid—however, don't get too persistent. If you haven't solved a programming problem in 30 minutes, you should call time-out and seek help or, at least, walk away from the problem and come back to it. Staying up all night trying to sort out a problem is not a good plan. It just makes you all irritable in the morning. If you go to bed, have a nice sleep, and then go back to the problem in the morning—you will be amazed how often you can fix it in minutes. (Later in this book, we'll cover what else you can do if a problem is being stubborn.)

Becoming a Great Programmer

You might think that great programmers can type at a thousand words a second, have a mega-sized brain, and are fitted with a socket that lets them connect directly to a computer. This is not true. Especially the socket bit. In my experience, the best programmers are the ones who are the most fun to be with. The ones who you enjoy talking to. The ones who don't get upset when you find a mistake in their programs and who will sometimes agree that your solution is better than the one that they had invented. I'd much rather work with someone like that than someone who can write a hundred lines of code a minute but who refuses to speak to me if I dare to suggest that one of those lines might be wrong.

Great programmers take care to find out that what they are doing is the right thing. If they are working for a customer, they will make sure that the customer gets what the customer wants. They will not assume that they know the best way to do it and just do it their way. They will make sure that what they produce is tested and comes with helpful documentation. They will work in the team, make coffee when it is their turn, and do whatever it takes to make sure that the project has a happy ending. Of course, they might also fill your office with beach balls, superglue your keyboard to the desk, or cover your chair with aluminum foil, but these are all done with a friendly spirit.

I have secured the services of a great programmer who will be adding Programmer's Points to our text. These are truly words of wisdom, so make sure to take note when you see them.

How the Book Works

Great scientists like Sir Isaac Newton and Benjamin Franklin performed experiments to discover how the world works. Then people like Thomas Edison came along and again experimented with what science and engineering could do to make things that everybody wants. You are going to take a similar experimental approach to learning about programming. By playing with XNA and writing tiny games, you are going to investigate how a computer works and how you can invent new kinds of computer games.

As you go through the text, you should never be more than a page or so away from making something happen with a program, so it helps if you have a computer system and an Xbox 360 nearby so that you can try things out. However, you can also read the book straight through because all the programs in the book will be laid out and explained.

Don't be afraid to experiment and try things out yourself. At certain points in the text, I will suggest ideas you might find fun to explore. Remember that learning by doing is one of the best ways to pick things up, so feel free to try stuff. One of the great facts about creating game programs is that even the code that you get a bit wrong can produce cool-looking results. You might even end up creating an entirely new type of game by mistake!

Remember that the great scientists did not always find it easy to immediately understand what is going on inside their experiments, and the same is true about programming. Some of the things that you do when you write programs will not seem to make much sense at first, so be prepared to have to work to understand what is going on inside the program.

> **Note**   Throughout the chapters, words appearing in *italics* are explained more fully in the Glossary at the end of this book.

C# and XNA

Before you go any farther, it is important that you consider exactly what this book is for. You are going to learn about the *programming language* C# and the XNA Game Studio 2.0 *software development kit*. Understanding the difference between the two is key. You are familiar with the idea of a computer program. At the moment, I'm using a word processor to create this text. I started the word processing program, and it is telling my computer to take each key I press and add it to the document I am writing. The program is the set of instructions that tells the computer what to do with the information it receives from the keyboard.

The C# programming language is a way of expressing that set of instructions. When you create your games, you'll write lines of C# to tell the computer how to make each game work. You can use C# to create programs that do many other tasks; you can even write your own word processor.

A Software Development Kit (SDK) is a set of prebuilt program components that you can use as part of other programs. XNA Game Studio is an SDK that provides program code that will draw things on the screen, play sounds, read the Xbox 360 gamepad, and do lots of other useful things. When you create games, the C# code you write will use these prebuilt features of XNA. Part of becoming a successful programmer is learning how to best use the features provided by an SDK. Experience with the XNA SDK will make it much easier for you to understand how to use other SDKs. A particular SDK will have an overall architecture that contains all the features that the SDK provides. This is often called a *framework*.

Getting Started

You are going to create programs on the PC and then either run them on the PC or send them into an Xbox 360 for execution. Either way, you need to install some tools on your PC.

Installing the Development Environment and the XNA Framework

When developers wanted to write a program on the very first computers, they had to take the back off and actually change the wires in the machine. Fortunately, things have moved on, and now you can use an *Integrated Development Environment* (IDE) to create your code. An Integrated Development Environment gets its name because it provides a single place where you can perform the entire creative process of code development. In an IDE, you can write a program by using the built-in text editor, you can run the program and see what it does, and you can also *debug* the program, which means you stop it and try to find out why it is not doing what you wanted it to. The IDE you are going to use is one of the Microsoft Visual Studio 2005 Express Editions, specifically the Microsoft Visual C# 2005 Express Edition. This is a version of the hugely powerful Microsoft Visual Studio product, which is used by professional developers all over the world. At this point I'm assuming that you have already installed Visual C# 2005 Express Edition and have it running on your machine. You can download it for free from *http://www.microsoft.com/express/2005/download/ default.aspx*. The setup procedure is quite straightforward, and at the end of the process you will be asked to register your copy. Registration does not cost you any money and actually gives you access to even more free resources. There are a number of other Express products that you can install. You can use these in addition to XNA Game Studio 2.0 but they are not required to create XNA games.

 Note   If you have other versions of Visual Studio on your machine, you can also use these to write XNA games as long as they include the C# development environment. However, you must make sure that your version of Visual Studio has the latest version of the service packs installed. The XNA Creators club website, *http://creators.xna.com*, has the most up-to-date information on service packs and Visual Studio versions.

Once you have got your development environment working, you need to install the XNA Framework. This binds itself to Visual Studio and provides it with all the extra libraries needed to create and deploy games. You can download the XNA Framework software from *http://creators.xna.com/Education/newtoxna.aspx*. The installation is straightforward.

Note   Once you install XNA on your system, you will find a customized version of Visual C# Express in your Program files under Microsoft XNA Game Studio 2.0. For the purpose of this text, every time I refer to XNA Game Studio 2.0 from now on, I really mean the customized version of Visual C# 2005 Express Edition.

Setting Up a PC to Run XNA Games

Once you have installed XNA on your PC you can use this to create and run games. If you just want to write games on the PC and run them on an Xbox 360, you don't need a very powerful machine. As long as it supports the minimum requirements for Visual Studio, you can create game software. To run XNA Framework games on a Microsoft Windows platform, your PC will need to be fitted with a graphics card that supports Shader Model 1.1 or greater and DirectX 9.0c. I recommend that you use a graphics card that supports Shader Model 2.0 because some samples and starter kits require this. To check that your graphics card supports Shader Model 2.0 you can search *http://microsoft.com* for "Check for Shader Model 2.0 Support" to find a procedure to do this.

XNA games can be controlled by the PC keyboard. If you obtain a wired Xbox gamepad you can plug it into a USB port on your computer, and after the New Hardware Wizard runs it will just work. Vista and later versions of Windows XP have the drivers for the gamepad already loaded. You can also obtain a special adapter that will let your PC communicate with wireless Xbox gamepads.

Setting Up an Xbox 360 to Run XNA Games

If you want the full game developer experience, there is no substitute for actually using a genuine console. In this section, you're going find out how to set up an Xbox 360 and make it ready to receive the games you are going to write.

To deploy games on your Xbox 360, it must be fitted with a hard disk. This is where the XNA Game Studio Connect application and the programs that you create will be stored. Your console must also be connected to the Internet, and you need to be signed up for a Silver Xbox Live subscription or better. You must also be a member of the XNA Creators Club.

XNA Creators Club

Xbox Live accounts can be made members of the XNA Creators Club. Creators Club members pay a membership fee on an annual or a quarterly basis. You can learn more at *http:// creators.xna.com*, where you can also find sample games and forums for club members. You can purchase an XNA Creators Club membership from the Xbox LIVE marketplace, where it is listed under Game Store, More..., Genres, and then Other. You don't need to join the XNA Creators Club to write and deploy XNA games for the PC.

Connecting an Xbox 360 to a Windows PC

When you are developing XNA programs and running them on an Xbox 360 the two machines use a network connection to communicate. There is a special procedure that you need to go through to set up both ends of the conversation between a Windows PC and an Xbox 360.

- Start up your Xbox and sign in using your Xbox LIVE account.

- Join the XNA Creators Club on your Xbox.

- Download and run the XNA Game Studio Connect application onto your Xbox from Xbox LIVE.

- Run XNA Game Studio Device Center on your computer.

- Connect your Xbox console to your computer.

A detailed description of these steps can be found in the Help information for the XNA Game Studio Device Center application, which is provided as part of your XNA installation. You can find the XNA Game Studio Device Center application on your Start menu, as shown in Figure 1-1.

Figure 1-1   Starting the XNA Game Studio Device Center application

The very first time that you run this application, there will be no Xboxes connected, and the display will look like the one shown in Figure 1-2.

Figure 1-2   The XNA Game Studio Device Center application

You can get detailed help on the procedure for connecting your Xbox to your PC by clicking the blue question mark on the right-hand side of the application.

Once you have completed the connection procedure, the PC and Xbox 360 will retain the settings that you entered; when you attempt to send a program to the Xbox 360, it should just work. This would be a really good time to take a coffee break.

Writing Your First Program

You are now going to start from scratch with your first program. It won't actually do much—you won't be writing your own version of Halo just yet—but it will give you an insight into what XNA does and how you can write your own C# bits to turn your Xbox 360 into a cool mood light.

Creating Your First Project

A computer game is not just a program—it is also lots of other bits and pieces that make playing the game fun and interesting. Just about every game has graphics, sounds, 3D models of game objects, and all sorts of other items that must be created along with the code. This means that when you make a game, you have to manage all these other resources too. The good news is that the XNA designers have thought of this, and they provide a comprehensive *content management* solution that looks after all these resources. You can just give your game resources to the content manager, and it will make sure that they are available to the programs that you write. Later on in the book, I'll show you how to add some content of your own so that you can use a picture of your mom or your dog as a game character.

The content management is part of the *project* mechanism provided by XNA Game Studio 2.0. What this means right now is that to create your first game program, you actually have to create an XNA Game Studio 2.0 project.

To create a project, first start up XNA Game Studio 2.0 if it is not already running. The application can be found on the Start Menu, as shown in Figure 1-1. Select New Project from the File menu, as shown in Figure 1-3. This will automatically create the entire project and the file into which you are going to put our code.

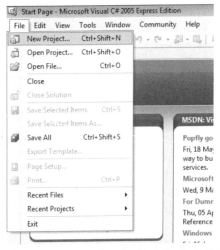

Figure 1-3   Opening the New Project dialog box

XNA Game Studio 2.0 can make a whole range of different projects, depending on what you actually want to build. The skeletons for each of these types of program are contained in project templates and Starter Kits. When you install XNA, you also install the SpaceWar Starter Kit. You can download and install other Starter Kits from the Creators Club Web site. You are going to use a template to create an empty XNA project.

Figure 1-4 shows all the possible types of projects that can be created. You need to select one of two projects: select the Xbox 360 game template if you want to run your program on the Xbox 360 or select the Windows game template if you want to run your program on a PC. Later in this chapter, I'll show you how you can create a workspace containing two projects, one for each target device. For now, you should just choose the one you want to use; the way that the program works is identical for both. Call the project "MoodLight" because that is what we are building first. You can use the Browse button to select an appropriate destination for the project. You should ensure that the Create Directory for Solution checkbox is checked so that all the files for this game will be held in one place. Once you have done this click OK to get XNA Game Studio 2.0 to build the project for you.

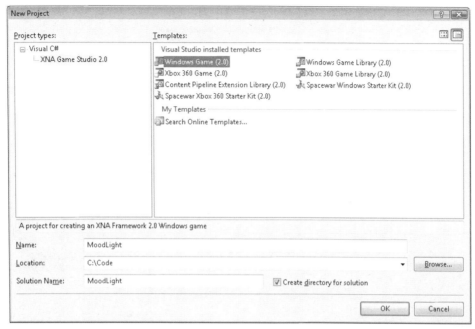

Figure 1-4   Creating a new project

When the project has been created, you should see a screen that looks like the one in Figure 1-5. Yours might not look quite the same (it certainly won't have an arrow pointing to the Start Debugging button), but it should look similar. There are a lot of controls that you can play with. At the moment quite a few are disabled and can't be used, but it still looks confusing the first time that you see it. The key here is not to panic. You are going to use only a few of the buttons to start with, and I'll explain the other ones as you need them.

Running Your First Program

If you are running your program on a PC, you can just press the Start Debugging button (as indicated by the arrow in Figure 1-5), and the program will run. If you are sending your program to an Xbox 360, you must go through the steps described earlier (in the "Setting Up an Xbox 360" section) to get to the Connect To Computer screen.

When you press the button to run the program, a number of things happen in quick succession:

1. XNA Game Studio 2.0 *compiles* the *source code* files. The source code of the program is all the lines of C# code that you and XNA Game Studio 2.0 create that actually describe what you want the computer to do. A compiler is a program that takes source code and creates a set of machine instructions that can be loaded into the computer's processor to control what the computer does. The C# language has a particular specification, and the compiler knows all about the rules in the specification. The compiler will reject any program that it thinks is not correct, and will tell you about the *compilation errors*. You are going to have to live with the fact that you will see a lot of these errors if you decide to become a computer programmer.

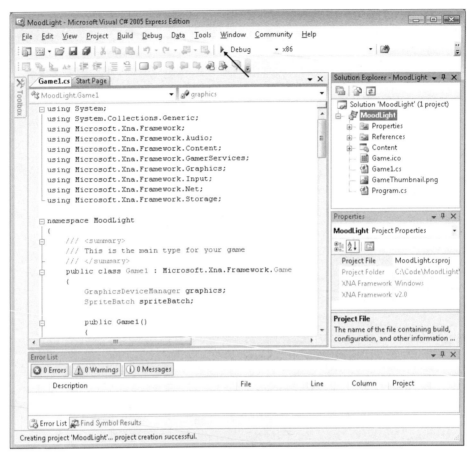

Figure 1-5   XNA Game Studio 2.0 and MoodLight

2. Your project might contain a large number of different source files; each of them must be compiled. If all the program source files compile correctly, they are then combined with any resources (e.g., images and sounds) that are part of the project.

3. If you are using an Xbox 360, these files are now transferred over the network into the Xbox 360.

4. Finally, XNA Game Studio 2.0 starts the program running either in a window on the PC or on the Xbox 360, at which point the window or target device is under the control of your program statements.

When XNA Game Studio 2.0 produces an empty project, it actually creates a program that will compile and run, so you can just hit the Start Debugging button (if you haven't already) and turn the program loose.

When you run the program, the Xbox 360 screen turns blue. That's it—nothing else. All that work to turn the screen blue? You could have done that with a can of paint in 30 seconds. The "empty" project from XNA just turns the screen blue, but in the next chapter you're going to add some code to make it do much cooler things. You're going to make a light that can display millions of possible colors, and an ever-changing mood lamp, and finally the world's first-ever color-changing game.

> **Note**   One slightly irritating thing about Visual Studio is that when the program is running, the organization of the controls in Visual Studio changes. This can confuse a first-time user because menus, toolbars, and panes suddenly don't seem to be where they used to be. If you carefully compare Figure 1-5 with Figure 1-6, you'll notice that a new toolbar has appeared that has buttons on it that you can use to pause or stop the program.

Stopping a Program

But before you do anything else, you need to stop the program. There are two ways to do this. You can press the Back button on an Xbox 360 gamepad to instruct the program to finish. If the program is running on the Xbox 360, XNA Game Studio 2.0 will display a message indicating that the remote connection to the device has been lost. Simply click OK on the message to dismiss it. Alternatively, you can stop the program from the XNA Game Studio 2.0 end by clicking the Stop button indicated by the arrow in Figure 1-6.

If you are using a PC and don't have an Xbox gamepad, you'll have to stop the program from XNA Game Studio 2.0. Later on, you'll see how you can improve the program so that you can use the PC keyboard to control an XNA program.

> **Note**   You should not normally stop your program by using XNA Game Studio 2.0. This is like turning off your Xbox 360 rather than quitting a game correctly. It stops the program, but because the program is interrupted, it might not save all the game data properly before it stops. When you make your own game, you should make sure that you provide the player with instructions on how to properly stop it.

Storing Games on the Xbox 360

Once you've created a game and run it on an Xbox 360 system, the game itself remains on the hard disk of the machine for you to load and play later, without the need for a PC to be attached. You can find the games you have created by selecting the Games Library, My Games, XNA Creators Club.

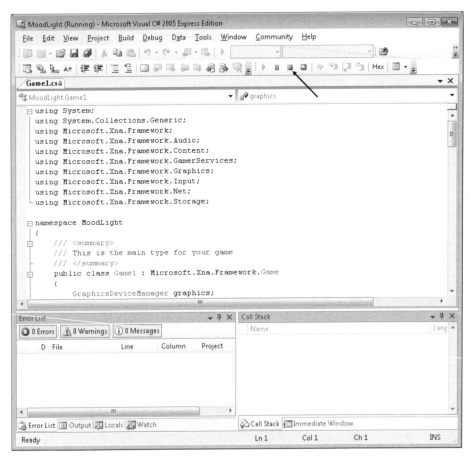

Figure 1-6   Stopping a running program

Using a PC or an Xbox to Run XNA Games

You can use a single XNA 2.0 workspace to hold two projects, one of which will run the game program on an Xbox and the other the Windows PC. You will find out more about projects and workspaces later in this book. The following example shows how a Windows PC project can be copied to produce an Xbox project.

Start by clicking the MoodLight project in the Solution Explorer of XNA Game Studio 2.0 so that it is selected. Then choose Create Copy of MoodLight for Xbox 360 from the Project menu, as shown in Figure 1-7.

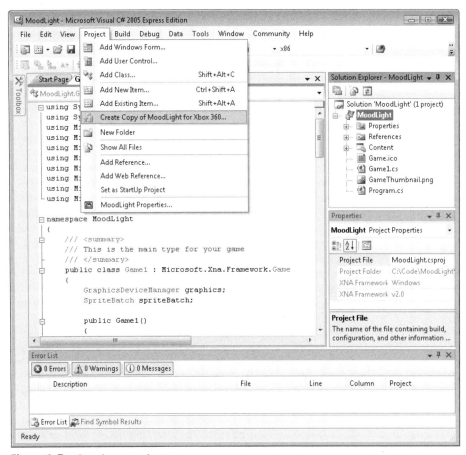

Figure 1-7   Copying a project

The warning screen in Figure 1-8 will be displayed. Clear this screen by clicking OK.

Figure 1-8   Create Copy warning screen

XNA Game Studio 2.0 will now copy the project and add the copy to the workspace. This means that there are now two projects in the workspace, as shown in Figure 1-9.

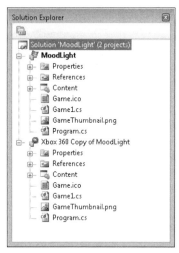

Figure 1-9   Solution containing two projects

 Note   It looks as if there are now two copies of everything concerned with the project. This is not actually the case. The copy uses links to the files in the original. This means that changes to the content of one project will be reflected in the other.

You can select which project is run by setting one of the projects as the StartUp Project. If you look carefully at Figure 1-9, you will see that the Windows version of MoodLight has the name of the project displayed in bold type. This means that it is the project that will run, and so the XNA program will run on the Windows machine. To set a project as the StartUp project, you right-click on the project and choose Set as StartUp Project from the menu that appears, as shown in Figure 1-10.

 Note   When a solution containing a project for both the Xbox 360 and a Windows PC is built, XNA Game Studio 2.0 will attempt to deploy the Xbox 360 version of the project to the console even if you have selected the Windows PC project as the StartUp project. You can select which platform you wish to deploy programs to by using the "Solution Platforms" combo box in Visual Studio.

Sample Code: Blue Screen of Life   The sample projects included on the companion media in the 01 BlueScreen folder for this chapter will draw a blue screen for you. They are exactly the same as an empty project that you might create. Sample versions of the code for running on both an Xbox and a PC are included.

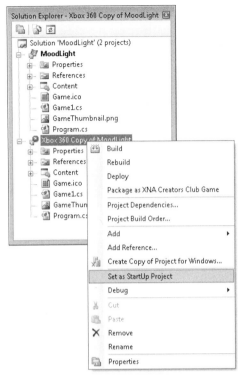

Figure 1-10   Selecting a StartUp project

Conclusion

Actually, you've done quite a lot in this chapter. You've learned about computers, what makes great programmers so easy to get along with, and the difference between C# (the programming language of champions) and XNA (the game development framework of champions). You've also got all your development tools sorted out, and you are now ready to roll. And you did manage to turn the screen a nice blue.

Pop Quiz

Every chapter will have a pop quiz at the end just to test you a little. There are no prizes, but you might find it useful to check that you know the answers to the questions before you go on to the next chapter. All the answers are either true or false, and you can find the answers by reviewing the chapter and looking in the Glossary. The list of answers for all the book's pop quizzes are at the back of the book. No peeking now.

1. The most important thing about being a great programmer is having a big brain.

2. You need an Xbox 360 to create games with C# and XNA.

3. XNA is a programming language.

4. XNA Game Studio 2.0 is an Integrated Development Environment.

5. The C# compiler produces an XNA output file.

6. C# is a framework.

7. You need a Creators Club membership to develop games on your Xbox 360.

8. The compiler runs your program.

9. The empty project created by XNA Game Studio C# 2.0 draws a red screen.

10. It is not possible to use an Xbox 360 gamepad on a PC.

Chapter 2
Programs, Data, and Pretty Colors

- Explore how games actually work.

- See how data is stored in a program.

- Discover how colors are managed on computers.

- Find out about classes and methods.

- Write some code that controls color.

- Write some code that makes decisions.

- Create a funky color-changing mood light.

Introduction

You now know how to create an XNA program and run it on an Xbox 360 or PC. The program only turns the screen blue, but you could call it a start. Next, you are going to figure out how game programs are constructed. Then you'll play with colors and find out how XNA stores color information and how C# stores data.

Program Project: A Mood Light

Your first project is going to be a program that turns an Xbox display (the bigger the better) into a mood light. These are the things that they have on spaceships, where a chandelier would actually not work very well. Instead, the spaceship will have a panel on the wall that can be set to glow in different colors and brightness levels or perhaps even change color over time. This is probably not a very efficient way of lighting a building—you are using one of the most powerful game consoles ever made to replace a lamp—but it will be a fun exercise and may even lead to a game idea or two along the way.

Before going any farther, you need to consider what a game program does. Computer programs in general read data in, do something with it, and then send data out. This is true whether the computer is working out the company wages or timing the ignition spark in a car engine. Figure 2-1 shows how this works with respect to games programs. The gamepad provides the input data to the game, and the display screen shows the output.

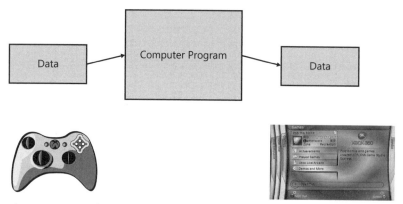

Figure 2-1   An Xbox game as a computer program

Later versions of games might have other inputs and outputs too; for example, if you are playing on Xbox Live, your console is receiving information about other players in your networked game. For now, start by considering only the output from your game. Later you'll take a look at where the input values come from.

Making a Game Display

To see how a game program can produce a display, you need to look inside one of the C# programs that XNA built. At the end of Chapter 1, "Computers, Xboxes, C#, XNA, and You," you used XNA Game Studio 2.0 to create a game program. Now you are going to take a look at this program and discover how it works.

The file that contains the game behavior is called, not surprisingly, **Game1.cs**. The name **Game1** was generated automatically when the project was created; the **.cs** part is the *file extension* for C# programs. If you want to take a look inside this file, start up XNA Game Studio 2.0 and open the solution you created in Chapter 1 from the Solution Explorer. You can find the Solution Explorer, as shown in Figure 2-2, in the top right-hand corner of the XNA Game Studio 2.0 screen. If you double-click the name of the file that you want to work with, the file opens in the editing window.

If you take a look at the content of **Game1.cs**, which drew that impressive blue screen, you can see how the program works. The program code that XNA Game Studio 2.0 created when you made an empty game contains the following method:

```
protected override void Draw(GameTime gameTime)
{
    graphics.GraphicsDevice.Clear(Color.CornflowerBlue);
    // TODO: Add your drawing code here
    base.Draw(gameTime);
}
```

Figure 2-2   Solution Explorer

A *method* is a named part of a program. In this case the method has the name **Draw** (you can ignore the **protected override void** part for now). All you need to know at the moment is that when XNA wants to draw the screen, it will use this method. You can change what gets drawn by altering the content of this method. At the moment you just get a blue screen; if you look at the second line of the preceding code, you can see where the blue screen comes from.

Statements in the Draw Method

The **Draw** method contains a block of statements. C# programs are expressed as a series of statements that are separated by the semicolon (;). Each *statement* describes a single action that your program needs to do. There are a number of different kinds of statements; you'll discover new ones as you learn more about programming. The statements are organized into a single block. A *block* is a way to lump statements together. The start of a block is marked with an open curly bracket character ({), and the end of the block is marked with a closing curly bracket (}). These curly kinds of brackets are sometimes called *braces*. The C# compiler, which is trying to convert the program text into something that the Xbox can actually run, will notice and complain if you use the wrong kind of bracket.

In the previous code, there is also a *comment*. Comments are ignored by the compiler; they let you put text into your program to describe the program or remind you to do things. In the pre- vious code, the comment is a "TODO," which tells the programmer they need to do something. In this case, the programmer must add drawing statements at that position in the program file.

> **The Great Programmer Speaks: Comments Are Cool**   Our Great Programmer likes comments. She says that a well-written program is like a story in the way that the purpose of each part is described. She says that she will be looking at our code and making sure that we put the right kind of comments in.

From the point of view of changing the color of your screen, the statement that is most interesting is this one:

```
graphics.GraphicsDevice.Clear(Color.CornflowerBlue);
```

Clear is a method that is part of XNA. You will see precisely how it fits into the framework later; for now, all you need to know is that the Clear method is given something that describes a color, and the method clears the screen to that color. At the moment, you are sending the Clear method the color CornflowerBlue, and it is clearing the screen to that color. If you want a different color, you just have to send a different value into Clear:

```
graphics.GraphicsDevice.Clear(Color.Red);
```

If you change the color as shown in the previous line and run the program, you should see that the screen is now set to red.

> **Sample Code: Red Screen of Anger**   The sample project in the 01 MoodLight Red Screen directory in the resources for this chapter will draw a red screen for you. You could run this when you felt particularly angry. You can change the color that you want to display by changing the colors used in the Update method; there are some comments in the code to help you with this.

You can set the background color to a range of preset ones, but you can also design colors of your own, which brings us to our first project.

Creating Your Own Color Values

You have seen that XNA has a set of colors built in, including one with the strange name of Teal (it is actually a rather boring blue/green). However, you want to make your own colors and use these in your program.

Storing Color Values

A particular color is represented by a structure that holds the red, green, and blue intensity values. A *structure* is used to hold a number of related data items in the same way that you might write your name, address, and phone number on a piece of paper. You want to create your own colors, and you need somewhere to store the color values you create. In programming terms, this is called *declaring* a *variable*. Figure 2-3 shows the anatomy of the statement that declares a variable to hold a value that represents a color.

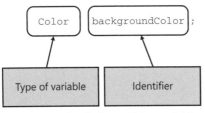

Figure 2-3   Declaring a Color variable called backgroundColor

The *type* of the variable is set as **Color**. This determines what you can put in your variable. Having seen this declaration, the C# compiler knows that you want to create a location with the name **backgroundColor** in the Xbox memory, which can hold color information. In programming terms, the name of a variable is called an *identifier*. The word **backgroundColor** is an identifier that I've invented. When you create something for you to use in a C# program, you have to think up an identifier for it. An identifier is made up of numbers and letters and must start with a letter. The identifier should describe what you are going to use the thing for; in this program, you are storing the color that is going to be used for the background, so it can be given the identifier **backgroundColor**.

> **Note**   The C# compiler uses the type of a variable to make sure that a program never tries to do something that would be stupid. The only thing that you can put in a **Color** variable is color information. If the program tries to put something else in the **backgroundColor** variable, such as a player name, then the program would fail to compile. This is rather like real life, where an attempt to put an elephant in a camera case would be similarly unsuccessful.

> **The Great Programmer Speaks: Pick Useful Identifiers**   Our Great Programmer says that there should be a special place in hell reserved for programmers who create identifiers like **X24** or **Cheese** or **count**. She says that these tell a reader of the program code nothing about what the variable is being used for. She really likes identifiers like **CarSpeed**, **backgroundColor**, and **accountBalance**.

Setting a Color Value

You now have a variable that can hold the color of your background. At the moment it is not set to anything useful. So next you have to write a statement that will cause the game program to put a value into this variable. You start by creating a new **Color** that contains a particular amount of red, blue, and green. Figure 2-4 shows the anatomy of an assignment that makes a new **Color** value and then places it in the variable.

The thing that is going to be assigned is on the right-hand side of the equals. In this case you are making a new **Color** value. Don't get confused with an equals that might be used to compare two things. You should regard the equals above as being what I call a "gozzinta" operator. The value on the right of the equals "goes into" the variable on the left. You'll investigate how to compare things later. Now that you have your variable, you can use it in the game program.

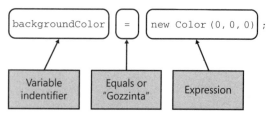

Figure 2-4   Assigning a new color value to backgroundColor

```
graphics.GraphicsDevice.Clear(backgroundColor);
```

This statement calls the **Clear** method and feeds it the value of **backgroundColor**. This will cause the screen to be cleared to the new color you created. If you put these statements together, you'll get a **Draw** method that creates the **backgroundColor** variable, sets it to a value, and then clears the screen using it.

```
protected override void Draw(GameTime gameTime)
{
    Color backgroundColor;
    backgroundColor = new Color(0,0,0);
    graphics.GraphicsDevice.Clear(backgroundColor);
    base.Draw(gameTime);
}
```

If you want to find out what color you get if you make one with no red, no green, and no blue, you can run a program that uses this **Draw** method. But I don't think I'm giving too much away when I tell you that this would produce a black screen. The actual color values are given in the order red, green, and blue, and each must be in the range 0 to 255 (you'll see why this is later). By using different values when you set the **Color**, you can experiment with different displays. The color combinations obey all the rules of color combinations (for light rather than for paint) that you would expect.

```
backgroundColor = new Color(255, 255, 0);
```

This statement would set **backgroundColor** to a color value that has the red and green values at maximum, which would be displayed as yellow.

> **Sample Code: Yellow Screen of Peril**   The sample project "02 MoodLight Yellow Background" creates a yellow background color and fills the screen with it. You can change the numbers in the Update method to make any color you like.

Controlling Color

At this point you can see that you add C# statements to the **Draw** method to change what is drawn on the screen. You also know that XNA makes use of a **Color** structure to lump together information that describes a particular color and that you can create your own `Color` variables that contain a specific amount of red, green, and blue. Finally, you have managed to make a program that uses a color variable to set the screen to any color you like.

Next you want the light to change color over time, to get a nice soothing mood light effect. This sounds like hard work, and like every great programmer, I really hate hard work, but actually it turns out to be quite easy. To discover how to do this, you have to find how XNA is connected to the game programs that you write. The way this works makes use of C# classes.

Games and Classes

The game program is actually a *class* called `Game1`. A class is a collection of abilities (methods) and data (variables) that forms part of a program. You can put as much stuff as you like inside a single class. A class is usually constructed to look after one particular part of a system. Later on in this book you'll use classes called `GameSprite`, `Player`, and `Card`. In the commercial world, you'll find classes called `Receipt`, `Invoice`, and `StockItem`.

When XNA Game Studio 2.0 created our project, it gave the game class the name `Game1`. You can rename this if you wish; you'll see how to do this later in the book.

Classes and Behaviors

A behavior is something that a class can be asked to do. A particular method performs a particular behavior. You used the `Clear` behavior of the `GraphicsDevice`. When you use `Clear`, this causes the code in the `Clear` method to be obeyed to clear the screen. You don't need to know how `Clear` works; you just need to know that you can feed it with information to tell it what color you want to use. The `Game1` class provides `Update` and `Draw` behaviors (among others) so that XNA can ask `Game1` to update the state of the game and draw it on the display. Figure 2-5 shows how the `Update` and the `Draw` methods are part of the `Game1` class.

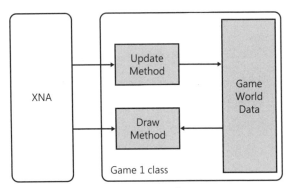

Figure 2-5   The Game1 class and XNA

The job of the `Update` method is to update the values in the game. The job of the `Draw` method is to use these values to draw the display. The XNA system will call `Draw` and `Update` at regular intervals when the game is running. You have already used methods provided by other classes; you know that the **Clear** method can be called to clear the display to a particular color. **Draw** and **Update** are methods that you provide for use by XNA.

Classes as Offices

You can think of **Update** and **Draw** as two people sitting in an office called **Game1**. Each has their own telephone. Every now and then, Mr. Draw's phone rings, and a voice on the other end of the line tells Mr. Draw that a sixtieth of a second has gone by. Mr. Draw then jumps up, gets the value of the background color from the desk, and then uses his phone to dial the number of the Ms. Clear in the **GraphicsDevice** office down the hall and asks her to clear the screen to that color. She has a set of paint cans and can fill the screen with any color that she is asked to use.

At a similar interval, the **Update** phone in the **Game1** office rings and tells Mrs. Update that a sixtieth of a second has gone by. She jumps up, goes up to the table in the office, and updates the information on the bits of paper on it. You can see how this would look in Figure 2-6.

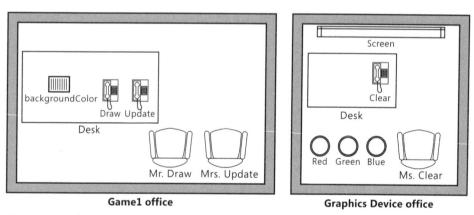

Figure 2-6   The **Game1** and **GraphicsDevice** classes as offices

The people/methods in our office/classes perform actions for each other, and data is just information that the class stores within itself. When a class wants to use a method, it calls it.

In our first version of the **Game1** class, the information on the table will be the color that Mr. Draw will use to color the graphics display. You change what happens when the screen is drawn by changing what Mr. Draw does (the content of the **Draw** method). You change what happens when the game itself is updated by changing what Mrs. Update does (the content of the **Update** method).

Note that nobody has to know exactly how the other methods work. Mr. Draw has no idea about cans of paint and displays, but he does know that if he asks Ms. Clear to clear with yellow paint, this will result in a yellow screen being drawn. A call of a method is equivalent to calling up someone in an office and asking them to perform their task.

Game World Data

You've seen that the actual state of the game is also held in the **Game1** class. In a driving game this state would include the speed of the car the player is driving, the car position on the track, and the position and speed of the other cars. This could be called the game world data. The game world data that you are going to use in the mood light is simply the red, green, and blue intensity values that will be used to color the screen. These variables can then be used by methods in the class.

```
class Game1 {

    // The Game World - our color values
    byte redIntensity;
    byte greenIntensity;
    byte blueIntensity;
    // TODO: Draw method goes here
    // TODO: Update method goes here
}
```

This code declares three variables inside the **Game1** class. These are part of the class; they are often called *members* of the class and can be used by any methods that are also members of the class. They have the identifiers `redIntensity`, `greenIntensity`, and `blueIntensity`. You can think of these as separate pieces of paper on the desk in the **Game1** office. Figure 2-7 shows how a class can contain members.

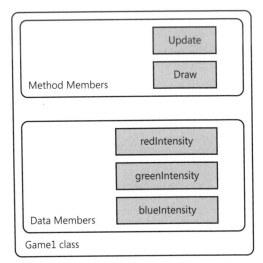

Figure 2-7   The Game1 class and its members

There are two kinds of members: methods (which do something) and data (which hold information). The **Game1** class you are working on has both kinds of member; it has the **Draw** method and the **Update** method and also the three data members, which are going to be used to hold the color values for the changing background. The data members are of type **byte**.

If you refer back to Figure 2-3, you can see that a declaration is the type of the variable, followed by the identifier. Previously you have declared variables of type **Color** that can represent a color. Now you are using another type that can represent a numeric value.

Storing Data in Computer Memory

The data for each color intensity is being held in a variable of type **byte**. The byte type is interesting because it uses 8 bits of computer memory to hold the value that it is trying to represent. Computer memory is actually a huge number of such locations, each of which is 1 byte in size. The Xbox 360 has 512 megabytes of memory. This means that the memory inside the console has about 512 million storage locations, each of which can hold a single byte value. The memory is addressed by number, and the compiler generates a program that uses a particular memory location when it accesses a particular variable. Figure 2-8 shows how this might work. The compiler has decided that **blueIntensity** is to be held in memory byte number 1003, **greenIntensity** in memory byte number 1004, and so on.

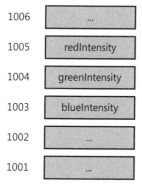

Figure 2-8   Storing the color intensity values in memory

When the program runs, the statements that work with **redIntensity**, **blueIntensity** and **greenIntensity** will be directed to these locations in memory. Each data type uses up a particular amount of computer memory; a **byte** uses a single memory location. The **Color** type uses at least 4 bytes of memory; other types can use a lot more. When the program needs to hold a **Color** value, the compiler will allocate a number of adjacent memory locations.

> **Note**   In XNA you never have to worry about precisely where the compiler chooses to put things. These issues are managed automatically and hidden from the programs. In fact, the way things really work is a little more complex than the explanation here, but for now it's important for you to remember that computer data is held in memory locations of a particular size and that a particular number of memory locations are available for a program to use.

The same memory locations that store data can also be used to hold program instructions. When an Xbox game is running, it might be that half the memory space holds the game program code (the methods) and the other half the data that is being used (the variables). When a game is showing the dreaded "Loading" screen, the Xbox is actually transferring program code and data values from the game disk into its memory.

Drawing by Using Our Color Variables

The color variables that you have created will represent the amounts of red, green, and blue that the mood light will have. You can use them in your **Draw** method to create the color to be used to clear the screen.

```
class Game1 {

  // The Game World - our color values
  byte redIntensity;
  byte greenIntensity;
  byte blueIntensity;
  protected override void Draw(GameTime gameTime)
{

    Color backgroundColor;
    backgroundColor =
        new Color(redIntensity, greenIntensity, blueIntensity);
    graphics.GraphicsDevice.Clear(backgroundColor);
    base.Draw(gameTime);
}
 // TODO: Update method goes here
}
```

This **Draw** method looks very much like the previous one, except that it uses member variables to define the color that is created rather than specifying particular values. Note that the actual assignment has been spread over two lines. The C# compiler is quite happy with this.

> **The Great Programmer Speaks: Don't Try to Fit Everything on One Line**   Our Great Programmer is very keen on sensible program layout. This means not letting program lines extend off the end of the page. She says that if the line gets too long, you should break it at a sensible point (not in the middle of an identifier) and then continue on the next line, slightly indented. She has personally checked all the program listings in this book to make sure that the layout meets her exacting requirements.

Updating Your Colors

When the program starts, the values of byte data members are automatically set to 0. If you run a program with the **Draw** method given previously, you'll see that the screen just goes black, as a color with all the intensity values set at 0 is created and then used to clear the display. What you now need to do is get control of the **Update** process and change the colors. When an empty project is created, XNA Game Studio will create an empty **Update** method that just contains a TODO comment that tells the programmer to add the required code.

```
protected override void Update(GameTime gameTime)
{
    // Allows the game to exit
    if (GamePad.GetState(PlayerIndex.One).Buttons.Back==ButtonState.Pressed)
        this.Exit();
    // TODO: Add your update logic here
    base.Update(gameTime);
}
```

The **Update** method is rather similar to **Draw** but has an extra couple of statements in it, one of which starts with the word **if**. This is the part of the code that decides when the game should end. When you ran your program, you'll have noticed that pressing the Back button on the gamepad stops the game. These two statements are the ones that give that behavior.

The first statement says "if the back button on the gamepad for player 1 is pressed, do the next statement" and the second statement says "exit the program." Put those together, and you get a behavior that means that when the **Update** method is called, if the Back button is pressed the program will exit. You are going to spend some time on conditions later, but for now just remember that if you delete these two lines from your program, it will be impossible to stop it via the Xbox gamepad. So don't.

You may be wondering who calls **Update** and how often. The answers at the moment are "the XNA engine" and "sixty times a second." Whenever your game is active, it will need to update the game world. This has to happen repeatedly for a game to be any fun. The XNA engine calls the **Update** method to give it a chance to perform. In a full-blown game this will involve reading the gamepad, moving all the objects in the world, checking to see if any have collided, and so on. In the mood light, the **Update** method will just change the color values that **Draw** will use to draw the display.

Update and **Draw** are completely separate methods, and you don't know when they are called in relation to each other. The job of **Update** is to update the values that represent the game world. The job of **Draw** is to produce a display that shows a view of that game world. This is exactly how every game works, whether it is a driving game, where the game world contains the position and speed of the car and the layout of the landscape it is driving through, or a shoot-'em-up, where the game world contains the position of all the players and any bullets they may have fired. Once you understand this principle, you are well on the way to understanding how games work. The **Update** method sets values up, and the **Draw** method uses them. To start with, you are just going to make a mood light that gets steadily brighter over time, so the first version of the **Update** method will increase the value of the red, green, and blue intensities by 1 each time that it is called.

```
protected override void Update(GameTime gameTime)
{
    // Allows the game to exit
    if (GamePad.GetState(PlayerIndex.One).Buttons.Back == ButtonState.Pressed)
        this.Exit();
```

```
    // Make each color brighter
    redIntensity++;
    greenIntensity++;
    blueIntensity++;

    base.Update(gameTime);
}
```

The **Update** method works by using the ++ *operator*. An operator is something in the program that tells the compiler that you want to perform an operation on a particular item. In this case you're using the operator ++ on each of the intensity variables. The thing an operator works on is called an *operand*. Sometimes operators work by combining operands, and sometimes they work on a single operand. The ++ operator works only on a single operand. The **Update** method uses it three times so that each color intensity gets one bigger. This means that each time the **Update** method is called, the display should get a little bit brighter.

If you run the program with this **Update** method, you'll see that the display does get steadily brighter for about 4 seconds. Then it goes black again. This does not seem right. One of the additions would seem to be making the value much smaller rather than increasing it. To understand why this is, you need to take a look at how numbers are stored in computers.

Memory Overflow and Data Values

You have already seen that byte values are actually represented by 8 memory bits. Now you need to understand what this means and the problems that it can cause.

A *bit* is the smallest unit of data that you can have. A bit is either on or off; in other words, it can store just two different values. The two values are often referred to as true or false. Each value will be represented by a particular voltage in the memory of the Xbox, but you need need worry about that in detail.

Think of a bit as a coin on a table. The coin can be either heads or tails, that is, in one of two possible states. If you put a second coin on the table, the two coins in combination now have four possible states: head-head, head-tail, tail-head, and tail-tail. Each coin that you add to the table doubles the number of possible states (that is, when you add the coin, you can have all the previous states with the new coin on heads plus all the previous states with the new coin on tails).

If you do the math with eight coins, you find that they can occupy 256 different states. So 8 data bits can hold 256 different values. One of these values is 0 (all false), which means that the largest possible integer value a byte can hold is 255 (all true). When the ++ operator tries to increase the value of 255, it will produce the value of 256, which cannot be represented by 8 bits. The addition process should set the value of a ninth data bit to 1 so that it can represent the value of 256, but there is no ninth bit to set, so the other eight bits are cleared to 0. This causes the value to wrap around, which means that the value in the byte goes back to 0 again. The result of this is that the screen goes from maximum brightness to minimum brightness in a single step. The technical name for this is *overflow*.

One very important thing to note here is that no error messages are produced. The computer doesn't "know" that it has done anything wrong. Sometimes if your program does something stupid, you'll get an error, and your program will stop. However, in this case the Xbox does not seem to notice that you have just fallen off the end of a byte and will continue to run. Your program may well do the wrong thing, though. This means that your program has a bug in it. When you create the finished mood light code, you need to make sure that the values never "wrap around" like this.

Note   Note that you have not "run out of memory." Rather, the program has tried to put too much information in a single memory location. The Xbox can work with values much larger than 256; it does this by using multiple storage locations to hold a single item. As an example, you have seen that the information to describe a color fills at least four memory locations.

The Great Programmer Speaks: The Computer Doesn't Care   Our Great Programmer finds it very amusing when people say "the stupid computer got it wrong." She says this is not what happens. What really happened was that the person who wrote the program did a bad job. She has been known to roll around on the floor laughing when people ask her, "But why didn't the computer notice it was wrong?" She knows that the computer really doesn't know or care what a program actually does. The job of the computer is to follow the instructions the program gives it. The job of the programmer is to write instructions that are correct in every scenario.

Sample Code: Fade from Black   The sample project in the 03 MoodLight Fade Up directory in the source code resources for this chapter will perform the fade up shown previously. It will then wrap around to black as the values in the bytes overflow.

Making a Proper Mood Light

The fade-up part of the mood light is very good, but you don't want it to suddenly change from white to black each time around. What you would like is for it to fade smoothly up and down. If you were telling Mrs. Update what to do, you would say something like this:

"Make the value of `redIntensity` bigger each time that you are called. When the value reaches 255, start making it smaller each time you are called until it reaches 0, at which point you should start making it bigger again. Do the same with blue and green."

Mrs. Update would think about this for a while and decide that she needs to keep track of two things for each color: the current intensity value (in the range 0 to 255) and something that lets her remember whether she is counting up or counting down for that color. Then each time she is called, she can follow a sequence like this:

1. If you are counting up, increase the value of `redIntensity`.

2. If you are counting down, decrease the value of `redIntensity`.

3. If `redIntensity` is 255, change to counting down.

4. If `redIntensity` is 0, change to counting up.

This is an *algorithm*. It provides a sequence of operations that is used to solve a problem. In this case you wanted to make the value of `redIntensity` move up to 255 and down again in steps of one.

Of course, Mrs. Update is not a person but a C# method, so now you have to convert the previous steps into C#. The first thing you need to do is work out what data you need to store. You need the intensity value and also a way of remembering if you are counting up or down.

```
// The Game World - our color values
byte redIntensity = 0;
bool redCountingUp = true;
```

You have seen the `redIntensity` variable before; what you haven't seen is the way that you can set it to 0 when you declare it. The `redCountingUp` variable is new, though. It is of a new type (There are loads of different types, you'll be pleased to hear). This is the `bool` type, which is special because it can hold only two possible values: `true` or `false`. It allows programs to perform what is called *Boolean algebra*, which consists of calculations involving only the values `true` and `false`. Such calculations are usually used to drive decisions along the lines of "If `itIsRaining` is `true` and `robWillBeGoingOutside` is `true`, I should call the `takeMyUmberella` method."

In this case the `bool` type is perfect since `redCountingUp` will be either `true` or `false` and nothing else. The program will use it to make decisions in the `Update` method so that it can behave according to the data. It is this ability to make decisions that makes computers truly useful in that they can change what they do in response to their situation. To make decisions in your programs, you have to use conditional statements.

Making Decisions in Your Program

You have seen two kinds of statement so far. One calls a method to do something (you use this to call the `Clear` method), and the other changes the value of a variable (you use this to increase the intensity of our colors). Now you are going to use a conditional construction that can change what the program does depending on the particular situation.

Creating Conditional Statements

Figure 2-9 shows how a conditional construction fits together. Conditional constructions start with the word `if`. This is followed by a condition in brackets. The condition will produce a

Boolean result, which can be either true or false. You can use a variable of **bool** type directly here.

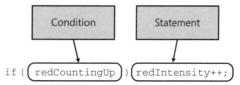

```
if ( redCountingUp ) ( redIntensity++; )
```

Figure 2-9   The **if** condition in action

If the condition is **true** (that is, in this case the variable **redCountingUp** holds the value **true**), the statement following the condition is performed. The result of this is that when this statement is obeyed, the value of **redIntensity** will get bigger if the program is counting up. The condition can be any value that gives a Boolean result, including this rather stupid code:

```
if (true) redIntensity++;
```

This code is completely legal C# code and will compile with no problem. When the program runs, the condition will be **true**, and the statement will increase the red intensity value. This is very stupid code, though, as the test might as well not be there. You could also write the following:

```
if (false) redIntensity++;
```

In this code the statement following the condition will never be obeyed because the condition is always **false**. This C# code will compile okay, but if you look very closely at the XNA Game Studio 2.0 display, you might notice that it is trying to tell you something, as shown in Figure 2-10.

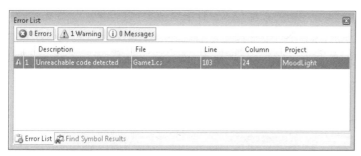

Figure 2-10   Compiler warnings

If the Error window in Figure 2-10 is not displayed, you can open it by selecting Error List from the View menu. Alternatively, you can use the key combination Ctrl+W followed by E.

When the compiler has finished trying to convert your C# source code into a program that can be run on the computer, it will tell you how many mistakes it thinks it has found. There are two kinds of mistakes. An *error* is a mistake that prevents what you've written being made into a program. Errors are really bad things like misspelled identifiers, using the wrong kind of brackets, and the like.

The other kind of mistake is called a *warning*. This is where the compiler thinks you may have done something stupid, but it does not prevent your program from running. Figure 2-10 shows the warning message for a program with a test for (**false**) in it.

What the compiler is telling you is that it has managed to work out that the statement after the test will never be reached. This is because it's impossible for the value **false** to be true. The compiler is warning you that although the code is legal C# code, what it does might actually not be what you want.

> **The Great Programmer Speaks: Warnings Should Always Be Heeded**   Our Great Programmer has very strong opinions on compiler warnings; she reckons that your code should compile with no warnings at all. Warnings usually mean that your solution is imperfect in some way, and you should always take steps to investigate and resolve them.

Adding an Else Part

The condition you have created is only half correct. If the program is not counting up, it must make the value of **redIntensity** smaller. You can use the -- operator to do this, but you need to add extra code to the condition. You need to add an *else* part. Figure 2-11 shows another form of the **if** condition, with the **else** part added.

The two statements are separated by a new key word, **else**. The new code means that if the program is counting up (that is, **redCountingUp** is **true**), the value gets bigger, but if the program is counting down (that is, **redCountingUp** is **false**) ,the value gets smaller. The **else** part is optional; you must add one only if you need it.

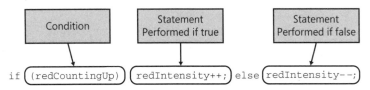

Figure 2-11   The **if** condition with an **else** part

Testing Values

The program must also manage the value in **redCountingUp** so that when it reaches the upper limit, it starts to count down, and when it reaches the lower limit, it starts to count up again. In other words,

1. When **redIntensity** reaches 255, set **redCountingUp** to **false**.

2. When **redIntensity** reaches 0, set **redCountingUp** to **true**.

To do this you need another kind of condition, one that performs a comparison. Figure 2-12 shows how such comparisons are created. This performs the first of the previously mentioned two tests.

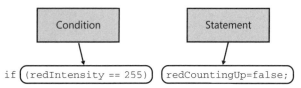

Figure 2-12   Performing a comparison using the `if` condition

The key to understanding what is happening is the = = comparison operator. When the program evaluates this condition, the values on the left and right of the = = operator are compared. If they are the same, the result of the comparison is true, and the statement that follows the condition is performed. If they are different, the result of the comparison is false, and the statement that follows the comparison is ignored.

The sequence = = is the comparison operator. It is completely different from the = operator, which we know as the "gozzinta." It is important that you don't get these two confused. Unfortunately, you have both a gozzinta and a comparison taking place in the `if` statement because you want to put a new value into **redCountingUp** if the comparison succeeds.

Fortunately, the compiler can usually detect when you use the wrong operator and produce a message.There are other comparison operators that can test to see if one value is greater or less than another; these are discussed later. An `if` statement that uses a condition can have an **else** part if required; it's just that we don't need one here. The final code to make our red intensity value move up and down ends up as follows:

```
if (redIntensity == 255) redCountingUp = false;
if (redIntensity == 0) redCountingUp = true;
if (redCountingUp) redIntensity++; else redIntensity--;
```

Note that the program needs a second test to change the direction of the counting when the bottom limit of the intensity value is reached. The tests are performed before the intensity value is updated so that if the very first value of **redIntensity** is either 0 or 255, the program will perform the wrong calculation.

> **Note**   Pay very careful attention to the previous three statements. Go back and read the original instructions to Mrs. Update and make sure that you are absolutely clear how these have been converted into C# statements that will perform the job.

The Completed Mood Light

You now have the code that lets you create a smoothly pulsing mood light:

```
// The Game World - our color values
byte redIntensity=0;
bool redCountingUp = true;
byte greenIntensity = 0;
bool greenCountingUp = true;
byte blueIntensity=0;
bool blueCountingUp = true;
protected override void Update(GameTime gameTime)
{
    // Allows the game to exit
    if (GamePad.GetState(PlayerIndex.One).Buttons.Back ==
        ButtonState.Pressed)
        this.Exit();
    // Update each color in turn
    if (redIntensity == 255) redCountingUp=false;
    if (redIntensity == 0) redCountingUp=true;
    if (redCountingUp) redIntensity++; else redIntensity--;

    if (greenIntensity == 255) greenCountingUp = false;
    if (greenIntensity == 0) greenCountingUp = true;
    if (greenCountingUp) greenIntensity++; else greenIntensity--;

    if (blueIntensity == 255) blueCountingUp = false;
    if (blueIntensity == 0) blueCountingUp = true;
    if (blueCountingUp) blueIntensity++; else blueIntensity--;
    base.Update(gameTime);
}
protected override void Draw(GameTime gameTime)
{
    Color backgroundColor;
    backgroundColor =
        new Color(redIntensity, greenIntensity, blueIntensity);
    graphics.GraphicsDevice.Clear(backgroundColor);
    base.Draw(gameTime);
}
```

These versions of **Update** and **Draw** will produce a program that smoothly fades the Xbox screen between black and white.

Sample Code: Mood Light   The project in the 04 MoodLight directory in the source code resources for this chapter contains the previously mentioned **Update** and **Draw** methods and provides a smoothly changing mood light that goes from dark to light and back again.

A Proper Funky Mood Light

Going from black to white and back is all very well, but it would be nice to add some additional variety to our light. It turns out that this is very easy to achieve. At the moment, the red, green, and blue intensities are all the same values, counting up from 0 to 255 and back down again. This just gives shades of gray. What you want is different combinations and the color intensities going up and down at different times. You can do this by changing the starting values of the intensity values and update directions:

```
byte redIntensity=0;
bool redCountingUp = true;
byte greenIntensity = 80;
bool greenCountingUp = false;
byte blueIntensity = 160;
bool blueCountingUp = true;
```

Rather than all the colors starting at 0 and counting up, the green value now starts at 80 and counts down, and the blue value starts at 160. This means that instead of just different shades of gray, you now have lots of other colors being presented. This provides a very groovy display. If you change the values in your program to the ones shown in the previous code, you can get a much more interesting-looking display. You can even try values of your own and see what they look like.

For a much longer-lasting display, you need to change the rate at which the three colors are updated. This is not actually very hard to do, so I've written an "Ultimate Mood Light" that you can take a look at.

ENTER PREFIX TEXT IN EDD   The project in the 05 Ultimate Mood Light directory in the source code resources for this chapter contains a new version of **Update** that changes the red, green, and blue intensities at different speeds, resulting in a display that never seems to actually repeat (although it does eventually). Take a look at the code and see if you can understand how it works.

Finding Program Bugs

Your younger brother has been reading this book and typing in the programs on his computer. He has just told you that the book is rubbish because the programs don't work. He has written an **Update** method and is complaining that for him, the red value only ever gets brighter. You ask him to show you the code and see this:

```
if (redIntensity == 255) redCountingUp=true;
if (redIntensity == 0) redCountingUp=true;
if (redCountingUp) redIntensity++; else redIntensity++;
```

At a first glance, it looks fine, and the C# compiler is quite happy that it's legal, but obviously it's not working. There is a bug in the program. Note that the bug is not there because the computer has made a mistake, so the instructions themselves must be faulty. You don't want to bother the Great Programmer, as she seems to be busy playing Halo on her Xbox, so you take a look, bearing in mind something she said recently.

> **The Great Programmer Speaks: Run Programs by Hand to Find Bugs**   A good way
> to find out what a program is doing is to behave like the computer and "run" the program
> yourself. By working through the statements by hand, keeping track of the variables, and
> making the changes to them that the program does, you can often find out what is wrong.

Your younger brother has actually made two mistakes in copying the program from these
pages. See if you can find them by working through the statements. Think a bit about the
answer before taking a look at my solution, shown in Figure 2-13:

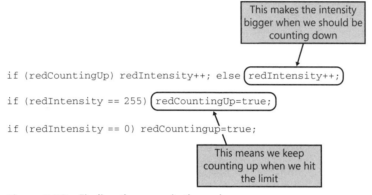

Figure 2-13   Finding the errors in the code

I marked out the errors; see if you can understand why they had the effect they did.

Conclusion

You have learned a lot in this chapter. You now know the fundamentals of C# programs and
the XNA framework. You have seen how to identify and create variables that store data and
also how to write statements that change the values of these variables. You have seen that the
data in a variable is held in a location in memory, which is a certain size and has a particular
capacity. If you exceed this, the value will not fit and will be changed in unexpected ways.

You know that in C#, programs are broken down into classes, each class having things it can
do (methods) and things it can hold (member variables). Classes are like offices, where
workers (methods) can be asked to do things. You also know that that an XNA game is a particular kind of class that contains an **Update** method that's used by XNA to update the state of
the game world and a **Draw** method that's used to draw the current state of the game world.
You have seen how our programs can be made to make decisions and change what they do,
depending on the values of the data they hold.

Pop Quiz

Time for another pop quiz. Have a go at the questions before you move on. When you learn to program, you find that each step builds on the last, so it's important that you understand what is in this chapter before you move on to the next. Again, all the answers are either true or false, and you can work them out from this chapter and the Glossary.

1. A program is a sequence of variables.

2. Programs are always held in a file called Program.prog.

3. An identifier is a name that you give to something you want to use in a program.

4. Methods tell the computer how to do something.

5. The `Draw` method updates the game.

6. A block of statements is made of wood.

7. The compiler checks code comments for accuracy and spelling.

8. A `Color` value is held as a single byte.

9. The type of a variable determines what kind of data can be put into it.

10. An identifier is a name built into C# to identify things.

11. A variable has an identifier and a type and holds values that your program wants to work with.

12. A variable of type `bool` can hold only the values 0 and 1.

13. Conditional statements start with the word `when`.

14. An `if` condition must have an `else` part.

15. An algorithm is like a recipe.

16. The operator = is used to compare two values and test if they are the same.

17. A class holds method members and data members.

18. A good identifier for a class would be `PlayGame`.

19. A good identifier for a method would be `Explode`.

20. A byte holds a single bit of data.

21. The ++ operator works between two operands.

22. The C# compiler detects if a variable overflows when the program is running.

23. Boolean values can be either `true` or `false`.

Chapter 3
Getting Player Input

- Find out how XNA represents the Xbox gamepads and keyboards.

- Discover the C# languages structures that let you get player input.

- Write some really silly games and scare people with them.

Introduction

You now know the basics of computer game programming. You know that a program is actually a sequence of statements, each of which performs a single action. You have seen that statements are held inside methods, each of which performs a particular task, and that methods are held in classes along with data. The program itself works on data values, which are held in variables of a particular type, and the program can make decisions based on the values that the variables have. (If none of this makes much sense, reread Chapter 2, "Programs, Data, and Pretty Colors," until it does.)

Now you are going to expand your understanding to include how to get input from the outside world so that games can actually react to what the player does. You'll see that once we have done this, a number of possibilities open up, and you can create some truly silly games, including "Color Nerve," "Mind Reader," "The Thing That Goes Bump in the Night," and "Gamepad Racer."

Program Project: A Mood-Light Controller

In the previous chapter you made a light that changes color over time. I also mentioned that this is the kind of thing that will be used in the starships of the future. A color-changing light is not all that useful for reading books, but it's great for setting moods; what your starship

> captain really needs is a light that he can set to any color. So now you are going to make a
> lamp that can be controlled by an Xbox gamepad. The user will press the red, blue, green,
> and yellow buttons on the gamepad to increase the amount of that color in the light. To
> make this work, you'll have to discover how to read the gamepad.

Before you start looking at gamepads, though, you need to decide how the program will
actually work. Consider the following statement of C# from the previous mood-light program,
which is part of the **Update** method:

```
if (redCountingUp) redIntensity++;
```

This is one of the tests that controls the intensity of the red part of the color. What it is saying
is "If the Boolean value **redCountingUp** is **true**, increase the value of **redIntensity** by one."
The statement is processed each time **Update** is called (at the moment that is 60 times a
second), and so this means that if **redCountingUp** is **true**, the red component of the screen
gets progressively brighter over time.

You want to write some code that says "If the red button on gamepad 1 is being pressed,
increase the value of **redIntensity** by one." Then, if the player holds down the button, the
screen will get redder. So all you have to do is change this test to read the button on the
gamepad, and you can easily create a user-controlled light.

Reading a Gamepad

The gamepads are actually very complex devices. They are connected to the host device either
by a Universal Serial Bus (USB) cable or by a wireless connection. As far as you are concerned,
the way that programs work with gamepads does not depend on how they are connected. The
connection to a gamepad can be used to read the buttons and joysticks and can also be used
to send commands to the gamepad, for example, to turn the vibration effect on and off. The
Xbox and XNA provide support for up to four gamepads connected simultaneously.

Gamepads and Classes

The gamepad information is represented in XNA by means of a class called **GamePadState**.
The job of this class is to provide the connection between the program and the physical
gamepad that the player is holding. To understand how you are going to use this, you have to
learn a bit more about how classes work.

You have already seen what a class is. A class contains data (variables that can hold stuff) and
methods (code that can do stuff). You can think of a class as an office, with a desk holding the
variables and people acting as the methods. Figure 3-1 shows the office plan for the class
Game1.cs, which you have seen is the basis of an XNA game.

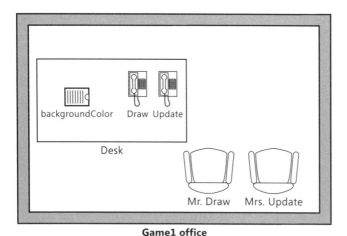

Game1 office

Figure 3-1 The Game1 class as an office plan

This class contains some variables on the desk (in this case the background color intensities) and two methods, which we have called Mr. Draw and Mrs. Update. Each method has a corresponding telephone. Programs can place calls to the telephones to request that the method perform the required task.

> **The Great Programmer Speaks: Classes Are Not Really Offices** Our Great Programmer has been reading these notes and finds them quite amusing. She reckons that classes are not exactly like offices, but she thinks that for the purpose of getting an understanding of how programs are constructed, it's okay to regard them as such.

When an XNA game starts, the XNA system makes an *instance* of the Game1 class that it can then ask to **Draw** and **Update**. When an instance of a class is created, the statements for the methods it contains are loaded into memory, and space is set aside for the data variables that the instance holds.

The class files that you write give the plans for the class so when the program runs instances of each class can be created. In real life you would make a game office by building a room, putting a desk and some telephones in, and then hiring a Mr. Draw and a Mrs. Update. The process of making an instance of a class is similar. However, to save memory, the running program will only use one copy of the method code that is shared between all the instances of a class.

> **Note** It's important to remember that this happens when a program runs. The process of creating instances of classes is not performed by the compiler. The job of the compiler is to convert your C# source code into instructions that the computer or Xbox can run. By the time that your program has control, the compiler has done its job, and the computer or Xbox is just running the machine language output that the compiler produced.

Finding a Gamepad

XNA also looks after a lot of other things when a game is running, and one of these is the **GamePad** class connected to all the gamepads. You don't have to know how the gamepad is actually connected; for all you know, it might use tiny pixies traveling up and down the wires carrying pixie notes written on pixie paper saying "Master has pressed the Red Button," but then again it might not. Figure 3-2 shows how the **GamePad** class would look if it were an office.

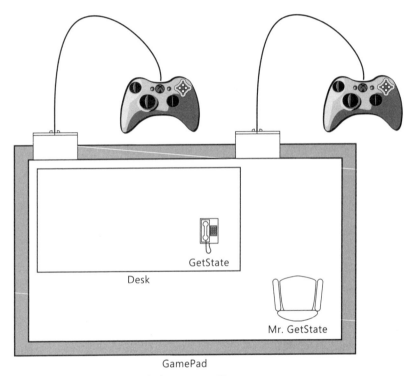

Figure 3-2   The GamePad class as an office

The **GamePad** class contains a method called **GetState** that will get the state of one of the gamepads. When **GetState** is called, it looks at one of the gamepads, reads its settings, and then sends information back.

The **GetState** method is supplied with a *parameter* that identifies the gamepad to be read. A parameter is a way that a call can give information to a method. You have seen these before; in your very first programs, you were passing **Color** parameters into the **Clear** method to select the color of the screen that you wanted.

In the case of the **GetState** method, the parameter identifies the gamepad that you want to read. If you're thinking in terms of offices, you can think of a parameter as part of the instructions that come down the telephone. When the phone rings and Mr. GetState answers it, he is asked to "get me the state of gamepad 1." The information about the state of the gamepad is sent back in a `GamePadState` structure, which is shown in Figure 3-3.

GamePadState	
Buttons	
A	*ButtonState.Pressed*
B	*ButtonState.Released*
X	*ButtonState.Released*
Y	*ButtonState.Released*
Start	*ButtonState.Released*
Back	*ButtonState.Released*

Figure 3-3   GamePadState structure with the green A button pressed

You can think of this as a set of items filled in on a form if you wish, but actually it's a C# structure that contains the data members, shown in Figure 3-3, as well as some other data.

So, if Mrs. Update wants to know the state of one of the gamepads on the Xbox, she calls the `GetState` method in the `GamePad` class and asks "Can you give me the state of the gamepad for Player 1 please?" Mr. GetState jumps up and fills in a "GamePadState" form and sends it back to her. Figure 3-4 gives the breakdown of the C# statement that will get the state of a gamepad into a variable of type `GamePadState`.

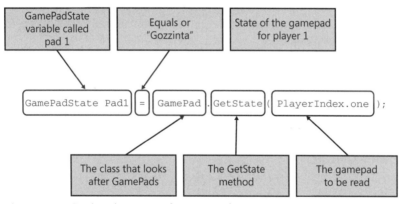

Figure 3-4   Getting the status of a gamepad

Testing the Gamepad Status

Now that you have the status, you can use it in the program to see if a button has been pressed. Figure 3-5 shows the breakdown of the C# statement that will perform the test.

This compares the state of the red button B with the value `ButtonState.Pressed`. If the two are equal, this means that the button is down, and the `Update` method must make the red intensity bigger. You can then use the same principle to manage the blue and green values, which means that you now have an **Update** method that looks like the following:

```
protected override void Update(GameTime gameTime)
{
    // Allows the game to exit
    if (GamePad.GetState(PlayerIndex.One).Buttons.Back == ButtonState.Pressed)
        this.Exit();

    GamePadState pad1 = GamePad.GetState(PlayerIndex.One);
    if (pad1.Buttons.B == ButtonState.Pressed) redIntensity++;
    if (pad1.Buttons.X == ButtonState.Pressed) blueIntensity++;
    if (pad1.Buttons.A == ButtonState.Pressed) greenIntensity++;

    base.Update(gameTime);
}
```

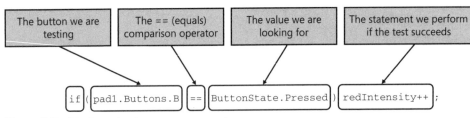

Figure 3-5   Testing a button on a gamepad

The only problem with this **Update** method is that the program doesn't handle the yellow button yet. When this is pressed, the program needs to increase the green and the red intensity; that is, it must perform two statements if the condition is true. It turns out that this is very easy; you can just put the two statements into a block that is controlled by the condition, as shown here:

```
if (pad1.Buttons.Y == ButtonState.Pressed)
{
    redIntensity++;
    greenIntensity++;
}
```

You have seen blocks before; the body of a method (the bit that does the work) is a block. In C# terms, a block is a number of statements that are enclosed in curly braces. The previous code will perform both statements if the condition is true since they are in a block controlled by the condition.

The Great Programmer Speaks: Blocks Rock   Our Great Programmer tends to use blocks after **if** conditions even when she doesn't actually need to. She says that it makes the program text clearer and that it is much easier to add extra statements later if you need to.

If you put the preceding statements into the **Update** method of one of your earlier mood-light programs, you'll get compiler warning messages because the new version of **Update** doesn't use all the variables that were created for previous versions of the program. To get rid of these warnings, you must delete the statements that create the unused variables. The Great Programmer doesn't like it when programs have variables in them that are not used; she says this looks unprofessional, and I agree with her.

> **Sample Code: Manual MoodLight**   The sample project in the 01 Manual MoodLight directory in the resources for this chapter implements the **Update** method as shown previously. You can increase the brightness of the colors on the screen by pressing the buttons on the gamepad.

Game Idea: Color Nerve

Every now and then you are going to try out a game idea. These will start out very simply and then build up to more complicated and interesting games. You can use the Manual MoodLight code to create your first game. The game makes use of something we saw in Chapter 2. You noticed that if you keep on making a value bigger, there comes a point where it won't fit in the memory store allocated for it, and it will overflow. This is what caused the screen to go from bright white to black. However, you can use this to create your first "Very Silly Game," which makes use of this.

Color Nerve is a game for two or more players. Each player takes a turn to press one or more buttons on the gamepad (the other players must watch carefully to make sure that they actually do press a button). Each player can press as many buttons as they want for as long as they like in their turn, but if the screen changes suddenly (because one of the color values has gone from 255 to 0), they are out, and the game continues. The last player left in the game is the winner.

This game can be very tactical. Players can press the buttons for very short times, or at the start of the game they can show their nerve by holding the buttons down for longer, trying to cause problems for the next player. They can also try to work out which color has wrapped around so that they can press that button when it is their turn. The game works very well at parties, any number of people can take part, and the rules are very easy to understand. Later you will improve the game to add pictures as well as a plain screen.

Using the Keyboard

XNA will work with keyboards as well as with gamepads. You might be surprised to learn that you can plug a USB keyboard into an Xbox 360 and use it just as you'd use the keyboard on the PC. If you want the program to work with the keyboard, you can add code that does this, as shown here:

```
KeyboardState keys = Keyboard.GetState();
if (keys.IsKeyDown(Keys.R)) redIntensity++;
if (keys.IsKeyDown(Keys.B)) blueIntensity++;
if (keys.IsKeyDown(Keys.G)) greenIntensity++;
if (keys.IsKeyDown(Keys.Y))
{
   redIntensity++;
   greenIntensity++;
}
```

Note that the process is very similar to how the gamepad works, but there are slight differences. You don't need to tell the **GetState** method on the **Keyboard** which keyboard to read because XNA supports only a single keyboard. The **KeyboardState** item that is returned from the call is not actually a piece of paper; instead, it is an instance that provides methods that the program can use to discover whether a particular key is pressed. Rather than seeing if the state of a button is set to the value **ButtonState.Pressed**, the program can call the method **IsKeyDown**. You supply the **IsKeyDown** method with a parameter that identifies the key you are interested in.

```
if (keys.IsKeyDown(Keys.R)) redIntensity++;
```

This code is a conditional statement that will increase the value of **redIntensity** if the R key is pressed. The method **IsKeyDown** returns **true** if the key is down or **false** if not. You can therefore use it to control the update of the **redIntensity** value.

Using Gamepad and Keyboard at the Same Time

If you want to use both gamepad and keyboard, you have to test for both. This means that the **Update** method now looks like this:

```
protected override void Update(GameTime gameTime)
{
   // Allows the game to exit
   if (GamePad.GetState(PlayerIndex.One.Buttons.Back == ButtonState.Pressed)
      this.Exit();

   GamePadState pad1 = GamePad.GetState(PlayerIndex.One);

   if (pad1.Buttons.B == ButtonState.Pressed) redIntensity++;
   if (pad1.Buttons.X == ButtonState.Pressed) blueIntensity++;
```

```
    if (pad1.Buttons.A == ButtonState.Pressed) greenIntensity++;
    if (pad1.Buttons.Y == ButtonState.Pressed)
    {
        redIntensity++;
        greenIntensity++;
    }
    KeyboardState keys = Keyboard.GetState();
    if (keys.IsKeyDown(Keys.R)) redIntensity++;
    if (keys.IsKeyDown(Keys.B)) blueIntensity++;
    if (keys.IsKeyDown(Keys.G)) greenIntensity++;
    if (keys.IsKeyDown(Keys.Y))
    {
        redIntensity++;
        greenIntensity++;
    }
    base.Update(gameTime);
}
```

This is not good code. The problem is that you are doing the same thing twice, just triggered in a different way. The Great Programmer, if she ever saw this, would not be impressed. Fortunately C# provides a way that a program can combine two conditions and then perform some code if either condition is true. This way of combining conditions is called the OR logical operator since it will be true if one thing or the other is true and is written in the program as two vertical bars (| |).

```
GamePadState pad1 = GamePad.GetState(PlayerIndex.One);
KeyboardState keys = Keyboard.GetState();

if (pad1.Buttons.B == ButtonState.Pressed || keys.IsKeyDown(Keys.R))
{
    redIntensity++;
}
```

The OR logical operator is placed between two Boolean expressions that can be either true or false. If one or the other expression is true, the combined logical condition works out to be true. In the previous code, if the red button is pressed on the gamepad *or* the R key is pressed on the keyboard (or both), the **redIntensity** value is increased. This is exactly what you want, and it means that Color Nerve can now be played with the gamepad or the keyboard (or both at the same time). Logical operators are so called because they produce logical rather than numerical results. There are other logical operators that you will use later.

> **Note**   If you find this logical operator stuff hard to understand, just go back to the problem that you are trying to solve. You want the program to perform a statement (**redIntensity++**) if the red key is pressed on the gamepad *or* the R key is pressed on the keyboard. So you use the OR operator (| |) to combine the two tests and make a condition that triggers if one or the other condition is true.

> Sample Code: Color Nerve   The sample project in the 02 Color Nerve directory in the resources for this chapter implements the game. You can adjust the colors of the screen by pressing the gamepad buttons or a key on the keyboard.

Adding Vibration

The communication between the gamepad and the game works in both directions. Not only can you read buttons on the gamepad, but you can also send commands to the gamepad to turn on the vibration motors. Again, you don't have to know exactly how these messages are delivered; all you need to know is the features of XNA that are used to control this vibration effect.

This means that you can make your Color Nerve game even more exciting by making the gamepad vibrate when the intensity values are getting close to their limits. It is interesting how features like this can enhance even a simple game. You will be using the vibration effect on the gamepads quite a lot in the next few games.

Controlling the Vibration of a Gamepad

The GamePad class provides a method called SetVibration that lets a program control the vibration motors:

```
GamePad.SetVibration(PlayerIndex.One, 0, 1);
```

The SetVibration method uses three parameters. The first one identifies which gamepad you want to vibrate. The second parameter is a value between 0.0 and 1 that controls the vibration of the left motor. The bigger the number, the more it vibrates. The third parameter controls the right-hand motor in the same way as the left one. The previous statement would set the right-hand motor of gamepad 1 vibrating at full speed. The left-hand motor is the low-frequency vibration, and the right-hand motor is the high-frequency vibration.

If you think of the GamePad class/office having a man called Mr. SetVibration, this means that he would be told which gamepad to vibrate and the settings for the left and right motors. Once the method has been called, the gamepad will start to vibrate, and it will keep vibrating until you call the method again to change its setting. In other words, you can think of the SetVibration method as a switch that can be set to a number of different positions. Initially both the gamepad motors are set at 0, which means no vibration.

Testing Intensity Values

The game needs to decide when to turn on the vibration. To do this, it must test the intensity values and turn on the vibration motor if they are getting too large. The program can decide to turn on the motors if any of the red, green, or blue intensity values are greater than 220. To do this, the program must test the intensity values:

```
if (redIntensity > 220)
{
   GamePad.SetVibration(PlayerIndex.One, 0, 1);
}
```

This shows another form of condition. In the previous ones the conditions have been checking to see if two values are equal. This code tests if one value is greater than another. The greater-than sign (>) is another logical operator. Placed between two values, it will return true if the value on the left is greater than the value on the right and false if not. That is exactly what you want.

Using the previous code, the gamepad will start to vibrate using the right-hand motor when the red intensity value goes above 220. If you add this code to the Update method in the Color Nerve game, you will find that if you increase the red value, the gamepad will start to vibrate. Unfortunately there is a bug in our program. When the red intensity value wraps around back to 0, the vibration will not stop. You need to add some code that turns off the motor when the intensity value is less than 220. It turns out that this is very easy to do; you can add an **else** part to the condition.

```
if (redIntensity > 220)
{
    GamePad.SetVibration(PlayerIndex.One, 0, 1);
}
else
{
    GamePad.SetVibration(PlayerIndex.One, 0, 0);
}
```

The statement after the **else** is performed if the condition is found to be **false**. You can add an **else** part to any **if** condition that you create. This means that when the red intensity value wraps around, the vibration will stop. You can extend the tests using OR so that the program will test all the intensity values:

```
if (redIntensity > 220 || greenIntensity > 220 || blueIntensity > 220)
{
    GamePad.SetVibration(PlayerIndex.One, 0, 1);
}
else
{
    GamePad.SetVibration(PlayerIndex.One, 0, 0);
}
```

Now the vibration is controlled by all the intensity values. As an improvement to the game you might want to experiment with different kinds of vibration for different colors, perhaps by using the low-frequency motor as well. This is controlled by the other value in the call of **SetVibration**:

```
GamePad.SetVibration(PlayerIndex.One, 1, 0);
```

This line of code would turn on the low-frequency vibration. You might also want to experiment with the thresholds at which the vibration starts.

There is still one more problem with the program. If you run it and make the gamepad vibrate, when the program finishes, the gamepad doesn't always stop vibrating. You need to add code that will stop the vibration when our game ends. The game stops when the player presses the Back button on the gamepad. The test for this is in the **Update** method. If the Back button is pressed, the **Exit** method is called to stop the game.

```
if (GamePad.GetState(PlayerIndex.One).Buttons.Back == ButtonState.Pressed)
    this.Exit();
```

The **Exit** method removes the game display and shuts the game down in a tidy fashion. What the program must do is turn off the gamepad motors before **Exit** is called. To do this, the program needs to perform more than one statement if the Back button is pressed. To do this, you must create another *block*:

```
if (GamePad.GetState(PlayerIndex.One).Buttons.Back == ButtonState.Pressed)
{
    GamePad.SetVibration(PlayerIndex.One, 0, 0);
    this.Exit();
}
```

Now, when the player presses the Back button to end the program, the vibration motors are turned off.

The Great Programmer Speaks: When in Doubt, Make Sure Yourself   The Great Programmer says that if you are in a situation where you are not sure whether something is always the case, you should add code to remove all possible doubt. Testing the previously discussed vibration behavior, I discovered that the gamepad is left vibrating on the earlier versions of XNA but not on some newer ones. To make absolutely sure that the vibration is stopped wherever your game runs, you should include the code to stop the vibration yourself.

Sample Code: Vibration Color Nerve Game   The sample project in the 03 Color Nerve with Vibes directory in the source code resources for this chapter holds a version of Color Nerve that has the vibration effect enabled.

Game Idea: Secret Vibration Messages

Once you see that it is easy to read gamepad buttons and drive the motors, you can start to have more fun with XNA, particularly with wireless gamepads. You can create mind-reading games where your assistant seems to know exactly what you are thinking. What the audience doesn't know is that both of you are holding Xbox gamepads in your jacket pockets and using them to send signals back and forth using the vibration feature. The code to do this is actually very simple, and you should be able to understand what it does.

```
protected override void Update(GameTime gameTime)
{
 // Allows the game to exit
 if (GamePad.GetState(PlayerIndex.One).Buttons.Back == ButtonState.Pressed)
 {
     GamePad.SetVibration(PlayerIndex.One, 0, 0);
     GamePad.SetVibration(PlayerIndex.Two, 0, 0);
     this.Exit();
 }
 GamePadState pad1 = GamePad.GetState(PlayerIndex.One);
 GamePadState pad2 = GamePad.GetState(PlayerIndex.Two);

 if (pad1.Buttons.A == ButtonState.Pressed)
 {
     GamePad.SetVibration(PlayerIndex.Two, 0, 1);
 }
 else
 {
     GamePad.SetVibration(PlayerIndex.Two, 0, 0);
 }

 if (pad2.Buttons.A == ButtonState.Pressed)
 {
     GamePad.SetVibration(PlayerIndex.One, 0, 1);
 }
 else
 {
     GamePad.SetVibration(PlayerIndex.One, 0, 0);
 }

 base.Update(gameTime);
}
```

The **Update** method reads the A button on the gamepad for player 1. If this is pressed, it turns on the fast vibration motor in the gamepad for player 2. It then repeats the process the other way, sending signals from gamepad 2 to gamepad 1. This gives you a way to send wireless signals from one gamepad to another. Note that both conditions have **else** parts so that if the button is not pressed, the vibration is turned off.

You could also use this for practical jokes; just leave a gamepad underneath your victim's bed and then wait until they turn the light off and settle down. Then give the vibration a quick blast for maximum scare factor. Just don't blame me if you never get the gamepad back!

Sample Code: Vibration Messages   The sample project in the 04 Mind Reader directory in the source code resources for this chapter holds a version of the vibration message program. Just remember to use it wisely. The program also turns the display screen black so that it is not obvious that there is a program running.

Game Idea: Gamepad Racer

The final game idea in this chapter is really silly, but it can be great fun. The first thing you need to do is find a large, smooth table. Put a couple of books under the legs at one end so that the table is not horizontal anymore but sloping. If you put a wireless Xbox gamepad at the top of the table and make the gamepad vibrate, it will slide down the table toward the other end. You may need to experiment with the angle, but I've found that with care you can arrange things so that a gamepad will take around 30 seconds to slide all the way down the table with vibration at full power. If you line up four gamepads on the top of the table, players can pick the one they think will win, and then you can race them down the slope.

The code for this game is very simple indeed; the **Update** method just turns on all the vibration motors in the gamepads:

```
protected override void Update(GameTime gameTime)
{
// Allows the game to exit
if(GamePad.GetState(PlayerIndex.One).Buttons.Back==ButtonState.Pressed)
{
    GamePad.SetVibration(PlayerIndex.One, 0, 0);
    GamePad.SetVibration(PlayerIndex.Two, 0, 0);
    GamePad.SetVibration(PlayerIndex.Three, 0, 0);
    GamePad.SetVibration(PlayerIndex.Four, 0, 0);
    this.Exit();
}

GamePad.SetVibration(PlayerIndex.One, 1, 1);
GamePad.SetVibration(PlayerIndex.Two, 1, 1);
GamePad.SetVibration(PlayerIndex.Three, 1, 1);
GamePad.SetVibration(PlayerIndex.Four, 1, 1);
base.Update(gameTime);
}
```

The only complication is that when the game ends, you must turn off all the vibrations. Put all the gamepads at the top of the slope and then run the program. Press the Back button on gamepad 1 to stop the game.

Sample Code: Gamepad Racer   The sample project in the 05 GamepadRacer directory in the source code resources for this chapter holds a version of the gamepad racer program.

Note   By careful tuning of vibration values, it would be possible to "knobble" gamepads and make sure that the same one wins each time. Note that I do not condone such behavior.

Program Bugs

Your younger brother is still trying to learn to program, but he keeps having problems. He is still claiming that this book is faulty because the programs don't work properly when he types them in. He is trying to get "Color Nerve" to work, but every time he runs the program, the red intensity gets brighter whether he presses the button or not. You take a look at his program and find the following code in the **Update** method:

```
if (pad1.Buttons.B == ButtonState.Pressed || keys.IsKeyDown(Keys.R));
{
    redIntensity++;
}
```

This is the only part of the program where the red intensity is being increased, and it seems that the condition is being ignored.

This looks perfectly okay, and it seems to compile and run correctly, but it seems to be making the red intensity brighter every time. At this point it is a good idea to take a look at Visual Studio and see if the compiler is trying to tell you anything about the code. Figure 3-6 shows your brother's code after he has compiled it.

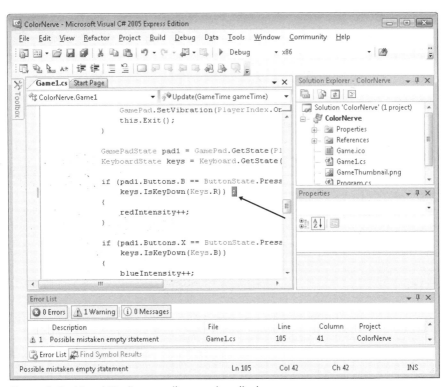

Figure 3-6   Visual Studio compiler warning display

Your attention is drawn to the bottom left-hand corner and the message "Possibly mistaken empty statement." If you double-click on this message, you find that the cursor moves to a point just after the `if` condition (I've indicated it with an arrow in Figure 3-6).

The C# compiler is trying to tell you something about this statement. If you go back to the original listing, you find that your brother has added an extra semicolon at the end of the condition. The problem is that this ends the statement controlled by the condition. So if the R button or the R key is pressed, the program will decide to do nothing (an empty statement) and then go on and do the next statement regardless, leading to the effect that you are seeing. Figure 3-7 shows how this happens.

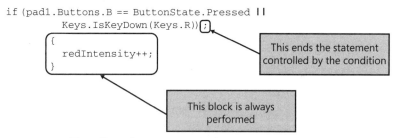

Figure 3-7   The effect of an extra semicolon

You remove the semicolon, the warning goes away, and the program works fine. Your younger brother is now starting to revise his opinion of you and offers to take out the trash that night, even though it is your turn.

> **The Great Programmer Speaks: Helping Other People Is a Good Plan**   The Great Programmer has been watching all this with approval. She reckons that it is always a good idea to try to help people who are stuck with a problem. Sometimes when a programmer working on uncovering a bug has the chance to explain what is going wrong with a piece of code to an innocent bystander, that can be enough to allow the programmer to work out what is broken. That means you can get a reputation as a fearsome bug fixer by just being a bystander. Furthermore, seeing what mistakes other people make can give you hints on things that you need to look out for when your programs go wrong. Oh, and sometimes you get your trash taken out for free.

Conclusion

You have learned a lot in this chapter, and you have finally managed to make some games that players can have fun with. You have seen how XNA allows programs to interact with physical devices by calling methods on classes, and you have seen how a program can make decisions on the information that it receives from the devices and use this to make simple (and silly) games.

Pop Quiz

No chapter would be complete without a pop quiz. So here it is. You should know the routine by now; just decide on true or false and look the answers up in the back to find out whether you are a winner or a loser.

1. If a class is an office, a method is a desk.

2. The compiler creates all the instances of classes in a program.

3. An `if` statement must have an `else` part.

4. A parameter is used to feed information into a class.

5. The `else` part of an `if` statement is always performed.

6. The state of a gamepad is represented in an XNA program by a byte value.

7. The `GamePad.GetState` method can be used to see if a button is pressed on a gamepad (this is a tough question; you are allowed to look at the chapter to work it out).

8. A block is a number of C# statements enclosed in curly brackets.

9. The C# condition (`true || false`) means "true or false" and would work out to **true**.

10. The C# condition (`redIntensity > 220`) will evaluate to "true" if the value in `greenIntensity` is greater than 220.

11. The gamepad vibration is always automatically turned off when an XNA game stops running.

Part II
Using the XNA Framework

Chapter 4
Displaying Images

- Find out how the Content Manager lets you add pictures to XNA games.

- Discover how pictures are manipulated in game programs.

- Display your pictures on the screen.

- Make a better version of Color Nerve and an even groovier mood light.

Introduction

Your understanding of computers and programs should be coming along nicely. You are start-ing to get a grasp of classes, methods, and data as well as the C# constructions that let your programs make decisions depending on the values in your variables. You also know how to read information from the gamepad and the keyboard and how to use this information to change what a game does when it runs.

In this chapter, you'll learn how to use images in your programs, you'll improve Color Nerve so that it lets you use your own pictures, and you'll make an even more impressive mood light.

Program Project: Picture Display

Pictures in games are always nice. The Xbox is extremely good at manipulating images on the screen. Many games make use of image resources that are then used to generate the view the player sees. In this project, you'll display a picture on the Xbox screen. Once you have some of your images loaded into the Xbox, you can see about using them in games. Doing this very simple thing requires a lot of work:

1. You need to get the picture that you wish to draw into your game project so that it becomes part of the program when it is loaded into the Xbox.

2. Then you must add code to the program that will fetch the image into the program when it runs.

---

3. Next, you need to tell XNA where on the screen the image is to be drawn.

4. Finally, you can go ahead and draw the item.

The good news is that while you're learning how to do this, you're finding out a lot about how games, C#, XNA, and Xbox work.

Resources and Content

In the early days of computers, a program simply read in numbers and printed out results. Things have moved on a bit since then, and now computer programs can work with images, video, and sound. This is especially useful where games are concerned; a large part of the enjoyment of a game results from an attractive game environment. And sometimes the graphics themselves form part of the game play. If you want to become a game developer, you'll need to know how these resources are made part of your program. In fact, many programs today have significant graphical content in the form of splash screens, icons, and the like. So the first thing you need to do is get some images and incorporate them into your project. Later, I'll show you how to use other kinds of resources, including fonts (for writing text) and sounds.

Unfortunately, I won't be able to help you create your graphics for use in computer games. I have no artistic abilities whatsoever, although I do know how to use a camera. If you need artistic resources, my advice is to find someone who is good at art and commission him or her to do the drawings for you. The same goes for any music or sounds that you might need.

This means that you can concentrate on what you are supposed to be good at: creating the game itself. This is what professional game developers do. They have a team of programmers who make the game work and a team of artists and sound technicians who work on the sensory aspects of the game. Having said that, you might be good at graphic design as well as programming, in which case you can do both. However, I'd still advise getting an artist involved, as it helps spread the work around and provides you with a useful sounding board for ideas. It also makes it more fun.

Getting Some Pictures

At this point, you'll need some pictures. The Xbox screen is capable of showing high-resolution images. A high-resolution image is made up of a large number of dots, or pixels. Modern digital cameras can create images that are thousands of pixels in height and width. However, from a game point of view, you want to make the images as small as you can. This reduces the amount of memory they consume and also reduces the work required to move them around the screen. For the games you'll create, you don't always need very high resolution, so your pictures need to be no more than 600 pixels in each direction.

There are a number of different formats for storing pictures on computers. Your pictures should be in the PNG (Portable Network Graphics), BMP (Windows Bitmap), or JPEG (Joint Photographic Experts Group) format. The PNG and BMP formats are lossless in that they always store an exact version of the image. PNG files can also have transparent regions, which is important when you want to draw one image on top of another. The JPEG format is "lossy" in that the image is compressed in a way that makes its storage space much smaller but at the expense of precise detail. The games that you create will use JPEG images for the large backgrounds and PNG images for the smaller objects that will be drawn on top of them.

If you have no pictures of your own (which I consider highly unlikely), you can use the ones that I have provided with the sample files for this chapter, but the games will work best if you use your own pictures. Figure 4-1 shows my picture of Jake. I will be using this for my first Xbox graphics programs. You can use another picture if you wish.

Figure 4-1   Jake

I have saved the image in the JPEG file format with a width of 600 pixels. If you need to convert into this format, you can load an image using the Microsoft Paint program and then save it in this format. With the Paint program, you can also scale and crop images if you want to reduce the number of pixels in the image. For more advanced image manipulation, I recommend the program Paint.Net, which you can obtain for free from *http://www.getpaint.net*.

Content Management Using XNA

As far as XNA is concerned, *content* (images, sounds, 3D models, and video) is what makes games more interesting. XNA treats items of content in the same way that variables are created in programs. XNA can import a content item of a particular type (e.g., my file containing a picture of Jake) and give it an identifier. When the game program is running, XNA fetches the game content items as they are requested by name. These content items are sometimes referred to as *assets*. In the same way that a company has assets such as buildings, machinery, and staff, a game has assets such as sounds and images.

Working with Content Using XNA Game Studio 2.0

You use XNA Game Studio 2.0 to put content into your game. When the finished program is constructed, XNA Game Studio 2.0 will make sure the assets are available to your game. The good news is that you don't need to worry about any of this; you need only know how to load assets into XNA Game Studio 2.0 and get a hold of them from within your game programs.

XNA Game Studio 2.0 Solutions and Projects

You start making a game by creating a brand-new project. I called mine `JakeDisplay`. You create the project using the New Project dialog box as you've done for all your previous projects. Remember that the project you are creating is either a Windows Game (2.0) or an Xbox Game (2.0). You can see this dialog box in use in Figure 1-16 in Chapter 1, "Computers, Xboxes, C#, XNA, and You." Note that the Create Directory For Solution option is selected in this dialog box. Whenever you create a project, you should ensure that this option is selected. This will create a directory structure that contains the program and all the other items that are required to make the game work.

Figure 4-2 shows what is created when I make a new project called `JakeDisplay`.

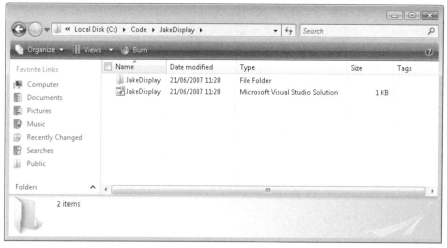

Figure 4-2   JakeDisplay solution directory

However, the file `JakeDisplay` that you can see in the directory is a solution. This might be confusing. You've used the `New Project` command in XNA Game Studio 2.0 and have ended up with a solution. In this case, XNA Game Studio 2.0 has created a solution called `JakeDisplay` and then added a single project to that solution. The project is also called `JakeDisplay`.

You can think of a *solution* as a "shopping list" of projects. Figure 4-3 shows how this works. The solution holds a list of the names of project files. Each of the project files holds a list of the names of the files used in that project. Each item on the list is often referred to as a *reference* to that item in that it will tell XNA Game Studio 2.0 how to get to it.

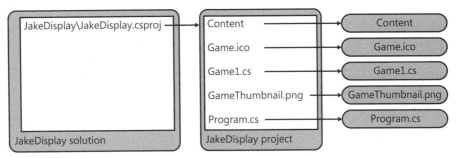

Figure 4-3   JakeDisplay solution

The solution file holds the name of the `JakeDisplay` project. The project file holds the names of the C# files in the project (Game1.cs and Program1.cs) and other resources used by the project, including the Content directory. At present, the only two resources are GameThumbnail.png, which is an image used as a thumbnail on the Xbox display when the game is stored on the Xbox, and Game.ico, which is the icon used for the game program file. When you add your image of Jake to the project, you'll add the name of the file to the project file so that XNA Game Studio 2.0 knows where to get the asset from. XNA Game Studio 2.0 displays the contents of the solution and project files as a diagram in the Solution Explorer, as shown in Figure 4-4. Note that the solution file and project files also contain other settings (the Properties and References) that you'll be using later.

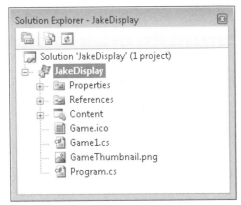

Figure 4-4   JakeDisplay in XNA Game Studio 2.0 Solution Explorer

Sometimes you may want to add additional projects to a solution so that you can separate your code into reusable portions or because you want to reuse code you already separated that way. For example, you might make a project called `HighScoreManager`, which would be in charge of displaying high-score tables for your game. High scores work the same way in many games, so it makes sense to write the code only once and then use it in those games. You would do this by creating a library project to deal with the high scores and then add this project to the "shopping list" of those projects. However, for now, you'll simply create games that are single projects.

> **The Great Programmer Speaks: Architecture Is Important**   Our Great Programmer is very keen on using projects to reuse code. The way she sees it, that way she can get paid several times for writing the same piece of software. When she starts work on a new system, she takes a lot of time to try to structure things into projects so that different parts of the system are in separate projects.

Adding Resources to a Project

An XNA Game Studio 2.0 project will contain references to everything that it uses. To keep things simple, you can keep everything used by a project in a single file directory. Figure 4-5 shows the content of the `JakeDisplay` project directory that XNA Game Studio 2.0 created for you when you made the new project. You can see the C# source files and also some other resources.

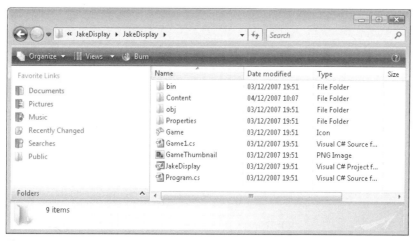

Figure 4-5   The contents of the JakeDisplay project directory

The project contains a Content directory. When you add an asset to this project, it will be stored in this directory. Figure 4-6 shows the JPEG image of Jake that I used in my Pictures directory. You need to place the picture you want to use into a directory somewhere on the computer.

Figure 4-6   My Jake image in my Pictures directory

You can either use one of the graphics images that are available in the sample projects or create your own picture at this point. Now that you have your graphics resource, you can tell XNA Game Studio 2.0 to use it. To do this, you need to add the content to the project. Resource references are added by using the Add Existing Item dialog box, which can be opened, as shown in Figure 4-7. Start by right-clicking the `JakeDisplay` Content item in Solution Explorer. From the menu that appears, select Add and then select Existing Item.

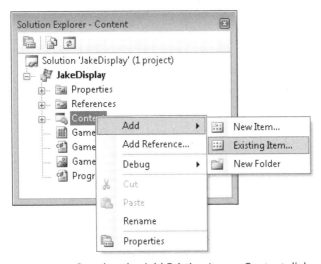

Figure 4-7   Opening the Add Existing Item – Content dialog box

Figure 4-8 shows the dialog box that you can use to select an item to add to the project.

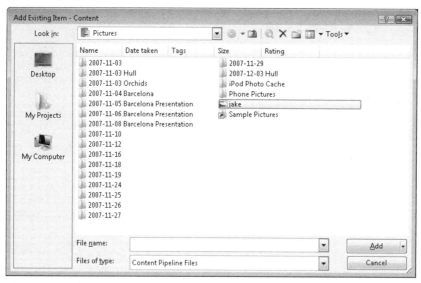

Figure 4-8   The Add Existing Item dialog box

Now you can select the image file that you want to use and click Add to add it. The project now contains the resource. Figure 4-9 shows the resource reference in the project once you've added it. You follow the same procedure to add other images to a game.

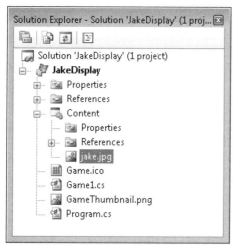

Figure 4-9   The JakeDisplay project containing the image resource

If you want to add more than one image to a project, simply repeat the process. Remember that each image is stored as part of the game program, so the more images you add, the larger your game becomes and the longer it takes to transfer it into the Xbox when it runs.

Adding Links to Resources

When you add a resource using the process described previously, XNA Game Studio 2.0 makes a copy of the resource and places the copy in the Content directory of the project. If you want several projects to share a single copy of a resource, you can instead add a link to it. You do this by clicking the down arrow at the right of the Add button in the Add Existing item dialog box, as shown in Figure 4-10. This will allow you to add the resource or add it as a link.

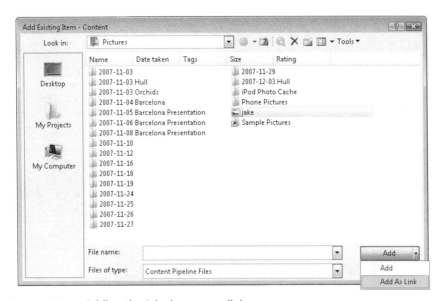

Figure 4-10   Adding the Jake image as a link

Each time XNA Game Studio 2.0 builds the game, it will follow the link to the resource to use it. If the resource is moved or deleted, the build process will fail.

The XNA Content Pipeline

This process of feeding resource in at one end and getting a complete game assembly out of the other is a bit like a *pipeline*. In fact, the XNA Framework refers to this part of the game-building process as the Content Management Pipeline.

Using Resources in a Game

You've done a lot of hard work, but your Xbox still can't draw any pictures. If you run the solution that you've created, you get the familiar blue screen. Next, you have to write some C# code that fetches the image resource and draws it on the screen at a particular position.

Loading XNA Textures

Within XNA, images that you want to draw in your games are called *textures*. Textures can be drawn as flat pictures, and they can also be wrapped around 3D models. You've already seen how to use the XNA **Color** type, which lets you manipulate color information. Now you'll use another type of XNA data variable so that you can work with your picture as a texture. XNA provides a range of types that are used to deal with textures. The type you'll use is called **Texture2D**. This holds a texture that you'll manipulate in two dimensions; that is, it will be drawn on the Xbox screen as if it were a flat surface.

You'll use the same program structure that you used for previous games. Members of your game class will represent the "game world." These will be updated by the **Update** method and used by the **Draw** method to draw the output.

However, you'll also make use of another method that lets the program get control when the graphics need to be loaded. Figure 4-11 shows how this works. It is a more detailed version of Figure 2-5 in Chapter 2, "Programs, Data, and Pretty Colors," which showed how XNA calls the **Draw** and **Update** methods as a game runs. It shows that there is also a **LoadContent** method that is called by XNA when a game starts running.

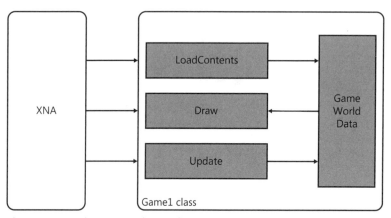

Figure 4-11 The Game1 class with the LoadContent method

You can think of **LoadContent** as another person in the Game1 office. That person has his or her own telephone. When the phone rings, that person is told whether he or she needs to load all the content and make it ready for use.

```
protected override void LoadContent()
{
    // Create a new SpriteBatch, which can be used to draw textures.
    spriteBatch = new SpriteBatch(GraphicsDevice);
    // TODO: use this.Content to load your game content here
}
```

In addition to loading the content that the game needs, the **LoadContent** method also creates a **SpriteBatch** for the program to use. You'll use this later to draw the texture on the screen. You've even been given a comment to tell you where to place the code that loads your texture. This is the place where the program must ask the Content Manager to fetch the texture.

```
Texture2D gameTexture;
...
protected override void LoadContent()
{
    // Create a new SpriteBatch, which can be used to draw textures.
    spriteBatch = new SpriteBatch(GraphicsDevice);
    gameTexture = this.Content.Load<Texture2D>("jake");
}
```

When the game starts, XNA will call the **LoadContent** method to fetch content for use in the game. The method will then perform the statement that loads the texture content.

```
gameTexture = Content.Load<Texture2D>("Jake");
```

The **Load** method is a kind of multipurpose tool called a *generic* method. Because it's generic, it can be used to fetch any kind of item, from textures to audio files to 3D models. You tell **Load** to fetch a **Texture2D** by placing the name of the type you want after the method name. You then give the method the asset that you want it to fetch. If you select the **Jake.jpg** item in Solution Explorer as shown in Figure 4-9 and then look in the XNA Game Studio 2.0 Properties pane (it should be in the lower right of the XNA Game Studio 2.0 window), you can see that the asset name has been taken from the file name of the resource. Figure 4-12 shows the property information for the Jake image resource.

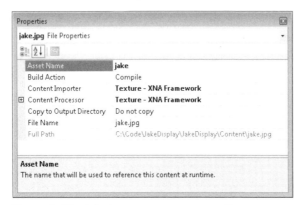

Figure 4-12   Jake image resource properties

This property information tells XNA Game Studio 2.0 where the image file is located, what to do with the file when the project is built, and the name to use in the program. So, once the **Load** method has completed, you have a copy of the image in the texture in your game. If the game had lots of different images, you would declare additional **Texture2D** items in your game world and load them using the **LoadContent** method as well.

If you get the name of the texture wrong, the game program will fail in this method, as it will be looking for an asset that is not there. The program fails by throwing an exception. Figure 4-13 shows the error that is produced if the asset name of a content item is incorrect.

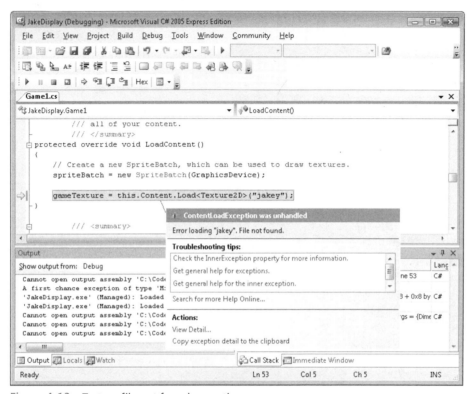

Figure 4-13   Texture file not found exception

Later, you'll find out how to get control when things go wrong like this; for now, you should make sure that the asset name you use in the call of **Load** matches the name of the content item.

> **The Great Programmer Speaks: Always Worry About Things Going Wrong**   Our Great Programmer spends a lot of time worrying about things that might go wrong. She reckons that in a commercial application, such as one that might be used in a bank, she has to write at least as much program code to deal with all the errors as she writes to do the actual job. Game programs are probably not as critical as bank code in that, if they go wrong, nobody will actually lose any money, but if a game constantly crashes, it will never become popular. Later, you'll see how to make sure that your program fails as seldom as possible.

Positioning Your Game Sprite on the Screen

In computer gaming terms, the image of Jake is a sprite. A *sprite* is a flat, preloaded image that is used as part of a computer game. Sprites can be large, such as background sky, or smaller, such as spaceships and missiles in a space shooter game. From the point of view of XNA, a sprite is an image resource along with location information that tells XNA where to draw the image. This means that you need a way to tell XNA where on the screen you want to put your sprite. You do this by using yet another XNA type, the `Rectangle`. This holds information about the position and size of a rectangle. You don't need to worry about how a rectangle works at the moment; you need to know only how to create one and set the size and position of it. Figure 4-14 shows how you use a rectangle to 2.0 where on the screen you want Jake to be drawn.

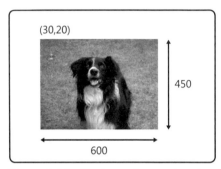

Figure 4-14   Placing a draw rectangle on the screen

The position of the rectangle is given by the coordinates of the top left-hand corner of the screen. You can regard the screen as a piece of graph paper. You express a position on the screen by giving an X coordinate value (the distance across the screen from the left) and a Y coordinate value (the distance down the screen from the top). This means that the position with the coordinate of (0, 0) is the top left corner. Note that this is not quite the same as graphs that you may have drawn in the past. In a conventional graph, the Y value increases as you go up the page. In computer graphics, the Y value increases as you move down the page.

In Figure 4-14, you can see that the top left-hand corner of the Jake sprite is at position (30, 20). This means 30 steps across and 20 down. The units are called pixels. *Pixel* is an abbreviation for "picture element" and refers to the smallest dot that can be drawn on the screen. The Xbox can drive displays with a range of different sizes, so the pixel at position (30, 20) may be a different physical distance across the screen, depending on the type of screen being used. Later, you'll find out how to write games that automatically scale themselves to fit any screen.

A rectangle is also used to give the width and height of the sprite. In Figure 4-14, I am drawing the sprite in an area that is 600 pixels wide and 450 pixels high. The good thing about this is that I don't have worry about the original size of the image; XNA will simply scale the image to fit in a rectangle that size. Later, you'll have some fun modifying the size. You can create a rectangle using **new**:

```
Rectangle spriteRect;
spriteRect = new Rectangle(30, 20, 600, 450);
```

This code declares a **Rectangle** variable and then sets it to one with the position and dimensions that you need. I've given the **Rectangle** variable the identifier **spriteRect**. This variable will be part of the game world. When the rectangle is created, it is passed the X, Y, width, and height values so that these can be held within the rectangle structure. This means that if you ever want to move the image or change its size on the screen, you need to change only one of the values that is held in the rectangle. These values are members of the **Rectangle** structure. In C#, members that hold values are called *fields*.

You can think of a field as a variable that has been declared inside of a structure or class. In the case of your **Game1** class, the game world data that you created (e.g., the color intensity values for your mood light) are fields of that class. Later, you'll see how to get hold of individual fields inside the **Rectangle** so that you can change its size and position.

The **Rectangle** needs to be created when the game program starts. You could do this in the **LoadContent** method, but XNA provides another place where it is more sensible, and that is the **Initialize** method. This is called when the game starts up. If all these methods are confusing, think about what happens when you have a party. This takes a number of steps:

1. Set up the tables and chairs.
2. Fetch the food and drink.
3. Repeatedly play music and dance.
4. Tidy up afterward.

When an XNA game runs, it goes through the same process:

1. Set things up: **Initialize**
2. Load game content: **LoadContent**
3. Repeatedly update the game and draw the display: **Draw** and **Update**
4. Free up all the content: **UnloadContent**

When the game ends, the XNA system will call the **UnloadContent** method. You can add statements to that method to explicitly release resources that your game has used, but for now you can leave this out.

In fact, you need not provide code for all these methods; they are there only so that you can get control at various points of the game's life cycle. The code that you put in the **Initialize** method needs to create a **Rectangle** with which to describe the destination of the draw operations:

```
Rectangle spriteRect;

protected override void Initialize()
{
    spriteRect = new Rectangle(30, 20, 600, 450);
    base.Initialize();
}
```

Sprite Drawing with SpriteBatch

You now have all the information about your sprite and are ready to draw it. Next, you need to take control in the **Draw** method and put your image onto the screen. But before you can do the drawing, you need to take some time out and discover more about how games consoles work.

A modern game console is not one powerful computer; in fact, it is several. Some of these run the game itself, while other special graphics processors drive the display. The graphics processor unit (GPU) contains optimized hardware to allow it to update the screen as fast as possible. When the **Draw** method runs, the method assembles a bunch of instructions for the GPU and sends the instructions into the GPU. The GPU then follows those instructions to put a picture on the screen. Complex games will contain many images that may be drawn at several different positions on the screen. It is important that the transfer of the position information and associated images is organized as efficiently as possible. XNA provides a special class called **SpriteBatch** to batch up a set of sprite-drawing instructions. Your program will call methods on a **SpriteBatch** variable to get the drawing done. This means that a **SpriteBatch** will need to be created for the program to use. When XNA Game Studio 2.0 creates a new project, it adds the statements to the **LoadContent** method that create a **SpriteBatch** for you to use. The variable is called **spriteBatch**.

> **Note**   It might look as if you have two items with the same name in your program. However, if you look carefully, you'll see that the class **SpriteBatch** has an uppercase "S" at the start, but the **spriteBatch** variable starts with a lowercase "s." This works because the C# compiler considers the case of the letter (whether it is large or small) as significant in an identifier. In other words, your program could have two variables, **Fred** and **fred**, and they would not be confused.

Now you can use **spriteBatch** to draw the sprite. You must tell **spriteBatch** when you've started drawing sprites and when you've finished.

```
protected override void Draw(GameTime gameTime)
{
    graphics.GraphicsDevice.Clear(Color.CornflowerBlue);
    spriteBatch.Begin();
    spriteBatch.Draw(gameTexture, spriteRect, Color.White);
    spriteBatch.End();
    base.Draw(gameTime);
}
```

You call methods on the **spriteBatch** variable to begin the draw process, draw the sprite, and then end the drawing. The **Draw** method is part of the **SpriteBatch** class and is given parameters that identify the image to be drawn, the rectangle to place it in, and the color of the light to "shine" on the texture.

> **Note**   The game class contains a **Draw** method that is used to draw the entire game, and the **SpriteBatch** class also contains a **Draw** method that is used to draw textures. While the methods have the same name and are both involved in the draw process, they actually do different things. However, both are performing a drawing operation in their own way, so it was appropriate for the designers of XNA to call them both **Draw** methods.

If you put a program together with the previously described methods, you can finally run a program that will display an image on the screen.

> **Sample Code: Jake Display**   The sample project in the 01 JakeDisplay directory in the resources for this chapter will draw a picture of Jake.

Figure 4-15 shows the output that you get when you run your program to display Jake on the screen.

Figure 4-15   Displaying Jake on a PC screen

If you change the content of the file Jake.jpg, you can make this program display other pictures.

Filling the Screen

It would be nice if the image that you display could exactly fill the screen. You've used values that will let you see the picture, but it does not completely cover the display, and if you run the program on differently configured Xbox systems, you'll notice that the picture takes up a different amount of space on the screen. It turns out that filling the screen is easy to do. Your program can ask the XNA environment the width and height of the screen and use this to set the size of the display rectangle:

```
spriteRect = new Rectangle(
    0,    // X position of top left hand corner
    0,    // Y position of top left hand corner
    graphics.GraphicsDevice.Viewport.Width,      //rectangle width
    graphics.GraphicsDevice.Viewport.Height);    //rectangle height
```

I've changed the layout of my call to construct the spriteRect variable. Rather than put everything on one line, I've spread the call out a bit and added some comments. This makes it easier to see what's happening. The code is constructing a `Rectangle` instance. When you do this, you can feed information into the construction process to set up the value. This particular call is feeding in the position of the top left-hand corner in the form of X and Y and the width and height of the rectangle that is required. I can get the width of the screen by using the following:

```
graphics.GraphicsDevice.Viewport.Width
```

This looks a bit scary but is easy to understand. It's rather like the way that we explain where things are. My office is on the third floor of the Robert Blackburn building on the Hull campus of the University of Hull. So you could express it as follows:

```
HullCampus.RobertBlackburn.ThirdFloor.RobMiles
```

The Hull campus contains a number of buildings, the Robert Blackburn building contains a number of floors, and so on. You can now find your way to my office by starting at the Hull campus, looking for the Robert Blackburn building, going to the third floor, and then finding the office with "Rob Miles" written on the door. The identifier is as follows: `graphics` `.GraphicsDevice.Viewport.Width` This means "start at the `graphics` variable, go to the `GraphicsDevice`, get the `Viewport`, and then get the `Width` field from it." The `graphics` variable is the Graphics Device manager for your program. It is created by XNA and contains methods and data that you can use in your program (you've already used the `Clear` method to clear the screen). The `graphics` variable contains a `GraphicsDevice`, which contains a `Viewport` and so on. Part of the skill of using XNA is knowing where these data items are.

Intellisense

You can find your way around the XNA framework by using the *Intellisense* feature, which is part of XNA Game Studio 2.0. Whenever you type an identifier into the editor, it will find the class, variable, or method that the identifier represents and offer you options based on that identifier. These options can save you a lot of typing. Figure 4-16 shows how it works. I have just typed the identifier **graphics** followed by the dot that separates it from the next item. Intellisense is showing me all the possible items that are valid in this context. I can scroll down the list, select the one I want by pressing Enter, and then move on to the next item.

```
protected override void Initialize()
{
    spriteRect = new Rectangle(
        0,                      // x position of top left corner
        0,                      // y position of top left corner
        graphics.
                    Disposed
    base.Init:      Equals
}                   GetHashCode
                    GetType
/// <summary>      GraphicsDevice
/// LoadConter     IsFullScreen              me and is the place to load
/// all of you     MinimumPixelShaderProfile
/// </summary:     MinimumVertexShaderProfile
protected over     PreferMultiSampling
{                   PreferredBackBufferFormat
    // Create                                 be used to draw textures.
    spriteBatch = new SpriteBatch(GraphicsDevice);
```

Figure 4-16   Intellisense for the Graphics Device manager

You can move quickly up and down the list of items by typing the first few letters of the item you want. Intellisense will also show you brief help snippets about the items. It makes writing programs much easier and reduces what you have to remember. The Great Programmer doesn't think she could write programs without it.

Sample Code: Jake Full Screen   The sample project in the 02 Jake Full Screen directory in the resources for this chapter will draw a picture of Jake that completely fills the screen.

Note   If you are using an Xbox that is connected to a TV, you might notice that not all the picture is visible. This is because TVs use an "overscanned" display, where only the middle part of the picture is displayed. You'll also find that if the shape of your picture does not exactly match that of the screen, the image will appear stretched. I'll discuss these problems of "aspect ratio" in a later chapter.

Game Idea: Color Nerve with a Picture

Now that you can display pictures, you can improve your Color Nerve game and display a picture rather than a blank background. This makes the game much more fun, especially if a familiar picture is used.

The key to this is the way that you select the color you'll use to "light" any sprite that you draw:

```
spriteBatch.Draw(gameTexture, spriteRect, Color.White);
```

When drawing this image, I used a white light so that the colors look natural. You can use light of any color, and XNA will process the image accordingly. If you want the image to be drawn more dimly, you can draw with the color gray; if you want to tint the image, you can simply change the color. You can use any color that you can create to tint your sprite:

```
protected override void Draw(GameTime gameTime)
{
  Color backgroundColor;
  backgroundColor = new Color(redIntensity,greenIntensity,blueIntensity);

  spriteBatch.Begin();
  spriteBatch.Draw(gameTexture, spriteRect, backgroundColor);
  spriteBatch.End();

  base.Draw(gameTime);
}
```

Rather than using white as the drawing color, this version of **Draw** uses the color it creates based on the red, green, and blue intensity values.

> **Sample Code: Jake Color Nerve**   The sample project in the 03 Image Color Nerve directory in the resources for this chapter is a version of Color Nerve that uses the picture of Jake. When you run the program, the image initially is completely black.

You can also use the same principle to make a picture mood light; this works especially well if you use a black-and-white image or one with really strong colors in it. You can also make a picture recognition game here where the aim of the game is to be the first one to recognize a picture as you slowly make it brighter.

> **Sample Code: Image MoodLight**   The sample project in the 04 Image MoodLight directory in the resources for this chapter is a version of the ultimate mood light that uses an image background. The image contains a pattern of blocks of different colors. One interesting challenge is to try to work out which of the blocks is white (only one of them is).

Conclusion

You have learned a lot in this chapter. You've seen how you can add graphical resources to XNA projects and use them in your game programs. You've also found out how images are positioned and drawn on the screen in XNA.

Pop Quiz

Just in case you thought you were having too much fun, here's a pop quiz to bring you back down to earth.

1. Images are managed by the C# compiler.

2. In an XNA program, an image can be held in a texture.

3. The `LoadGraphicsContent` method is used by XNA to load the graphics images onto the display.

4. A sprite is a small, pixie-like creature who lives with the fairies.

5. The `SpriteBatch` class is used to batch up sprites before they are drawn.

6. There is no need to add any code to the `Initialize` method to make an XNA game work.

7. The `Rectangle` has a `Width` field, which specifies how wide it is.

8. The XNA system can store only one image at a time.

Chapter 5
Writing Text

- Discover how text is drawn using XNA.

- Add some font resources to your XNA program.

- Draw some funky text.

- Create the biggest clock you've ever seen.

- Find out how to fake 3D images.

Introduction

Your programming skills are really coming along. Your programs can store different kinds of numbers, do things with them, and even make decisions. You also know how to add image assets to your games and place them on the screen.

Now you'll find out how to use some XNA features to make your games even better. Then you can move on to create fully formed games. The first thing you want to do is add some text output so that your games can talk to the players.

Program Project: Giant Clock

The Xbox and the PC each have clocks inside them so that they always know the date and time. You can use this to turn the entire display into a giant digital clock.

Text and Computers

In the early days of computers, the appearance of text that you could print was limited by the shapes built into a mechanical printer. Later, dot-matrix, laser, and ink-jet printers came along, giving high-resolution graphical displays that could draw any character design you wanted. The Xbox is capable of showing very high resolution images, and you can use this ability to display text.

Text as a Resource

Before you can start drawing text on the Xbox, you need to understand just how computers manage character designs. The design of the shape of the characters is described in a *font* file. Windows provides a very large number of these font files. The shape of the text that you are reading now is described in a font called "**Times New Roman**." Windows also provides a font called "**Arial**," used in this book for headings, and "`Courier New`," used here for program listings.

The font file gives the shape of each of the characters. When a character shape is needed for either printing on paper or drawing on the screen, the font data is used to draw this shape at the required size. To get an XNA program to display text in a particular font, you need to decide which font you want to draw and then add a reference to that font file to the program project. You then use the XNA Content Management System to bring the font into the program for use when you want to draw text.

Creating the XNA Clock Project

You create the project (called `BigClock`) using the New Project dialog box, as you've done for all your previous projects. You can see this dialog box in use in Figure 1-4 in Chapter 1, "Computers, Xboxes, C#, XNA, and You." Note that the Create Directory For Solution option is selected in this dialog box. Whenever you create a project, you should ensure that this option is selected.

Adding a Font Resource

When you want to use a picture, you need to add a reference to the picture. You use a font in the same way, except that you want to create the font reference as well as add it to the project. Figure 5-1 shows how to do this. Right-click the Content item in the `BigClock` project in Solution Explorer, then select Add and then New Item.

You can add a number of different kinds of new items to a project. Figure 5-2 shows the dialog box that lets you select the kind of item you wish to add.

The range of items that you can add to your project depends on how many other Visual Studio components you have installed. You might have more items available than those shown in Figure 5-2. If you select the Sprite Font item, you can create a sprite font reference.

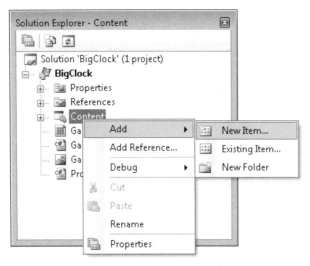

Figure 5-1   Adding a new item

When you do this, you'll find that XNA Game Studio 2.0 has filled in the Name information at the bottom of the dialog box with `SpriteFont1.spritefont`. This font doesn't exist; rather, it's simply a placeholder. You need to change the name of the font to one that's on the computer. I suggest that you use `Arial.spritefont`, as shown in Figure 5-2. This is the name of one of the fonts supplied as part of Windows. You can use a different font if you want. If the name you give does not match a font that's installed on your computer, you'll find that you won't be able to build your program, as the Content Manager will be unable to find the requested item.

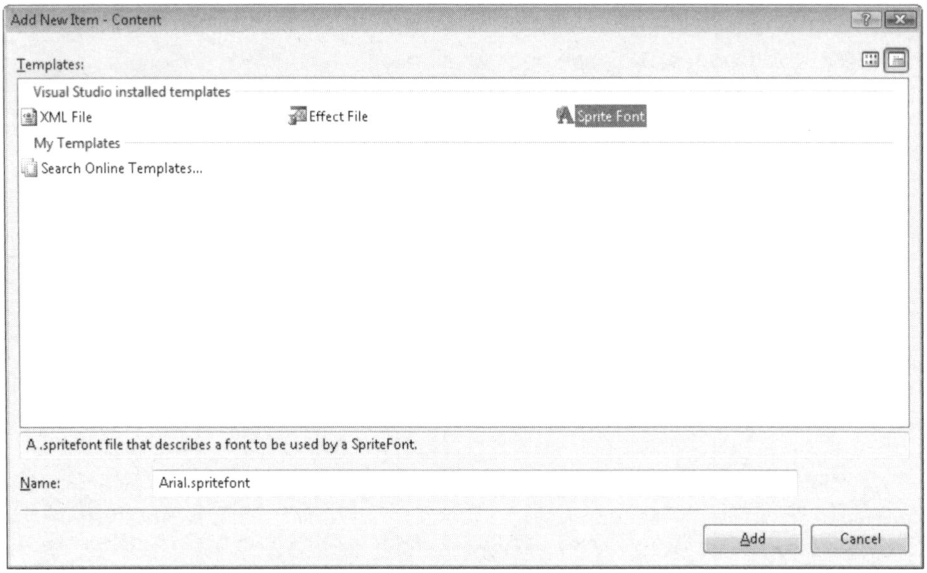

Figure 5-2   Selecting a new item

You can have more than one font in your game if required, but you need to add each font that you want to use as another resource. Remember, though, that adding extra fonts will make your output program bigger, as the character designs need to be made part of the program. The name that you give must match a font available on the computer that's being used to build the game because the XNA Content Manager will use the font file on the host computer to build the sprite design for use in your XNA program.

Figure 5-3 shows the font item in Solution Explorer in XNA Game Studio 2.0 as added to the project. If you select this item in Solution Explorer and open it by double-clicking it, you can see that it's a file describing the font that's to be used in your program.

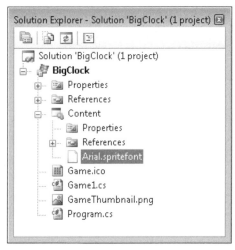

Figure 5-3   The font reference in the BigClock project

> **Note**   It's important you understand what's happening here. When you add a resource to a project, you simply add a reference to the thing that you want to use. You can think of the reference as an item on a shopping list. Just like an item on a shopping list would remind you to buy a new toothbrush the next time you were shopping, a resource reference tells the Content Pipeline that a certain resource must be fetched when the program is to be built.

When the project is built, the Content Pipeline follows the reference to the required item and then adds it to the program that's being built. The purpose of the resource information is to tell the Content Manager what to retrieve and how to use the resource in the project.

This reference file is not written in C#, nor is it plain text. It's written in a format called *Extensible Markup Language*, or XML.

The XML File Format

A markup language is one that's used to describe things. It contains the names of these things and information about them. XML is extensible, so you can use it to describe just about anything. As an example, a snippet of XML that describes a high score might look as follows:

```
<?xml version = "1.0" encoding = "us-ascii"?>
<highscore game = "Breakout">
   <playername>Rob Miles</playername>
   <score>1500</score>
</highscore>
```

This high-score information is for the game Breakout and shows the name of the player and the score the player reached. The format of the lines and the way that the open bracket (<) and close bracket (>) characters are used to denote the names of the values and the values themselves are defined in the XML standard. The first line of the snippet identifies which version of XML you're using for the rest of the data. The nice thing about XML is that it's easy to understand the content, and it's a very well-established way in which computer software can exchange information.

In the case of your font, the XML tells the Content Pipeline the name of the font to fetch, the size of the font, whether it's to be drawn as bold or italic, and other font-related information. You don't need to worry too much about what's in this file at the moment, but you can take a look if you wish. Later, you'll change the content of this file to change the size of the characters that are drawn.

Loading a Font

The XNA Content Manager will fetch a font and make it available for use in a very similar way to the images that you've used before. Each character design will be delivered to your program as a little image. You'll then use a **SpriteBatch** instance to draw the characters on the screen. For your clock, the game world consists of the **SpriteFont**, which you will have loaded. **SpriteFont** is yet another XNA type (there are many more). Your **SpriteFont** will hold information about a font that the Content Manager has loaded for you. You can declare the variable for the game world as follows:

```
// Game World
SpriteFont font;
```

The font can be loaded in the **LoadContent** method.

```
protected override void LoadContent()
{
   // Create a new SpriteBatch, which can be used to draw textures.
   spriteBatch = new SpriteBatch(GraphicsDevice);
   font = Content.Load<SpriteFont>("Arial");
}
```

At this point, you might be experiencing déjà vu or at least think you've seen this code before. The pattern is the same as when you loaded your images, and even the name of the method is the same. However, this time you're using the generic **Load** method to fetch a **SpriteFont** rather than a `Texture2D`. There is some strong programming magic at work here, but fortunately you don't need to worry about this at the moment; all you need to know is that the `Load` method will get whatever type it is asked to fetch. Later, you'll create some games that contain textures, fonts, and sounds, and for each type the `Load` method will behave in an appropriate manner.

Drawing with a Font

Now that you have your font, you can draw with it. Remember that when you used the textures in Chapter 4, "Displaying Images," you used a `Rectangle` to tell the `Draw` method where to locate the texture. However, when drawing text, you don't do this. Instead, you use a *vector*, which tells the `Draw` method where on the screen to start. "Vector" is a posh word for "direction and distance." You're using the 2D (X and Y value) version of the vector. Games that work in 3D space use values of X, Y, and Z (where Z is the depth value).

A 2D vector is given as two coordinates: the X value and the Y value. It's a bit like a treasure map that pirates used to use. A pirate would say, "Start ye at the Old Oak Tree and take ye two hundred paces East and three hundred paces South, and there ye shall find my treasure chest." The vector says, "Start at the origin and move 200 units across and 300 units down." If you think about it, this means that a vector indeed does specify a direction in that a very smart pirate could work out that he could "cut the corner" and get to the treasure more quickly by moving in the appropriate direction. Figure 5-4 shows how this would work, with a line showing the direct path to Blackbeard's treasure.

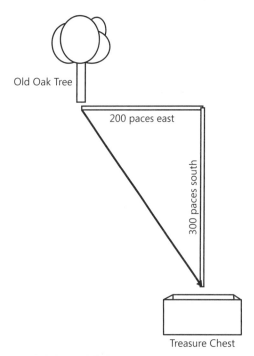

Figure 5-4   Vectors and directions

In a text-drawing program, you're using a vector like a coordinate in that it specifies the top left-hand corner of the text you're about to draw. You feed it into the **DrawText** method as follows:

```
protected override void Draw(GameTime gameTime)
{
    graphics.GraphicsDevice.Clear(Color.CornflowerBlue);
    Vector2 textVector = new Vector2(200, 300);
    spriteBatch.Begin();
    spriteBatch.DrawString(font, "Hello World", textVector, Color.Red);
    spriteBatch.End();
    base.Draw(gameTime);
}
```

You've placed the top left-hand corner of the text at the spot 200 pixels across the screen and 300 pixels down. The text that you're writing is the famous string "Hello World," which is, by one of the laws of the universe, what your first program that prints text should say. In a C# program, you enter a string as a sequence of characters enclosed in double quotation marks. You're printing the text in **Red**. If you run this program, you get the display shown in Figure 5-5.

Figure 5-5   "Hello World" on the big screen

While it is perfectly okay to make your first program print something other than "Hello World," I take no responsibility for any misfortune that you suffer as a result of offending the programming gods in this way.

> **Sample Code: "Hello World"**   You can make your "Hello World" program by creating an empty project, adding the font reference, and then adding the game world section and the **Initialize**, **LoadContent**, and **Draw** methods described previously. If you don't fancy doing that, you can load the sample project in the 01 Hello World directory in the resources for this chapter, which will write "Hello World" on the screen. Either flesh out your own BigClock solution or just open the **01 Hello World** method to continue with the rest of the chapter.

Changing the Font Properties

The program works okay, but you really wanted something larger than such small text. It is possible to scale text sprites, but at the moment it's easiest to get larger text simply by changing the XML in the **SpriteFont** resource file. This also means that if anybody asks you what you were doing today, you can say, "Oh, I hand coded some XML," which should impress them a bit. To get hold of the file that describes the font, open it by double-clicking it in Solution Explorer for the **BigClock** project. Figure 5-6 shows which item to select.

Figure 5-6   Selecting the Arial SpriteFont resource

The left-hand window in XNA Game Studio 2.0 will change to show you the XML that describes the font to be loaded. Figure 5-7 shows the XML; I've added boxes around the most important items.

You can change the name of the font that you want to use, the size of the font, the spacing between letters, and the style. You can change the **FontName** to select any font installed on your computer. Use Control Panel on your Microsoft Windows operating system to find out what fonts are available. Make sure you type the name correctly, including spaces and capital letters. The other values are fairly self-explanatory. Change them to whatever value you think best. When you next build the program, the new values are used. You'll need to adjust the font size depending on the font design that you select. I've found that a font size of 100 gives nice large text using the Arial font that you started with.

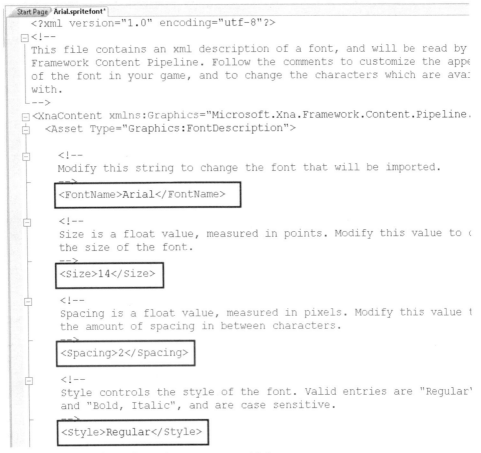

Figure 5-7   Modifying the SpriteFont resource XML

Getting the Date and Time

You can now display text on the screen in a variety of sizes and fonts. You could use this to write a program that simply displays messages on the screen. Next, you need a way to determine the correct time for the clock in your program to display. Both the PC and the Xbox have internal clock hardware that is used by some games to change the way they play so that, for example, if it's dark outside, it's dark in the game as well. To accomplish this, the XNA Framework must provide a way of finding the date and time.

The date and time values are held in a special structure called DateTime. You already know that XNA provides types that are tailored to different needs. You've seen the Color type, the Texture2D type, and the SpriteFont type, to name a few. The DateTime type holds all the information about the date and time of a particular instant. The structure is not part of XNA as such; rather, it's part of the Microsoft .NET Framework, which provides resources to all C# programs. Thus, when you want to manipulate dates and times in a C# program running on a Windows operating system, you can do it in exactly the same way.

For your clock you need a DateTime structure that's set to the current date and time. It turns out that DateTime provides a *property* that will create one for you. A property is a value or setting that an object in a C# program can expose for you to use. You've already seen these; when you used Color.CornflowerBlue, you were asking the Color structure to give you a color that represents that shade of blue. You use DateTime.Now in the same way. Later, when you start using structures and classes to design more complicated game programs, you'll get more of an insight into how all this works. For now, you'll simply get a DateTime value that holds the current time and use that to drive your clock.

```
DateTime dateTimeNow = DateTime.Now;
```

The Now property of the DateTime structure is always set to the current date and time. This works by taking values from an internal hardware clock, which means that after a while the value will be out of date. In fact, you could use a DateTime variable to record the time at which the game was started. Later, you'll see how to do calculations on dates and times so that you can tell how much time has gone by.

Once you have your DateTime variable, you can ask it to do things for you. One thing it can do is give you a string that contains the time in text form.

```
DateTime nowDateTime = DateTime.Now;
string nowString = nowDateTime.ToLongTimeString();
```

These two statements create a variable of type DateTime, which holds the current date and time, and then use this to create a string. A string does exactly what you would expect: it holds a string of text. The DateTime structure contains a method with the identifier ToLongTimeString. You know that objects contain methods; this method has the job of converting the date and time information inside the object into a string that you can put on the screen in text form. In fact, DateTime provides several methods that you can use (see Table 5-1).

Table 5-1   **Some DateTime String Methods**

Method Call	Output
ToLongTimeString()	7:07:07 AM
ToShortTimeString()	7:07 AM
ToLongDateString()	Saturday, July 07, 2007
ToShortDateString()	7/7/2007
ToString()	7/7/2007 7:07:07 AM

You can think of these methods as a number of different people sitting in the `DateTime` office. All of them have their own telephone and can be asked to deliver an appropriately formatted string of text. You can call any of these methods to get a string of text that describes the value being held by the variable **nowDateTime**. You can use them to add the date and time to your clock if you wish.

> **Note**   The precise format of the date and time produced depends on the *localization* of your system. Both Windows and the Xbox are configured to display the date and time in a manner in keeping with the country where they are being used. The previously given samples are for an Xbox in use in the UK. Yours might look slightly different.

Putting all this together, you can create a version of the **Draw** method that will display the current time on your screen.

```
protected override void Draw(GameTime gameTime)
{
    graphics.GraphicsDevice.Clear(Color.CornflowerBlue);
    DateTime nowDateTime = DateTime.Now;
    string nowString = nowDateTime.ToLongTimeString();
    Vector2 nowVector = new Vector2(50, 400);

    spriteBatch.Begin();
    spriteBatch.DrawString(font, nowString, nowVector, Color.Red);
    spriteBatch.End();

    base.Draw(gameTime);
}
```

I've changed the name of the vector to **nowVector** to make it better describe what it is used for. I've also moved the draw position so that if you set the font size to 100, this **Draw** method will give you a big clock on your Xbox that nicely fills the bottom of the screen.

> **Sample Code: Big Clock**   The sample project in the 02 Big Clock directory in the resources for this chapter contains an XNA Game Studio 2.0 solution for the program in this section. Note that both Xbox and PC versions are available. However, you should remember that because of localization differences, you might not see exactly the same display on each device.

Because the **Draw** and **Update** methods are called automatically for you by the XNA environment, the clock will be repeatedly redrawn with the up-to-date time.

Making a Prettier Clock with 3D Text

At the moment, your clock is very boring; it just displays the time in red on a blue background. You can make the text more interesting by changing the way that you draw the time. This kind of multiple drawing is performed a lot in computer games.

Drawing Multiple Text Strings

One way to make the display more interesting is to draw different-colored versions of the text at slightly different positions on the screen.

```
protected override void Draw(GameTime gameTime)
{
    graphics.GraphicsDevice.Clear(Color.CornflowerBlue);
    DateTime nowDateTime = DateTime.Now;
    string nowString = nowDateTime.ToLongTimeString();
    Vector2 nowVector = new Vector2(50, 400);

    spriteBatch.Begin();
    spriteBatch.DrawString(font, nowString, nowVector, Color.Red);

    nowVector.X = nowVector.X + 4;
    nowVector.Y = nowVector.Y + 4;

    spriteBatch.DrawString(font, nowString, nowVector, Color.Yellow);
    spriteBatch.End();
    base.Draw(gameTime);
}
```

This version of the **Draw** method is very similar to the original, except that **DrawString** is now called twice, first drawing in red and then in yellow. In between the draw operations, the values of the **X** and **Y** properties of the position vector are increased by 4 using the following statements:

```
nowVector.X = nowVector.X + 4;
nowVector.Y = nowVector.Y + 4;
```

Figure 5-8 shows how this works. The thing on the right-hand side of the "gozzinta" is an *expression*. This generates a result that is then placed in the destination.

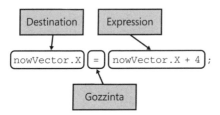

Figure 5-8   A statement that evaluates an expression and updates the value for a variable

The sequence of instructions that the compiler creates to work out the statement is as follows:

1. Fetch the value of the **X** property of **nowVector**

2. Add 4 to it

3. Store the value back in the **X** property of **nowVector**

The effect of adding 4 to the **X** and **Y** properties is to move the drawing position for the text across and down the screen. Figure 5-9 shows the result of these changes.

Figure 5-9   A more interesting time display

From this, you can see that when you draw on the screen, the images are laid on top of each other in the order they are drawn. The red version of the time string is overwritten by the yellow one. The nice thing about this approach is that it gives a good 3D effect. The human eye is happy to interpret the darker color as being in the "background," making the letters appear to stand out of the display. However, the 3D effect is not quite perfect. The image in Figure 5-10 is an enlargement of part of the text and shows that the red part is not actually "solid"; instead, it's simply a layer drawn behind the yellow one.

Figure 5-10   Detail of the overwritten text

If you want the 3D effect to be perfect, you need to draw lots more red versions to "fill in the gaps." You could do this by simply copying the code four times, but perhaps you remember reading somewhere that computers are supposed to make life easier, and this doesn't feel very easy at all. What you really want to do is perform a block of statements for a given number of times, and it turns out that C# provides a way to do this: it's called the **for** loop construction.

Repeating Statements with a for Loop

A program can do three things as it runs. It can perform a single action (a statement), it can make a choice of what to do (a condition statement), or it can repeat something (a loop construction). It might surprise you to learn that with these three programming constructions, you could write any program. You've seen how to write statements and conditions; now you need to discover how to create a loop. With a loop, you need to write the drawing instructions only once, and the loop construction will then perform them as many times as you like.

```
spriteBatch.Begin();
int layer;
for (layer = 0; layer < 4; layer++)
{
    spriteBatch.DrawString(font, nowString, nowVector, Color.Red);
    nowVector.X++;
    nowVector.Y++;
}
spriteBatch.DrawString(font, nowString, nowVector, Color.Yellow);
spriteBatch.End();
```

This code will perform four drawing operations with the red color. The code in the block controlled by the **for** will be repeated a given number of times. When the loop finishes, the final **DrawString** will put the yellow version on top of all the red ones. Note that the yellow **DrawString** is not repeated four times because it is not inside the block of code controlled by the **for** loop.

The loop itself is controlled by the three items in brackets that follow the keyword **for**. These are shown in Figure 5-11.

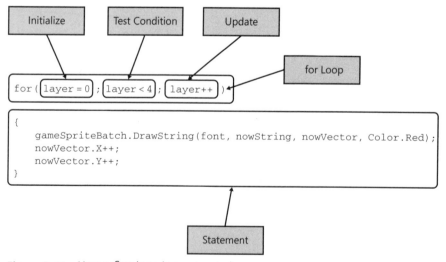

Figure 5-11   How a **for** loop is constructed

Each of the three items is used to manage the behavior of the loop, described in the following list:

- **Initialize**   This is a statement that is obeyed when the loop starts. In this example, you're using an integer variable called `layer` to count each of the layers that you're drawing. The loop must set this to zero at the beginning.

- **Test Condition**   The condition controls when the loop finishes. It can be either `true` (the loop continues) or `false` (the loop ends). The condition in your loop is `layer < 4`. You might not have seen the `<` operator before; it performs a "less than" comparison between the two operands. If the item on the left is less than the item on the right, the result of the comparison is `true`. If the item on the left is not less than the item on the right, the result of the comparison is `false`. C# provides a range of different comparison operators.

- **Update**   Each time the statements in the loop are completed, the update is performed. In this case, the update statement `layer++` makes the value in `layer` 1 larger each time. After the update has been performed, the test condition is evaluated to see whether the statements controlled by the loop are to be obeyed again.

The C# compiler has the job of producing the machine instructions that will perform the loop when the program runs. The precise sequence that's followed by the code that the compiler produces is as follows:

1. Perform the initialization statement to start the loop.

2. Perform the test and finish if the test is false.

3. Perform the statement in the loop body.

4. Perform the update statement.

5. Go to step 2.

This is not the only kind of loop construction that C# provides. It is also possible to perform loops while conditions are true.

> **Sample Code: 3D Big Clock**   The sample project in the 03 3D Big Clock directory in the resources for this chapter contains an XNA Game Studio 2.0 solution that uses a **for** loop to draw multiple versions of the time.

Other Loop Constructions

C# also provides two other loop constructions, called **do – while** and **while**. These are not really vital in that you can always get the looping behavior that you want by using an appropriately designed **for** loop, but they can be useful in situations where you don't want to go to the trouble of creating a **for** loop construction. You can find out more about these kinds of loops and when they would be useful in the glossary.

Fun with for Loops

You can test your understanding of the **for** loop behavior by looking at some **for** loops and trying to work out what they would do.

```
for (layer=0; layer > 4; layer++)
```

There's a mistake in this statement, but it's rather hard to spot. The mistake is that the test is now **layer > 4**. The > character means "greater than." This means that the test is now true only when the value of **layer** is greater than 4. Since **Initialize** sets the value of **layer** to 0, this condition will never be true. The result of this is that the code in the statement controlled by the loop is never performed.

```
for (layer=0; layer < 4; layer--)
```

There's another mistake here. The less-than character (<) is in the correct place, but rather than increasing the value of **layer** each time around, the update will make **layer** smaller by using the -- operator each time. This means that the value of **layer** will never become greater than 4, so the loop will never end. The result is that your program will appear to "get stuck" at this point.

You can write code to request this if you really want a loop that goes on forever.

```
for (layer=0; true; layer--)
```

Simply putting the value **true** in the position of the condition will cause the loop to never stop. If you're wondering what would happen if you ran a loop like this, you can try it if you like, but I can save you the trouble. If you run either of these never-ending loops, you'll eventually get the message shown in Figure 5-12. This is the message that XNA displays when it runs out of memory.

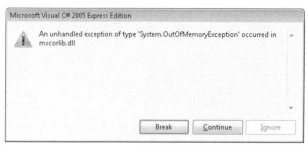

Figure 5-12   Out-of-memory error message

The reason you get this message is that each time the **DrawString** method is called in the body of the loop, it uses a small amount of memory to record what will be drawn. If you call the method a large number of times, it will eventually use up all the memory available for this purpose, and the program will stop. The good news is that this doesn't cause any damage to your Xbox or PC, but it will cause serious damage to your credibility if one of your programs ever does this.

One of the nice things about loops is that you can get a lot more work done by the computer simply by changing the values that cause them to stop.

```
for (layer = 0; layer < 40; layer++)
```

This version of the loop will draw 40 red time values before putting the yellow one on top. It gives rise to the rather funky display shown in Figure 5-13.

Figure 5-13   Funky time

This is nice, but you can do even better. You can make the display even more funky by using some other drawing tricks that XNA provides.

Creating Fake 3D

Lots of the graphics in games are faked. Rather than make something 3D, a game programmer will make something that looks 3D but turns out to be much easier to program. Now, you'll make some 3D text, but you won't use any complicated rendering or models (although the Xbox can do this kind of thing if required). You'll use only two principles:

Things that are 3D have shadows.

Things that have the light shining directly on them look the brightest.

This means that you'll need to draw your text in three stages. First, you draw the shadows, then the "sides" of the text, and finally the top layer of the text. This seems like a lot of work, but, as Figure 5-14 shows, I think it's worth the effort.

Figure 5-14   3D text that jumps out of the screen

Creating Shadows Using Transparent Colors

The first part of the text that you want to draw is the shadow at the back. You'll draw your picture from the back forwards and use the fact that each time you draw, you add to what's already there. You'll use another feature of XNA drawing: colors that cause things to be drawn slightly transparent (that is, with part of the background showing through). By drawing transparent colors on top of each other, you can get a nice blurry effect.

```
Color nowColor = new Color(0,0,0,20);
for (layer = 0; layer < 10; layer++)
{
   spriteBatch.DrawString(font, nowString, nowVector, nowColor);
   nowVector.X++;
   nowVector.Y++;
}
```

This code is very similar to the previous code that draws the 3D text, except that it creates the value for **nowColor** in a slightly different way. The **Color** is constructed from four values rather than three.

```
Color nowColor = new Color(0,0,0,20);
```

The first three values give the intensity of red, green, and blue, which you've set to 0 because you're drawing in black. The fourth gives the transparency of the color. In graphical terms, this is often called the "alpha" channel value. The bigger the number, the less the background will show through. Just like your color intensity values, the transparency value can range from 0 (completely transparent) to 255 (solid color). If you don't give a transparency value, the **Color** is created as solid.

A value of 20 means that a lot of the background will show through the color that you draw. Figure 5-15 shows the display produced by drawing 10 times using a transparent black value. Note that because each of the drawing positions is slightly different, you get a blurring effect.

Figure 5-15   Creating a shadow using transparent colors

This works rather well in that the text is nicely blurred around the edges, as a shadow would be. Now you know one way how video games achieve blur. They can do it by repeatedly redrawing the same scene in slightly different positions.

The next part of the drawing process uses the same technique you've used before, except that you use slightly different colors. The complete drawing method is as follows:

```
protected override void Draw(GameTime gameTime)
{
   graphics.GraphicsDevice.Clear(Color.CornflowerBlue);

   DateTime nowDateTime = DateTime.Now;
   string nowString = nowDateTime.ToLongTimeString();
   Vector2 nowVector = new Vector2(50, 400);
   int layer;

   spriteBatch.Begin();

   // Draw the shadow
   Color nowColor = new Color(0, 0, 0, 20);
   for (layer = 0; layer < 10; layer++)
   {
     spriteBatch.DrawString(font, nowString, nowVector, nowColor);
     nowVector.X++;
     nowVector.Y++;
   }

   // Draw the solid part of the characters
   nowColor = Color.Gray;
   for (layer = 0; layer < 5; layer++)
   {
     spriteBatch.DrawString(font, nowString, nowVector, nowColor);
     nowVector.X++;
     nowVector.Y++;
   }

   // Draw the top of the characters
   spriteBatch.DrawString(font, nowString, nowVector, Color.White);
   spriteBatch.End();

   base.Draw(gameTime);
}
```

This produces the display shown in Figure 5-14.

> **Sample Code: 3D Shadow Clocks**   The sample project in the 04 3D Shadow Clock direc-
> tory in the resources for this chapter contains an XNA Game Studio 2.0 solution that contains
> a program that shows the 3D time over a blue background. If you want to draw the time over
> a picture, you can take a look in the 05 3D Picture Clock directory, which draws the same
> clock over a picture of Jake. Finally, if you want to see the time over your mood light, you can
> take a look in the 06 3D Clock Mood Light directory.

Drawing Images with Transparency

Something else that's useful is that if you draw an image using a color that has a transparency value, the image is drawn transparently. This is how game programmers get pictures to slowly fade onto the screen. The image is repeatedly drawn with different levels of transparency to make it slowly appear over a background.

Conclusion

In this chapter, you've learned how to add font resources to your programs. You've also gained a bit of insight into how 3D effects can be created from 2D images. You've also seen how you can use the **for** loop construction to repeat code a particular number of times.

Pop Quiz

At the risk of being somewhat predictable, the chapter ends with another pop quiz.

1. A font describes the color of the text to be printed.

2. An XNA game can use only one font to draw text.

3. The Content Manager creates your fonts.

4. A resource in an XNA project is a reference to an item that must be included in the game file when the program is built.

5. XML stands for Xbox Machine Language and is used to design the font graphics.

6. A vector describes a direction and distance of movement.

7. The first program you write that can print should display "Hello Mum."

8. The Xbox requires a network connection to load the date and time.

9. Dates and times are printed the same all over the world.

10. The **DateTime** structure holds the value of a particular date and time.

11. A property of an object cannot be used outside that object.

12. You can call the **ToString()** method on an object to ask the object to supply a text description of itself.

13. A **for** loop construction always runs forever.

14. The C# code **for (layer = 0; layer < 4; layer++)** would repeat five times.

15. After a loop controlled by the C# code **for (layer = 0; layer <= 10; layer++)** has completed, the value in layer would be 10.

16. The C# code **for (layer = 4; layer < 0; layer++)** would repeat zero times.

17. The C# code **for (layer = 4; layer > 0; layer++)** would repeat infinite times.

18. Colors can be made "transparent."

Chapter 6

Creating a Multiplayer Game

- Discover how to detect and use individual key-press events in a game.

- See how to create and debug a complex program.

- Write one of the only 16-player games for the Xbox in the world.

Introduction

Now that you can write programs that process data, read input from the gamepad, and display text and graphics, you can move on to create some proper games. The first games that you are going to create are simple to use and play but are great fun, particularly if you have large numbers of people around to play them. While you create the behaviors for the games, you'll also learn some more C# constructions that can be used in any game.

> ### Game Idea: Button-Bashing Mob
>
> One very popular and easy-to-create game is one where a player has to press a button as quickly as possible. Players compete against each other, and the winner is the one who can press the button most in a given time. Because each gamepad has four buttons and the Xbox can support four gamepads, up to 16 players can take part for maximum button-bashing fun.

To get started, you'll need to create an empty project called ButtonBash. This will need to be able to display text. The best way to do this is to create a new project and then initialize and load the font as for the Hello World application in Chapter 5, "Writing Text."

To create the game, you'll first build a program that will count and display the presses of a single button on the gamepad. Then you can scale up the program and use more buttons. This is a very common programming technique. "Make a button-bashing game for 16 players" sounds a bit daunting, but "make a program that will count how many times the B button on gamepad 1 is pressed" is something you can probably do. Your program will need to keep track of the number of times the button has been pressed. You can use an integer to hold the value.

```
int count;
```

The range of an **int** variable in C# can go over 2,000,000,000. It's unlikely that anyone could press a button that number of times in a minute. The game could be started by pressing the Start button on the gamepad to zero the counter. You can do this in the **Update** method.

```
protected override void Update(GameTime gameTime)
{
    // Allows the game to exit
    if (GamePad.GetState(PlayerIndex.One).Buttons.Back==ButtonState.Pressed)
        this.Exit();
    GamePadState pad1 = GamePad.GetState(PlayerIndex.One);
    if (pad1.Buttons.Start == ButtonState.Pressed)
    {
        count = 0;
    }
    base.Update(gameTime);
}
```

When the Start button is pressed, the conditional statement in the **Update** method sets **count** to 0. You can use a variant of the clock program **Draw** method to display the value in **count**.

```
protected override void Draw(GameTime gameTime)
{
    graphics.GraphicsDevice.Clear(Color.CornflowerBlue);
    string countString = count.ToString();
    Vector2 countVector = new Vector2(50, 400);
    spriteBatch.Begin();
    spriteBatch.DrawString(font, countString, countVector, Color.Red);
    spriteBatch.End();
    base.Draw(gameTime);
}
```

Running this program will give you what you expect: the value 0 displayed on the screen. Now you need to add the statements to the **Update** method that will count the number of times that the B button has been pressed.

```
if (pad1.Buttons.B == ButtonState.Pressed)
{
    count++;
}
```

This seems to be what you want; if the condition is true, the counter will be incremented.

Sample Code: Broken Button Bash · The sample project in the 01 Broken Button Bash directory in the resources for this chapter contains an XNA Game Studio 2.0 solution that contains a program that uses the previously mentioned **Update** method in this section to implement a test button-bashing program.

You might have gathered from the example's title, "01 Broken Button Bash," that this won't work. This is because the **Update** method is called 60 times a second. If you hold down the button, you'll find that each time **Update** is called, the value of **count** gets one bigger, so the score goes up at a rate of 60 times a second. This is impressive (and might be the basis of other games in the future), but it won't give you the game you want. You need to find a way of detecting when the button has moved from the up to the down position. Your program must increase **count** only when this happens, not when the button is simply in the down position. Figure 6-1 shows the sequence of events when the button is pressed. The **Update** method is being called at regular intervals. At some point, the B button is pressed. This means that when **Update** is called the first time in the figure, it detects that B is up, and the second time it is called in the figure, it detects that B has been pressed.

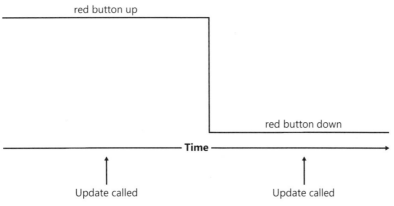

Figure 6-1   Time line for **Update** calls and the red button

This means that the **Update** method must perform a test along the lines of "if the button was up last time and is down now, the counter must be increased." The **Update** method needs to know the state of the button the last time it was called. It can then test to see if the button state has changed since it was called the last time. You can declare a **GamePadState** variable to hold this information and create an **Update** method as follows:

```
GamePadState oldpad1;
protected override void Update(GameTime gameTime)
{
    // Allows the game to exit
    if (GamePad.GetState(PlayerIndex.One).Buttons.Back==ButtonState.Pressed)
        this.Exit();

    GamePadState pad1 = GamePad.GetState(PlayerIndex.One);
    if (pad1.Buttons.Start == ButtonState.Pressed)
    {
        count = 0;
        oldpad1 = pad1;
    }

    if (oldpad1.Buttons.B == ButtonState.Released && pad1.Buttons.B == ButtonState.Pressed)
    {
        count++;
    }
    oldpad1 = pad1;
    base.Update(gameTime);
}
```

The variable **oldpad1** holds the previous state of the gamepad; at the end of the method you store the current pad state in it. The test for the edge makes use of the AND (**&&**) logical operator. Only if the previous state of the button was up AND the current state is down is the **count** value increased. You've already seen the OR (**||**) logical operator, which causes a condition to be true if one or the other condition is true (or both are true). The AND operator is used in the same way but produces a true result if the conditions on each side of it are both true. When the player presses Start to begin the game, the value of **oldPad1** is set to the current pad state so that only changes to the gamepad after Start was pressed are registered.

> **Note**   This code is quite simple, but you need to understand exactly how it works. Make sure that you can follow what is going on: the way that **Update** is called 60 times a second and the way the method makes a copy of the previous gamepad settings at the end of each call.

If you had a *really* fast player who could press and release a button more than 60 times a second, your program would not detect this, as the up and down events would occur in between two calls to the **Update** method.

Level and Edge Detectors

The code in the previous section is an edge detector in that it detects a change from one state to another. This is the kind of code that you would use to detect when a game player selects an option or presses a switch. Up until now, you have used the buttons as level detectors in that only whether a button is up or down has been significant. When you design the controls for a game, you need to decide what kind of input you're using for the control. If you're creating a driving game, you'd use a level-based signal to control whether the accelerator was pressed and perhaps an edge-triggered signal to control the gear selections made by the player.

Constructing the Complete Game

Now that you know how to make edge detectors, you can go on and create the button-counting code for all 16 buttons in the game. The best way to organize these is to track and examine each controller in turn. For each controller, you'll need some variables to hold information about the gamepad and the buttons.

```
// Gamepad 1
GamePadState pad1;
GamePadState oldpad1;
int acount1;
int bcount1;
int xcount1;
int ycount1;
Vector2 apos1 = new Vector2(150, 250);
Vector2 bpos1 = new Vector2(200, 200);
Vector2 xpos1 = new Vector2(100, 200);
Vector2 ypos1 = new Vector2(150, 150);
```

The top two variables hold the gamepad states. The variable **pad1** holds the state of the gamepad during a call of **Update**. The variable **oldPad1** holds the value from the previous call of **Update**. Then there are counters for each of the buttons on the gamepad. Finally, there are four vectors that will position the counters on the screen. The code that runs in the **Update** method is a variation on the edge detector that you saw previously but is extended to handle all the buttons on the gamepad.

```
pad1 = GamePad.GetState(PlayerIndex.One);
if (pad1.IsConnected)
{
    if (pad1.Buttons.Start == ButtonState.Pressed)
    {
        acount1 = 0;
        bcount1 = 0;
        xcount1 = 0;
        ycount1 = 0;
        oldpad1 = pad1;
    }

    if (oldpad1.Buttons.A == ButtonState.Released &&
        pad1.Buttons.A == ButtonState.Pressed)
    {
        acount1++;
    }

    if (oldpad1.Buttons.B == ButtonState.Released &&
        pad1.Buttons.B == ButtonState.Pressed)
    {
        bcount1++;
    }

    if (oldpad1.Buttons.X == ButtonState.Released &&
        pad1.Buttons.X == ButtonState.Pressed)
    {
        xcount1++;
    }

    if (oldpad1.Buttons.Y == ButtonState.Released &&
        pad1.Buttons.Y == ButtonState.Pressed)
    {
        ycount1++;
    }

    oldpad1 = pad1;
}
```

This code makes use of the **IsConnected** property of the **GamePadState** structure. This property is true only if the gamepad is active, meaning that the program will update the values for the gamepad only when it is connected. Now that you have the game behavior working, you need to add the display part of the game code in the **Draw** method (and remove the **countString** and **countVector** variables declared earlier).

```
spriteBatch.Begin();

if (pad1.IsConnected)
{
   spriteBatch.DrawString(font, acount1.ToString(), apos1, Color.Green);
   spriteBatch.DrawString(font, bcount1.ToString(), bpos1, Color.Red);
   spriteBatch.DrawString(font, xcount1.ToString(), xpos1, Color.Blue);
   spriteBatch.DrawString(font, ycount1.ToString(), ypos1, Color.Yellow);
}

spriteBatch.End();
```

This code uses the vectors that were set up at the beginning of the program to position the count values in the correct place on the screen. The code also draws the counters only if that gamepad is connected.

> **Sample Code: Button Bash**   The sample project in the 02 Button Bash directory in the resources for this chapter contains an XNA Game Studio 2.0 solution that contains a program that you can use to play "16-player button bash."

If you look at the sample program, you'll notice that there's a lot of repetition. The same code is used four times in a row, once for each gamepad. In addition, the statements for each gamepad are fundamentally similar. It turns out that you can use more advanced features of C# to make this program much smaller and easier to understand. However, the game works well, and the more people who take part, the more fun it is. Simply begin the game by pressing Start on gamepad 1, and then all the players must bash their particular button as many times as possible in a certain amount of time. This turns out to be a test of stamina as much as anything else. Later, you might return to this code and add an automatic clock to time the games.

> **The Great Programmer Speaks: Make Sure You Can Test Your Code**   The Great Programmer has been looking at the code that you've been writing. She has noticed that your program is quite long and reckons that she could do the job with fewer statements. But since your game works and she enjoys playing it, she thinks it's a good solution. However, she's worried about one thing. The only way that the program can be tested completely is by using four Xbox gamepads. If you don't have four gamepads in hand, you can't prove that all the counter and display code works properly. In many of the programs that she has written, it's been very difficult to test parts of the code, particularly the bits that deal with errors. She therefore thinks that you need to work out a way that you can test the program without needing to have all the hardware present. I'll show you how to do that next.

Adding Test Code

If you have four gamepads, you can simply connect them and play the game. However, if you have only one, you need a way to use it to test the code for the other gamepads as well.

The simplest way to do this is to copy the state of **gamepad1** into the other gamepads during the **Update** method.

```
pad2 = GamePad.GetState(PlayerIndex.Two);
// test code - copy the value of pad1 into pad2
pad2 = pad1;
if (pad2.IsConnected)
{
    // code for gamepad 2
}
```

The test code copies the value of **pad1** into **pad2**. This means that the button presses on this gamepad are now copied onto the counters for this pad, too. If you also copy this information into the other two gamepads, you can test all of them with only a single gamepad. Figure 6-2 shows you the display produced by a test version of the program. I found some faults in the positioning of the counter displays by using this program on a PC with only one Xbox gamepad attached.

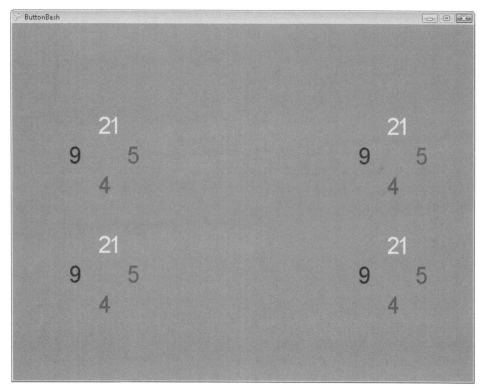

Figure 6-2   Test gamepad counter displays

Once the code has been tested, it's important that these tests are removed from the program. It turns out that C# provides a mechanism called *conditional compilation*, which lets you ask the compiler to ignore parts of a program. This provides a way that you can mark statements of program code that are to be ignored and that do not become part of the program when it is built but that you can keep around for testing when you later update your code.

To understand what's going on here, you have to take the lid off the compiler and find out a bit more about how it works. The job of the compiler is to take the C# statements that you write and convert them into machine instructions for the Xbox or PC. The compiler opens the source file on the computer that holds your C# and reads it in a line at a time. It finds all the variables, makes sure they are used correctly, looks for all the statements, and generates low-level instructions that are to be used when the program runs.

The part at the very front of the compiler that reads in the C# file is called the *preprocessor*. If you built a machine to make apple pies, you'd have to have a part at the front that peeled the apples, discarded any rotten ones, and got them ready for cooking. The preprocessor does this peeling job for the compiler. It takes the program source, removes all the comments (which the compiler should not see), discards blank lines and empty space, and passes on clean statements. However, the C# compiler preprocessor can also be told to do things to the source that it sees.

```
#if test
   // test code - copy the value of pad1 into pad4
   pad4 = pad1;
#endif
```

Commands to the preprocessor have a # at the start of the line and are called *directives*. What the previous statements say to the preprocessor is, "If the **test** symbol has been defined, pass on the following statements to the rest of the compiler; otherwise, ignore them." The statements to be passed on are between the **#if** and the **#endif** directives.

If you want to switch these lines on, you simply need to define the symbol at the top of the source file as follows:

```
#define test
```

If the symbol **test** has been defined, all the test statements are compiled into the main program. Deleting the **#define** directive will keep the designated statements from being compiled.

> **Sample Code: Button Bash Test**   The sample project in the 03 Button Bash Test directory in the resources for this chapter contains an XNA Game Studio 2.0 solution that contains a program that you can use to test the button-bashing program with only one gamepad.

If you use XNA Game Studio 2.0 to open the code file Game1.cs in the 03 Button Bash Test sample project, you'll see that the test code is "live." If you go to the top of Game1.cs and delete the **#define** line, you'll see that all the code controlled by the **test** symbol goes light gray in the editor to indicate that this code is no longer live. If you run the program, it will now work with four gamepads as it should.

> **Note**   It's very important that you understand what's happening here. The program is not making a decision what to do when it runs; this decision is taking place when the program itself is built. If the symbol is not defined, the statements are not even part of the machine language program itself.

You can create as many symbols as you like, so if you wanted to, you could turn on and off different parts of the program. This is one of the ways that games manufacturers make "demo" versions of their games. Some game levels are conditionally compiled in the source so that they can make a limited version of the program just by recompiling with some of these symbols missing.

> **The Great Programmer Speaks: Remember to Charge for Testing**   The Great Programmer is one of the most expensive programmers you'll ever meet. She charges a lot of money for her work, but her customers are happy to pay because they know they are getting a properly tested program, and they never get any nasty surprises. She says that if you're asked how much a job will cost and how long it will take, you must make sure that you include the time it will take you to test your solution as well as the time it will take to actually write the program that does the job. She's very careful to include the cost of these parts of the work in her prices, and her software is always very well tested and works the first time, so she makes the big bucks.

Conclusion

In this chapter, you've discovered how to detect edges on button presses and how to use this to create a good party game. Finally, you've seen the importance of testing and found a mechanism, conditional compilation, that makes testing easier.

Pop Quiz

At the risk of being somewhat repetitive, the chapter ends with another pop quiz.

1. Only the Start button can be used as edge triggered.

2. You need to have the previous state of the gamepad if you want to detect an edge.

3. Edge-triggered inputs only work if the button is held down.

4. Conditionally compiled code is discarded when the program runs.

5. The preprocessor produces the output file from the compiler.

Chapter 7
Playing Sounds

- Use the XACT tool to prepare sounds for inclusion in XNA projects.

- Incorporate sounds into XNA.

- Play the sounds from C# within your programs.

Adding Sound

Now that you can display pictures and text, it's time to make some noise. Then you can set about making a proper gaming experience for your players. You add sound to a game in the same way as you add other resources, but the sounds themselves must be specially prepared for inclusion into the game. You can't just grab your favorite sound sample and drop this into the XNA Game Studio 2.0 project as you did for the graphics resources. Instead, you need to use something called the Microsoft Cross-Platform Audio Creation Tool (XACT) to create the library of sounds that you want to use, insert the library into your game, and then create a sound engine in the game program to play those sounds at the appropriate times.

> ### Program Project: Drum Pad
>
> The first program you are going to make creates a very simple drum kit that is controlled from an Xbox gamepad. Each button is assigned a different drum sound, enabling you to, use your console to play the drums.

Creating the DrumPad Project

You'll create the project (called **DrumPad**) using the New Project dialog box, as you've done for all your previous projects. You can see this dialog box in use in Figure 1-4 in Chapter 1, "Computers, Xboxes, C#, XNA, and You."

Projects and Folders

Whenever you write a program, you need to consider how things will be organized. At the moment, all the files related to a particular game program are stored in a single directory in the file store of the PC. You should be familiar with using directories, or *folders* as they are sometimes called. The Microsoft Windows operating systems provide folders for your documents and pictures so that you can easily group documents and pictures together. When XNA Game Studio 2.0 creates a new XNA project, it will make a new folder that will hold all the information for a particular solution. This folder will contain other folders, reflecting the way that XNA Game Studio 2.0 organizes things.

Because you're about to add a whole bunch of sound files to the DrumPad project, it would make sense to put these all together in a particular place. You can get XNA Game Studio 2.0 to create such a location. You'll create a Sounds folder and put everything concerning sound in this single location. This will include all the sound samples and also the XACT project file that will create the content that will be loaded into the game program.

Figure 7-1 shows how you can use XNA Game Studio 2.0 to create a new content folder. Start by right-clicking the Content item in the DrumPad project in the Solution Explorer and find your way to the New Folder option, as shown.

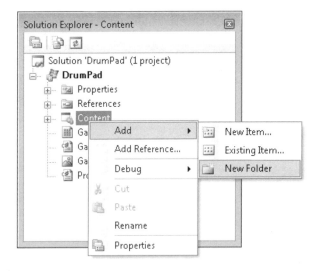

Figure 7-1 Creating a new content folder in XNA Game Studio 2.0

XNA Game Studio 2.0 will create a new folder with the original name New Folder. You can overtype this with a more appropriate name; I'd suggest Sounds. Once you've created the new directory, it takes its place in Solution Explorer for the project, as shown in Figure 7-2.

This has created a new folder, and the next step is to get some sound files and put them into that folder.

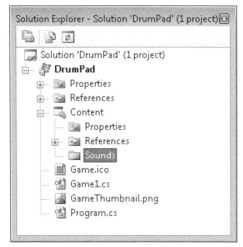

Figure 7-2 The new Sounds folder in Solution Explorer

Capturing Sounds with Audacity

You'll start with a few drum sounds. The samples that I used were captured using the microphone input in my notebook to record live drum sounds. I used a program called Audacity 1.2, which you can obtain for free from *http://audacity.sourceforge.net*. This program will capture live sound and provides a graphical interface that you can use to select portions of recordings and export them as WAV files. Figure 7-3 shows a wave form that has been captured and a portion marked off to be exported.

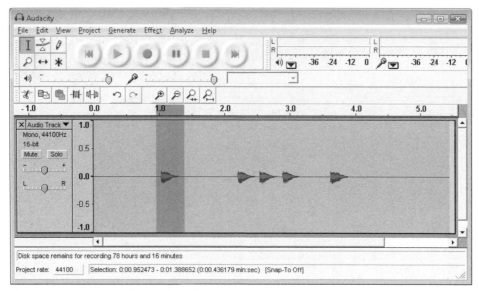

Figure 7-3 The Audacity user interface

Each time you click on the round, red, record button in the controls at the top of the screen, a new track is recorded.

Before you start recording, you should select the format of the sound that you are going to capture. The quality of a sound recording is controlled by the sample rate and the resolution of each sound sample. You need to be careful when recording sounds because the higher the quality of the sound, the more disk space and memory the sample will take up. I have found that a sample rate of 44,100 Hz and 16-bit resolution gives good-quality sounds that do not take up too much memory. You can select these by clicking the item on top of the track, as shown in Figure 7-4, where the sample rate is being selected. The resolution is set using the Set Sample Format menu item immediately above the Set Rate menu item, which appears expanded in Figure 7-4.

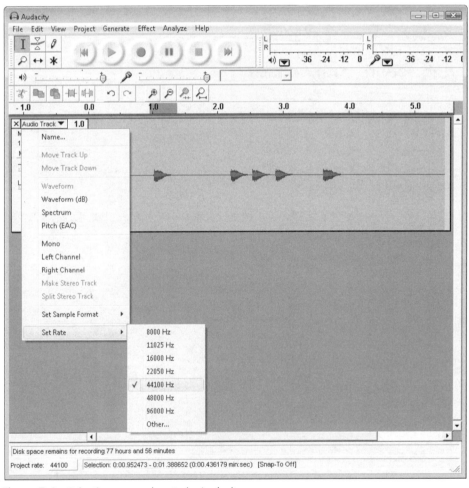

Figure 7-4 Selecting a sample rate in Audacity

Once you have recorded a sound, you can change the sound quality settings. If you are recording very long sounds, such as background music, you may decide to reduce the quality so that the sound files are smaller.

Note that with sound samples, as with other assets in your game, you must be careful to observe copyright laws. While it's very tempting to use parts of songs or TV shows as in-game sounds, you need to make sure that you don't get into trouble for doing this.

Sounds and File Types

When I had finished with the drums, I had some sound files that were WAV files. Today, you're more likely to have heard of MP3 or WMA files when storing sound. In these files, the sound information is compressed so that it takes up less space in your music player. The XNA Framework doesn't work with files compressed in this way; it can use only WAV files.

Storing Sounds in Your Project

To get the files into the Sounds folder, you can use Windows Explorer to drag and drop them into place. Figure 7-5 shows the Sounds folder with the drum sounds included.

Note that you do not add these files to the XNA Game Studio 2.0 project; you are just storing them in the Sounds folder. The only item that will be added to the game project will be the output from the XACT tool that we are using next.

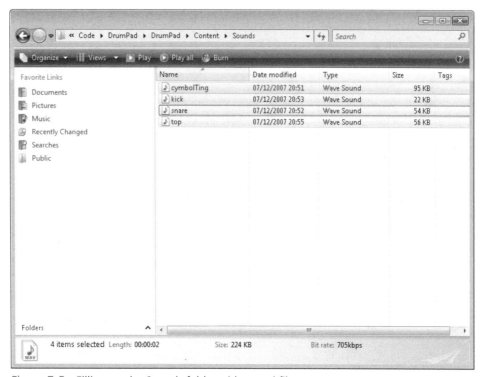

Figure 7-5   Filling up the Sounds folder with sound files

> **Note**   If you've installed any programs that work with sound files, you might find that your WAV files have different icons. The ones in Figure 7-5 are associated with Windows Media Player on my computer.

Now that you have the files, you can get them into a form that can be used in your XNA program. To do this, you must use the XACT tool that's supplied as part of the XNA game development framework.

Using the XACT Audio Creation Tool

When you start using the XACT tool, you get an impression of just what a professional world you're moving into. This is a full-blown, industry-ready audio creation tool for use by game developers. The downside is that this makes it rather complicated, but for what you want to do, you simply need to follow a sequence of actions to take your WAV files and include them in games. XACT organizes the sounds for a game as an XACT project that contains references to the sound files you want to use and instructions on how to use them in the game. When you build the project, XACT creates the resource files that will be picked up by XNA Game Studio 2.0 and used in the game program.

Starting XACT

When you install XNA Game Studio 2.0, you get some additional tools, including the XACT program. Figure 7-6 shows where you can find these tools in the All Programs list that you get from the Start menu.

The two tools that you'll use are XACT and the XACT Auditioning Utility. The Auditioning Utility lets you hear the sounds that are being edited. When you start creating audio, you should run both the XACT Auditioning Utility and XACT. The first time you run these programs, you might get a Windows Security Alert from Windows Firewall indicating that it has blocked these programs from accessing network ports. You should allow these programs to have access to the network if you want to be able to preview sounds.Once the tools are running, you can begin creating the sounds for your games.

Using XACT

Figure 7-7 shows how XACT appears when it first starts up.

This looks rather complicated, but you'll use only part of the XACT program to start with.

Creating an XACT Project

First, you need to create a new XACT project. This will be stored in the Sounds folder along with the sound samples. To create a new XACT project, choose New Project from the Files menu. Then use the New Project Path dialog box to navigate to the Sound folder of the DrumPad project and save the project with the name "GameSounds," as shown in Figure 7-8.

Figure 7-6   The XNA tools

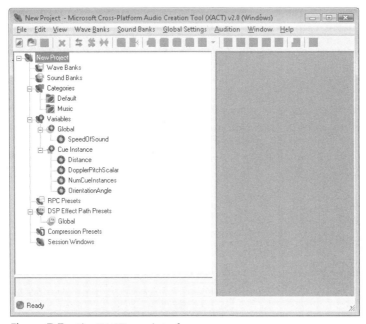

Figure 7-7   The XACT user interface

Now that you have your sound project, you need to create a "wave bank" to hold the sound samples you want your program to play.

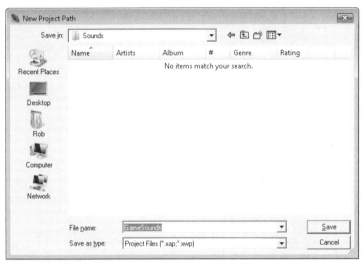

Figure 7-8   Creating the GameSounds project

XACT Wave Banks

You've seen how to create WAV files that contain the audio you might want to play in your games. Within XACT, a set of WAV files are stored together in a wave bank. A large game may use several wave banks. Some of them will contain short sounds used for spot effects, such as gunshots. These sounds need to be kept in memory because they are used frequently. Other wave banks will hold things like background music, which can be read from a storage device as it is played. To create a wave bank, choose New Wave Bank from the Wave Banks menu. Figure 7-9 shows what the empty wave bank will look like. This will have the name "Wave Bank" and appear in the left-hand tree under Wave Banks. It will also open in the right-hand pane.

To add wave files, choose Insert Wave File(s) from the Wave Banks menu. XACT will display the Open dialog box, as shown in Figure 7-10.

Select the wave files to be added. If you hold down the Ctrl key, you can select multiple files. Click Open to add the files. The sound bank that you create should look like the one in Figure 7-11.

Note that all the files are displayed in red at the moment. This indicates that although the files are part of the XACT project, they are not being used in any sounds. To use something in a wave bank, you need to create a sound, which is stored in a sound bank.

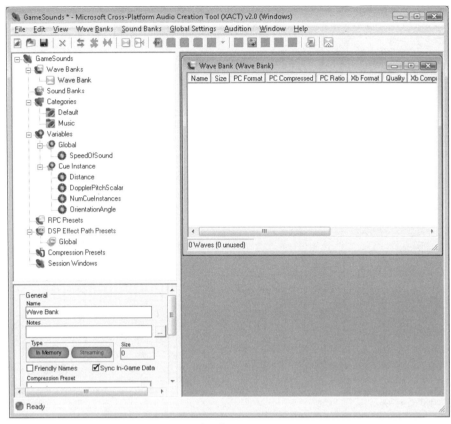

Figure 7-9   Creating an empty wave bank

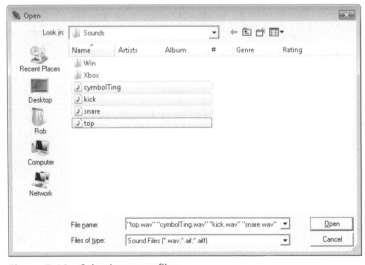

Figure 7-10   Selecting wave files

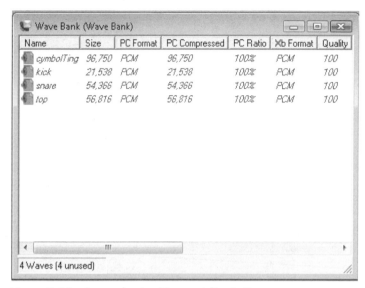

Figure 7-11   A wave bank with sound files in it

XACT Sound Banks

The sound bank is where you construct the sounds out of the waves. You can think of the wave bank as a kind of warehouse that holds the raw materials for audio output. A sound bank is where the raw materials are put together in a particular combination to make a sound. This is a good idea because one wave sample can be used in several different sounds and in conjunction with other samples.

A sound in a sound bank is made up of a number of tracks, each of which is based on a particular wave. If you want, you can combine a number of waves to get particular effects. If you want the sound of a gun firing followed by the bullet ricocheting off the wall, you can create a sound that first plays a "bang" wave followed some time later by a "ping" wave. You can also make a sound that automatically makes changes to the way that it plays the waves. In this way, game developers can provide a rich environment for players with a minimum number of waves.

To create a sound bank, choose New Sound Bank from the Sound Banks menu. XACT will create an empty sound bank to use. This will have the name Sound Bank and appear in the left-hand tree under Sound Banks. It will also open in the right-hand pane. Next, you'll move your sounds from the wave bank into the sound bank. The best way to do this is to drag them from one to another. This is easier if you arrange the windows in the right-hand area so that both are visible. To do this, choose Tile Horizontally from the Window menu. This should result in each window filling half the screen, as shown in Figure 7-12.

Now, you need to drag the sounds out of the wave bank into the sound bank. Click the name of one of the files in the wave bank and drag it into the Cue area of the sound bank underneath the Cue Name header. This will create a sound in the sound bank and also a cue for the sound.

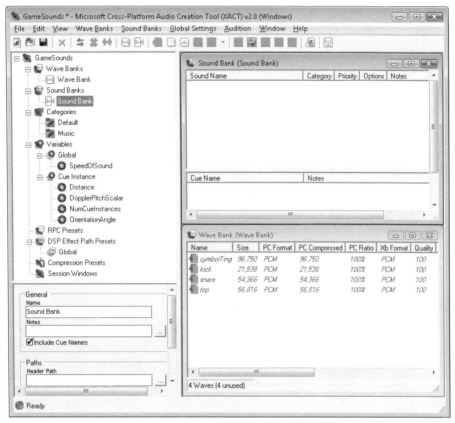

Figure 7-12   Using wave and sound banks in XACT

The cue is the item that's used by the software to start a sound playing. A single cue can play one or more sounds or pick a sound randomly from a list. For this example, you'll have one sound per cue, and you'll need a cue for each sound that you want to play. Eventually, you should have a screen that looks like that shown in Figure 7-13.

Cues can be created by dragging a sound from the sound bank into the Cue area. Duplicate cues or sounds can be deleted by selecting them, pressing the Delete key on the keyboard, and then confirming the operation.

Auditioning the Sounds

The XACT Auditioning Utility allows you to test the sounds that you are creating. You need to start the utility from the program group shown in Figure 7-6 and make sure that the firewall is not blocking ports. The XACT Auditioning Utility will display a command prompt with the text "Waiting for the XACT authoring tool to connect..." That means it's waiting for you to audition a sound from the XACT window. You can test any of your sounds, waves, and cues by selecting the one you want to test in the XACT window and then clicking the green Audition button on the toolbar at the top of the XACT window.

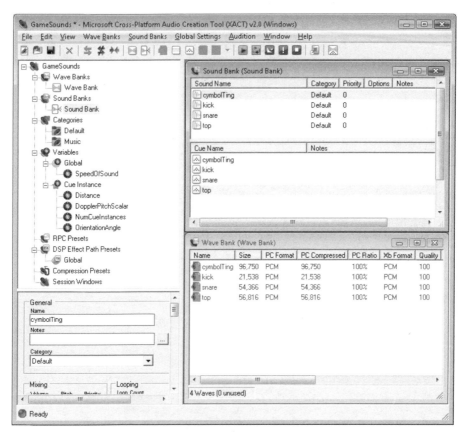

Figure 7-13   Waves, cues, and sounds in XACT

Note   If this fails to work, you might need to investigate the configuration of the computer you are using for development. If this machine is using Internet port 80 to operate as a Web server, then this will interfere with the connection to the auditioning server.

XACT will work with sound properties slightly differently depending on whether you're creating sounds for the PC or the Xbox. To change between these, choose View Xbox 360 Properties or View PC Properties from the View menu.

Building the Sound Project

The final thing you need to do is build the sound project. This is the point at which the sound and wave bank files are made into resources that can be used in game programs. To build the project, choose Build from the File menu. This brings up the Build Project dialog box. Click Finish to build the project and create the output files.

> **Note**   XACT builds different output files from the project depending on whether you're creating sounds for the PC or the Xbox. To change between these, choose View Xbox 360 Properties or View PC Properties from the View menu. Then, when you build the project, the correct files are created.

Once you have built the project, you should choose Save Project from the File menu to save the updated XACT project.

XACT and Sounds

At this point, it's worth reviewing what you've done so far. You wanted to play four sounds in your program. Each of the sounds is held in a WAV file. You used XACT to create a wave bank that contains references to those WAV files. You then created an XACT sound bank that contains four sounds, each of which refers to one of the waves in the wave bank. Each sound has a single cue associated with it that your XNA program will use to play the sound. You stored all this in an XACT project file that you're about to include in your game project so that you can write an XNA game that uses these sounds.

Using Sounds in an XNA Program

You're already familiar with how to include resources in XNA games. To play sounds, you add the XACT project file, which is then used to find all the other sound resources. The file is added in the same way that you added other resources in earlier chapters. Figure 7-14 shows how to add a resource.

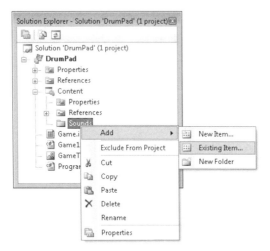

Figure 7-14   Adding a resource to the Sounds folder

You're adding the XACT project file in the Sounds folder held in the Contents folder of your XNA Game Studio 2.0 project. Figure 7-15 shows how to browse for this file. The figure also shows that the folder contains all the sound samples and two folders that XACT created when it built the projects for PC and Xbox.

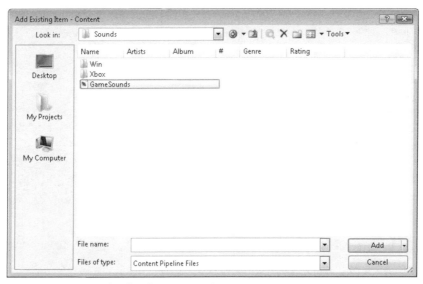

Figure 7-15 Browsing for the XACT project

The XACT project is now added to the content for the DrumPad project, as shown in Figure 7-16.

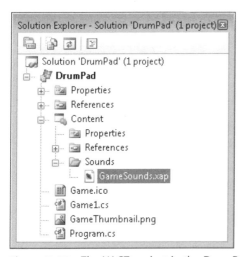

Figure 7-16 The XACT project in the DrumPad project

> **Note** If your program fails to run with the sound project included, make sure that you have used Build in XACT to create the required sound content and also that you have saved the GameSounds project from XACT.

At this point, you've done most of the hard work, and all you need to do next is write the program code to play the sound. This is slightly complicated in that the software you're using is designed for use in very advanced games, but after using XACT, I reckon you can do just about anything.

Creating an Audio Engine

When you start a game program, the XNA system automatically creates a content manager and a graphics device manager. This is because without content and a graphics device, you don't really have a game. However, as you've seen, it's perfectly possible to play a game without sound. The XNA developers leave it to you to create an audio engine to play your sounds. The best place to create the audio engine and the wave and sound banks that it needs is in the **LoadContent** method.

```
// Game world sounds
static AudioEngine audio;
static WaveBank waves;
static SoundBank sounds;

protected override void LoadContent()
{
    // Create a new SpriteBatch, which can be used to draw textures.
    spriteBatch = new SpriteBatch(GraphicsDevice);
    audio = new AudioEngine("Content\\Sounds\\GameSounds.xgs");
    waves = new WaveBank(audio, "Content\\Sounds\\Wave Bank.xwb");
    sounds = new SoundBank(audio, "Content\\Sounds\\Sound Bank.xsb");
}
```

This code creates an **AudioEngine** and then a **WaveBank** and a **SoundBank** that will be used in your game. The items in double quotation marks are strings that give the location of the resources that will be used. The **AudioEngine** is told where to find the XACT game settings, and the **WaveBank** and **SoundBank** are told which audio engine they are to use and which files contain their data.

At this point, you might be wondering where these files are. If you look in the Sounds folder in your XNA Game Studio 2.0 project, you won't find them there. This is because these folders are used when the program is running, not when it is built. Before your program is started, XNA Game Studio 2.0 makes sure that these files are in place for it to pick up. If you get the name of the files wrong, the program will compile, but it will fail when it tries to run.

Creating and Playing Sounds

Now you're at the point where you can play sounds in your program. You are going to make a program that plays different drums by pressing different buttons on the Xbox gamepad. You've already seen how to read the state of a gamepad and test for buttons, so the code is quite easy to write.

```
// Current state of the gamepad during the update GamePadState pad1;
// Old gamepad state. XNA initializes this to all
// buttons not pressed. After the first call of Update
// this holds the previous gamepad state GamePadState oldpad1;

protected override void Update(GameTime gameTime)
{
    pad1 = GamePad.GetState(PlayerIndex.One);
    if (pad1.IsConnected)
    {
        // allow the game to exit when back is pressed
        if (pad1.Buttons.Back == ButtonState.Pressed)
        {
            this.Exit();
        }
        // test if A has been pressed since the last Update
        if (oldpad1.Buttons.A == ButtonState.Released &&
            pad1.Buttons.A == ButtonState.Pressed)
        {
            sounds.PlayCue("snare");
        }
    }

    // record the current gamepad state for the next
    // call of update
    oldpad1 = pad1;

    // update the audio engine
    audio.Update();

    base.Update(gameTime);
}
```

This version of **Update** will play the "snare" sound when the A button is pressed on gamepad 1. It does this by calling the **PlayCue** method provided by a **SoundBank** object. The name given to **PlayCue** is the name of the sound cue that you want to play. You're using the same "edge detection" code that you used for the button-bashing game in Chapter 6, "Creating a Multiplayer Game," because you want to start the sound playing only when the button goes down.

Each call of **PlayCue** will start another drum sample playing, so if you just tested for the button being held down, you'd get lots of snare drums playing at once, which would not sound good. You can expand this code so that each of the buttons on the controller plays one of your four sound samples.

The `Update` method shown previously makes a call to `audio.Update()`. This lets the audio engine gets control at regular intervals. If you don't do this, you'll find that the audio might not play correctly.

> **Sample Code: 01 DrumPad**   The 01 DrumPad project in the resources for this chapter contains an XACT project and all the WAV files. It makes a different drum sound when each of the buttons is pressed. If you want to use your own sounds with this project, simply replace the WAV files in the sounds folder with yours, rebuild the XACT project, and rebuild the XNA Game Studio 2.0 project.

If you use sounds that are long enough, you'll find that you can get several versions of a given sound sample playing at the same time if you press the buttons very quickly.

> **The Great Programmer Speaks: Division of Labor Is Good**   You've been telling the Great Programmer all about how horrible XACT is and how you had to make all these sounds and waves and cues just so that you can get your program to play a sound. She doesn't agree with you. She reckons that in proper game studios, they have programmers and sound engineers. The way that XACT separates the tasks means that sound people can work on making sure that all the sounds fit the game properly, and the programmer just needs to know that when the grenade hits the ground, the "explodeGrenade" cue should be played.

Playing Background Music

You can also use the XNA sound system for playing background music. The technique described here could be used for engine noise or background sounds for a particular location. Unlike the sounds you've used so far, you want the music to repeat when it finishes playing, and you'd also like a way to stop and start the music from within your program. The actual music file will be a wave file like all the other sounds, but it may be somewhat larger. It is loaded in an XACT project in the same way as the other sounds that you saw earlier.

Making the sound repeat is easy. You simply need to alter a property of the sound in the sound bank. You do this by selecting the appropriate sound in the sound bank and changing the properties of the sound so that the `Looping` property is set to `Infinite`, as shown in the lower left of Figure 7-17.

If you create and build an XACT project to use this sound in your XNA game, you'll find that it will repeat indefinitely once you start playing it. (Make sure you rebuild and resave the XACT project after adding the music file.) However, you might want to have a way to stop and start it. This would be the case if you wanted to use a sound for an engine. The engine sound sample would be played as a loop when the engine is running, but the player will expect the engine sound to stop when the engine is switched off.

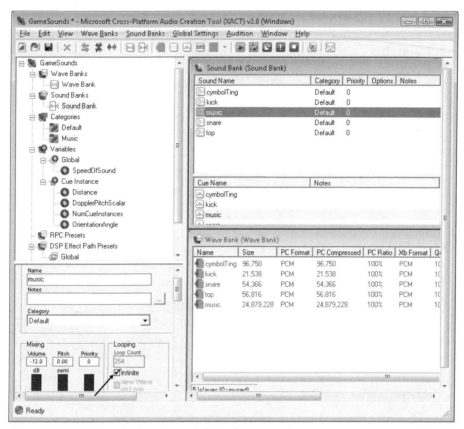

Figure 7-17   Setting the looping to infinite for a sound

Using Sound Cues to Control Playback

When you played the previous sounds, you called the method **PlayCue** on the sound bank to play the sound once. However, another way to control playing sounds involves getting hold of a cue that you can use to control the sound. The cue will be one of the variables in your game, and you can then call methods on this cue to control the sound's playback. The new code you need is shown in bold type in the following:

```
// Game world sounds
static AudioEngine audio;
static WaveBank waves;
static SoundBank sounds;
Cue musicCue;

protected override void LoadContent()
{
    // Create a new SpriteBatch, which can be used to draw textures.
    spriteBatch = new SpriteBatch(GraphicsDevice);
    audio = new AudioEngine("Content\\Sounds\\GameSounds.xgs");
    waves = new WaveBank(audio, "Content\\Sounds\\Wave Bank.xwb");
```

```
    sounds = new SoundBank(audio, "Content\\Sounds\\Sound Bank.xsb");
    musicCue = sounds.GetCue("music");
}
```

The cue is created by the SoundBank, which is given the name of the sound you wish to create a cue for. Once the program has a cue, it can then call methods on the cue to control it.

This code is a slightly modified version of the **LoadContent** method for the game. In addition to creating the audio engine, sound, and wave banks, it also sets the variable musicCue to a cue from the sound bank that you specify using the name "music". It then calls the method **Play** on that variable to start the music playback. You can use the variable musicCue to allow the player to control the music playback from the **Update** method.

```
// use the Start button to control the music playback
if (oldpad1.Buttons.Start == ButtonState.Released &&
        pad1.Buttons.Start == ButtonState.Pressed)
{
    if (musicCue.IsPlaying)
    {
      if (musicCue.IsPaused)
      {
          musicCue.Resume();
      }
      else
      {
          musicCue.Pause();
      }
    }
    else
    {
        musicCue.Play();
    }
}
```

The code uses the same edge detection method that you've seen before so that the Start button on the gamepad controls the sound playback. The musicCue provides Boolean properties that can be used to determine the state of sound playback. If the music is playing, the Start button will toggle the playback between pause and resume. If the music is not playing, the Start button will start playback.

> **Sample Code: 02 Drumpad with Music**   The 02 Drumpad with Music project in the resources for this chapter contains an XACT project and all the WAV files including a music file. The music can be controlled with the Start button on the gamepad. It also contains the drum pad code to make sounds when the buttons are pressed. I've modified the properties of the "cymbolTing" sound in the XACT project so that it makes random changes to the pitch of the sound each time it is played. You'll find that it makes quite a difference to the sound of the sample each time.

If you have the time, you can explore some of the more powerful features of XACT, including automatic random selection of different sounds for a particular cue and changing the pitch and volume of sounds as they play using events. You can also create "variables" in your sound projects that can be controlled by your program so that the sounds closely follow the game. I could write a thick book on the fun that you can have with the XACT tool, but you're here to learn how to write programs, not create sounds.

Conclusion

This has been an interesting chapter. You've seen how to capture sounds and store them on your computer. You've also explored a very powerful audio creation tool: getting the Xbox to make sounds and play music.

Pop Quiz

And now the ever-popular pop quiz. Some people say that for some things in life, there are no right answers. Well, I think that for these questions there is.

1. The XACT tool runs on the Xbox.

2. Games can use MP3 files for sound.

3. A sound bank in XACT contains the actual sound sample information.

4. A folder and a directory are the same thing.

5. You need an audio engine in your game for each sound that you want to play.

6. A particular cue brings together a number of sounds.

Chapter 8
Creating a Timer

- Find out how your program can measure the passage of time.

- Create a massively multiplayer reaction game.

- Use C# arrays to allow the program to determine who has won.

Making Another Game

You are now going to use your knowledge of XNA and C# to create another game. This builds on the party theme that you explored in Chapter 6, "Creating a Multiplayer Game," where you created a button bashing game.

Game Idea: Mob Reaction Timer

In this game, you'll test the reactions of your players. Each player is in charge of one button on a gamepad. The game will play a sound, and the player who presses his or her button the soonest after the sound starts playing will be the winner. Anyone who presses their button before the sound starts playing is out.

You will need to use a timer variable to keep track of time and a variable for each player to measure the reaction time of that player.

```
// Game World
int timer;

// Gamepad 1 scores
int ascore1;
int bscore1;
int xscore1;
int yscore1;
```

These are the variables for the timer and the first gamepad. The timer starts counting up from zero when the sound plays. Each time that XNA calls the **Update** method, the value in `timer`

131

is increased by one, and the program checks to see if the player has pressed his or her button. If the button has been pressed, the value of the timer is copied into the value for that button. The player with the lowest value is the winner. The first problem you have to solve is how to start the game. If the sound is produced as soon the game begins, the player who starts the game has an obvious advantage. The trick is to make the timer a negative number when the game starts and increase it each time **Update** is called. When it reaches the value 0, the sound is played and the game can start counting. Figure 8-1 shows how this works.

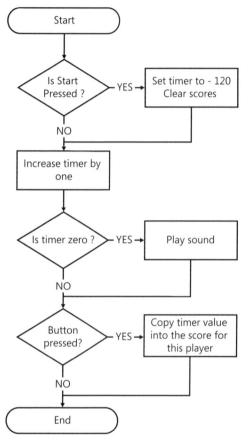

Figure 8-1   Flow diagram for a reaction timer

Each time **Update** is called, the flow in Figure 8-1 is performed. If the Start button is pressed, the timer variable is set to -120. Each time **Update** runs, the value in **timer** is made one bigger. When **timer** reaches zero, the sound is played. When a button press is detected, the program copies the current value of **timer** into the score for that button. If a player presses a button before the sound has been played, he or she will have a negative **timer** value. The player who gets the smallest positive value is the winner.

```
protected override void Update(GameTime gameTime)
{
    pad1 = GamePad.GetState(PlayerIndex.One);
    if (pad1.Buttons.Back == ButtonState.Pressed)
    {
        this.Exit();
    }

    // start a new game
    if (pad1.Buttons.Start == ButtonState.Pressed)
    {
        timer = -120;
        ascore1 = 0;
        bscore1 = 0;
        xscore1 = 0;
        yscore1 = 0;
    }

    // update the timer
    timer++;

    // play the sound at the start of the game
    if (timer == 0)
    {
        sounds.PlayCue("ding");
    }

    // if A is pressed copy the timer
    if (oldpad1.Buttons.A == ButtonState.Released && pad1.Buttons.A == ButtonState.Pressed)
    {
        ascore1 = timer;
    }

    // repeat for buttons B, X and Y

    oldpad1 = pad1;
    // repeat for gamepads 2, 3 and 4

    base.Update(gameTime);
}
```

You should look carefully at this method because, although it is not very large, it is somewhat complicated. Remember that the **Update** method is called 60 times a second, so when the Start button is pressed and **timer** is set to −120, this means that there will be a 2-second delay before the sound plays. The code runs and works well. In fact, I'm rather proud of it. Unfortunately, it has a rather nasty bug in it.

Sample Code: 01 Broken Reaction Timer Game   The 01 Broken Reaction Timer Game project in the resources for this chapter contains a version of the game using the **Update** method from this section. Have a go with it and see if you can find out where the bug is.

Reaction Timer Bug

You first notice the bug in the program when you find that your younger brother is beating everyone at the game. He seems to have amazing reflexes. Or he is cheating. It turns out to be the latter. He has noticed that although you get a negative (and therefore invalid) score if you press your button before the sound plays, you can press the button again later and have another go. What he does is press the button up and down very rapidly until he hears the sound and then stops. This usually results in his winning.

If you look at the code in the Update method, you'll find that there's nothing to stop a naughty player from pressing his or her button lots of times. There's no penalty for pressing the button before the sound plays because the player can just press the button again. You've designed the game without allowing for the fact that players might cheat and seem to have reckoned without your younger brother.

You need to change the program to fix the problem. At this point, you're doing proper programming. You've used an *algorithm* that gives a set of steps to make the game work, but you've found that it's faulty in some circumstances. Therefore, you need to either improve your solution or find a better one.

Since I wrote the first version, I'm going to start by asking you to work out what is going wrong. This might seem a little unfair, but I'm going to give you some help by suggesting things that might be the cause. Pick the one you think is the most sensible and then read on.

1. The problem occurs because you're not detecting when the player releases the button as well as when it's pressed.

2. The problem occurs because you should be using level detection on the buttons, not edge detection.

3. The problem occurs because you want to register only the first press of the button.

4. The problem occurs because you need to reset the gamepad after it's been read.

If you look carefully at the flow diagram in Figure 8-1 and the code, you can simulate these ideas to see which makes the most sense. If this feels a bit like solving a puzzle, you're very close to what this part of programming is all about. If you get stuck trying to solve a programming problem, the best thing to do is to go back and consider what it is you're trying to achieve. What you mustn't do is just add lines of code in the hope that one of them fixes the problem.

Your younger brother is winning by pressing his button more than once. Since you can't physically stop him from doing this, you have to find a way to prevent later button presses having any effect on the score of the player. From the previous list, option 3 is the best one to take a look at. So the problem now becomes; How can you tell if the button has been pressed more than once? Take a look at the flowchart and try to decide what the program could test to decide if this is the first or second time that the button has been pressed in a game.

It turns out that this is easy. The program works by copying the value of the timer into the score for each player. When the Start button is pressed, the program loads zero into the score values for each of the players. The very first time the player presses his or her button, the zero will be replaced with a time value. Next time he or she presses the button, the score will not be zero, so you should not update this value.

```
// if A is pressed and ascore1 is 0 copy the timer
if (oldpad1.Buttons.A == ButtonState.Released &&
    pad1.Buttons.A == ButtonState.Pressed && ascore1 == 0)
{
    ascore1 = timer;
}
```

The program now contains a condition that tests whether the score is zero and sets the score only if it is. If the score is not zero (that is, the button has already been pressed), then the score will not be stored.

> **Sample Code: 02 Fixed ReactionTimer**   The 02 Fixed ReactionTimer project in the resources for this chapter contains a mended version of the game using the **Update** method as fixed in this section.

Finding Winners Using Arrays

Your younger brother is now rather cross with you. The bug fix means that he can't always win at the game anymore, and this has upset him somewhat. So he has taken to claiming that the game is rubbish anyway "because it doesn't tell you who won."

Unfortunately, he has a point. When the game has finished, the players must look at the screen and decide who the winner is. This doesn't seem right, bearing in mind that computers are supposed to make our lives easier. So now you have to work out a way of deciding who has the winning score. Any scores less than or equal to zero must be ignored since those players either pressed their buttons before the sound played or never pressed their buttons at all. Of the remaining scores, you want the one with the lowest value. You could write some complicated code like this:

```
if (ascore1 > 0)
{
    if (ascore1 < bscore1 && ascore1 < xscore1 && ascore1 < yscore1)
    {
        // if we get here button A of Gamepad 1 has won
    }
}
```

This code works only for the A button of gamepad 1. The first **if** statement checks to see if the score is greater than zero. If it is, the second condition is performed. This is a rather complicated **if** statement that checks to see if the score for the A button is less than the score for the other buttons on the gamepad. If the score is less than all of them, that button is the winner. You need to write three other conditions for the other buttons on the gamepad. This is a lot of work, and it gets even worse when you consider the possibility of four gamepads.

Creating an Array

What you need is a way of working through a list of scores using your program. In C#, a variable that holds a list of values is called an *array*. The type of values you want your array to hold are integers, and it will be "single dimensional" in that it will have only one list of values. You can create such an array in C# using a couple of statements:

```
int[] scores = new int[4];
```

This declares an array variable called **scores** that can refer to one-dimensional integer arrays and makes it refer to a new 4 element array instance. You can think of an array as a row of numbered boxes, each of which can hold a single value. A single "box" in an array is called an *element*. Figure 8-2 shows how this works.

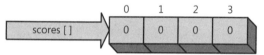

Figure 8-2   Array reference and array instance

The size of the array is set when you create it. In the previous code, you made an array with four elements. If you want a different size, you simply change the 4 to a different number.

> **Note**   You may have noticed that I'm talking about "array instances" and that arrays are created using the key word new. I have used these terms before when I was talking about objects. This means that arrays are implemented in C# as objects, and you can ask them to do things for you. Later, you'll see how you can use array properties and methods to make your life easier.

Using Data in an Array

Now that you have your array, you need to be able to get hold of individual elements. If you take a look at Figure 8-2 again, you'll see that each element has a number above it. This is called the *subscript* or *index* of that element in the array. You can regard a subscript as telling the computer how far "down" an array to go to get to the element that is required. In this respect, array elements are similar to house numbers on a street (except that no houses have the number zero). To use a particular element in an array, you simply give the subscript of the element you want. The following code shows how this works. The value of the subscript is enclosed in square brackets.

```
if (scores[0] > 0)
{
   if (oldpad1.Buttons.A == ButtonState.Released &&
       pad1.Buttons.A == ButtonState.Pressed && scores[0] == 0)
   {
      scores[0] = timer;
   }
}
```

This C# code works in the same way as the original code, except that it uses the first element in the array, **scores[0]**, instead of a variable called **ascore1**. You can use **scores[1]** as **bscore1**, the score for the B button on gamepad 1, and so on.

At this point, it doesn't seem that creating an array has made life much easier; you've only found a quick way of declaring more than one variable. However, the real power comes when you use variables in your array subscripts:

```
for (int i = 0; i < 4 ; i++)
{
   scores[i] = 0;
}
```

This is a **for** loop construction that takes the value of i from **0** to **3** (remember than when the value of i reaches **4**, the test "i less than 4" will fail, and the loop stops). The value of i is used as a subscript for the array access. This means that the first time around the loop, the statement will set **scores[0]** to zero. The next time around the loop, the assignment will be made to **scores[1]** and so on up until the end of the array. This is how you'd set the scores array elements to zero at the start of a game.

> **Note**   The previous code uses an additional C# feature of the **for** loop that lets you declare the counter variable (in this case a variable called i) in the loop itself. This variable exists only for the duration of the loop, being local to the **for** loop block. The Great Programmer thinks this is the right thing to do here, as you need the variable only for the duration of the loop block.

In this case, you want to work with only four elements, so the code doesn't look that much shorter than your original. However, if you needed to set 1,000 values, the code would contain the same statements, except that you'd change the limit value so that i goes up to 999.

> **Note**   If you have a mind like your younger brother, at this point you'll be wondering what would happen if you tried to use silly subscript values like **scores[101]**. Your younger brother would no doubt be hoping that this would cause the computer to crash or, better yet, allow access to secret memory locations. The boring answer is that if you step outside what are called the *bounds* of an array your program will be stopped in its tracks by an exception because this is just not allowed to happen in a proper language like C#. This form of naughtiness was not always detected in older computers, however, and was once one of the standard ways that a virus program could attack a system.

Scanning an Array

Now you need to use an array to help you find the best score. Figure 8-3 shows typical arrangement of the values.

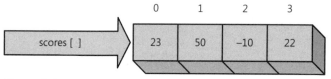

Figure 8-3   Sample scores

You now need to write some C# that will work through the array and find the best score. At this point, you have a problem. If I ask you, "Which element in Figure 8-3 has the winning time in it?" you would glance at the page and say, "The element with subscript 3." And you'd be right. The problem is that you won't necessarily be able to tell me precisely how you worked it out. You simply looked along the row, and that number was the smallest number that wasn't negative. It was obvious.

Unfortunately, you can't say to the C# compiler, "Look along the row and find me the winner." You need to set things out in simpler and much more boring steps. The program must look at each element in turn and see if it wins. At any given point in the process, the program would have an idea of the best result it has seen so far. If it sees a value that is better, it now has a new winner and so on.

If you think about it, this is what people really do, particularly if they are working through 1,000 numbers instead. In that case, they would take care to remember the best result that they had seen so far as you went through and probably write it down on a piece of paper. With all this in mind, consider the following code:

```
int winningValue = 120;
for (int i = 0; i < 16; i++)
{
   if (scores[i] > 0)
   {
    if (scores[i] < winningValue)
    {
        winningValue = scores[i];
    }
   }
}
```

This code uses a variable called winningValue to hold the smallest value it has seen so far. It starts by setting it to a large value that is guaranteed not to be a winner. It then compares winningValue with each element in the array in turn. If the element is smaller than the current smallest, it sets winningValue to the new value. Before it tests winningValue, the code makes sure that the count is a valid one in that the button must have been pressed.

At the end of the pass through the loop, the variable `winningValue` will have the value of the winning score.

Now that you know the winning score, you can write some code to display the winner:

```
string winnerName;
if (scores[0] == winningValue)
{
   winnerName = "Gamepad 1 button A";
}
if (scores[1] == winningValue)
{
   winnerName = "Gamepad 1 button B";
}
```

This code selects the winning string for the A and B buttons on gamepad 1. The string `winnerName` is set with the name of the winning button and gamepad and can be displayed on the screen at the end of the game. You could write more statements for each of the other buttons and gamepads.

> **Note**   You need to be careful to make sure that when you check the buttons, you set the correct elements in the array; otherwise, the wrong names will be displayed.

Using an Array as a Lookup Table

The previous code will produce a string that contains the name of the winning gamepad and button. But you still need to perform all those conditional statements to decide the string to display. However, you do have a way to make your life easier, and it starts by finding out the position in the array of the winning score.

```
int winningValue = 120;
int winnerSubscript = 0;
for (int i = 0; i < 16; i++)
{
   if (scores[i] > 0)
   {
    if (scores[i] < winningValue)
    {
       winningValue = scores[i];
       winnerSubscript = i;
    }
   }
}
```

This is the same loop as before, but you now have a variable called `winnerSubscript` that will hold the position in the array of the winning value. Note that the program copies the value of `i` into the `winnerSubscript` when it finds a new winning value. Remember that when you find a new winning value, the variable `i` will hold the subscript in the array where that value is stored.

Now that you have the subscript value of the winning score, you can use it in another array to find the string that describes that player. The array is set up as shown in Figure 8-4.

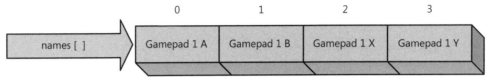

Figure 8-4   Player lookup table

This is an array of strings of text. There is an element in the array for each of the buttons on gamepad 1, and the names are lined up with the buttons that are tested. Now, to get the description of the winner, you simply need to look up the name in your table:

```
winnerName = names [winnerSubscript];
```

You need to have a way of setting up the lookup table with the correct strings. C# provides a way that you can create an array and set the initial values in it.

```
string[] names = new string[] {
  "Gamepad 1 A",
  "Gamepad 1 B",
  "Gamepad 1 X",
  "Gamepad 1 Y"
};
```

This creates an array with the preset values that you give. Note that you don't need to tell C# how long the array is since it can work this out automatically.

Displaying the Winner

You now have code that you can use to display the winner. Now you need to work out how you'll add this to the program. A good time to display the winner would be 2 seconds after the sound was produced, which is when the timer value reaches 120. By then, all the players should have pressed their buttons.

```
protected override void Update(GameTime gameTime)
{
    pad1 = GamePad.GetState(PlayerIndex.One);
    if (pad1.Buttons.Back == ButtonState.Pressed)
    {
        this.Exit();
    }

    // start a new game
    if (pad1.Buttons.Start == ButtonState.Pressed)
    {
      for (int i = 0; i < 16; i++)
      {
        scores[i] = 0;
      }
```

```
     winnerName = "";
   timer = -120;
}


// update the timer
timer++;

// play the sound at the start of the game
if (timer == 0)
{
   sounds.PlayCue("ding");
}

// if A is pressed and scores[0] is 0 copy the timer
if (oldpad1.Buttons.A == ButtonState.Released &&
      pad1.Buttons.A == ButtonState.Pressed && scores[0] == 0)
{
   scores[0] = timer;
}

// Repeat for other buttons and gamepads
if (timer == 120)
{
   int winningValue = 120;
   int winnerSubscript = 0;
   for (int i = 0; i < 16; i++)
   {
      if (scores[i] > 0)
      {
         if (scores[i] < winningValue)
         {
            winningValue = scores[i];
            winnerSubscript = i;
         }
      }
   }

   if (winningValue != 120)
   {
      winnerName = names[winnerSubscript];
   }
   else
   {
      winnerName = "**NO WINNER**";
   }
}
   base.Update(gameTime);
}
```

This version of **Update** will work out who has won 2 seconds after the game has been played. It places the name of the winner in the variable **winnerName**, which can then be displayed in the **Draw** method. When the game is started, the **winnerName** is set to an empty string so that the name appears only when it has been calculated.

There is one further improvement to this code, which is that if all the players have pressed their buttons before the sound, there will be no winner. The program checks to see if the winningValue has been changed by the search for the best time. If no value better than 120 was found, it means that everyone pressed their button too early, and the program displays "**NO WINNER**".

> **Sample Code: 03 ReactionTimer with Winner Display**   The 03 ReactionTimer with Winner Display project in the resources for this chapter contains a fully working version of the game that displays the winner.

Conclusion

This has been an interesting chapter. You've created another party game and discovered how to measure time and trigger events. You've also started to work with arrays as a means of allowing your programs to work much more effectively with collections of data.

Pop Quiz

And now yet another popular pop quiz. Is this a quiz your father could answer? We ask.

1. The C# code `int [] scores;` would create an array that could hold four integers.

2. An array can hold any type of data.

3. An array is an object.

4. The first element in an array has the subscript 1.

5. It doesn't matter if your array subscript values are out of range.

Chapter 9
Reading Text Input

- Discover how the keyboard works in XNA.
- Use enumerated types.
- Use arrays and references.
- Work with strings of text.
- Create message board program.

Using the Keyboard in XNA

The Xbox itself does not have a keyboard. But you can plug any USB keyboard into an Xbox, and the keyboard will work. XNA programs use the keyboard in the same way whether they are running on an Xbox or a Windows PC. In this chapter, you'll explore how you can use the keyboard in your XNA games. At the same time, you'll find out more about how C# programs can manipulate text.

Program Project: Message Board

The next program you'll make won't be a game as such but rather an extension to one of your earlier programs. You'll create a message board that can be used to display text for all to see. You can use this to tell people where you are (really cool kids might have one on the outside of their bedroom door to show when they are free/busy and leave helpful messages for parents like "Please clean"). Or you could use it in the living room on the big-screen TV to avoid having to talk to people.

Creating the Message Board Project

You can use an earlier project, the BigClock project in the 06 3D Clock Mood Light directory in the resources for Chapter 5, "Writing Text," as the starting point of your message board. This provides a clock (which would be a nice thing to have on the message board) and also has the code that lets you display text on the screen.

Registering Key Presses

You've used the keyboard before in the Color Nerve game in Chapter 3, "Getting Player Input." You used it alongside the gamepad:

```
GamePadState pad1 = GamePad.GetState(PlayerIndex.One);
KeyboardState keys = Keyboard.GetState();

if (pad1.Buttons.B == ButtonState.Pressed || keys.IsKeyDown(Keys.R))
{
    redIntensity++;
}
```

This code increases the intensity of the red part of your color if the B button on the gamepad is pressed or the R key is pressed on the keyboard. The **IsKeyDown** method is provided with a parameter that tells it which key to test for. If that key is pressed, the method returns true. By calling **IsKeyDown** with different parameters, you can check to see whether particular keys are pressed. In a game situation, this is particularly useful because a player might be pressing several keys at once, such as holding down an arrow key to move while pressing the spacebar to fire a weapon.

The previous code is using inputs in a *level*-sensitive mode, meaning that as long as the R key is held down, the intensity value will increase. However, you've seen that this is not always how you want to use inputs. Sometimes you want them to be *edge triggered* so that you register an event only when something changes. You used edge-triggered events to detect button presses to create the button-bashing games in Chapter 6, "Creating a Multiplayer Game," and also in the reaction timer game in Chapter 8, "Creating a Timer." For a keyboard to be useful, it must be edge triggered; you want to know only when the key changes from up to down. You can't just say that a key has been pressed if **IsKeyDown** says it's down at any particular time.

There are two reasons that you can't do this. The first is that if you test the keyboard 60 times a second, your program might decide that a particular key has been pressed 60 times a second. The second reason is that when people type, they often press several keys at once. When I type the word "the," I find that as I press the "h" character, I still have the "t" held down. This is called "rollover," and hardware designers have been dealing with this ever since keyboards were first used with computers. So you need to write some kind of keyboard edge-triggered code.

> **Note** At this point, it's worth mentioning that reading text from a keyboard in XNA is a lot trickier than reading text in other programming environments. This is because in XNA, the keyboard handling is really designed for playing games.
>
> In conventional programming, there are commands that let you read in a line of text that the user enters. If you write programs to run in the Microsoft Windows environment, you can request that a method be called each time the user presses a key. However, you're using XNA, so you'll just have to live with writing more basic code to read text input. The only good news is that writing this type of code does provide a good way to learn some fundamental programming principles along the way.

Detecting When Keys Are Pressed

You can detect a key being pressed by comparing the current state of the keyboard with the state it had previously. If a key is shown as being in the down position and it was previously up, it must have been pressed, and you need to register it. You could do this on an individual key basis:

```
if (keyState.IsKeyDown(Keys.R) && oldKeyState.IsKeyUp(Keys.R))
{
    // if we get here the key R has just been pressed
}
```

This code tests to see if the R key has just been pressed. The variable **oldKeyState** holds the previous state of the keyboard, and the variable **keyState** holds the current state. The problem with this approach is that you would need to perform this test for every single key on the keyboard—code that would take a while to write. Fortunately, there's a slightly easier way to do this. The **KeyboardState** structure provides a method named **GetPressedKeys** that gives you an array of the keys that are currently pressed. You've seen arrays before; you made one to hold the score values of the reaction timer game in Chapter 8. This time, the array is being used to allow a method to return a set of answers, each of which identifies a key that is currently pressed. The elements in the array are of type **Keys**.

> **Note** There is potential for confusion here. You can use a key on a keyboard to type a character. In this case the word *type* means the action of typing. However, within the C# language, the *type* of a variable determines what kind of information the variable can be used to hold.

The Keys Type

Part of the fun of programming is deciding the best way to store the things that a program must work with. You've seen that you can use the **byte** type to hold small integer values (in the range 0 through 255) and the `int` type to hold integer values in a wider range. You have also seen that XNA provides a variety of types that can hold game-specific things like textures and colors. The designers of XNA needed a way to represent a key on the keyboard so that programmers can write programs that react to a particular key being pressed. You've already used values of type `Keys` in your programs; `Keys.R` is used in the previous code to ask `IsKeyDown` to test whether the R key is being pressed.

Enumerated Types

The `Keys` type is a kind of type I haven't mentioned yet. It's an *enumerated type*. The word *enumerate* means to "count" or "number" items. Enumerated types are created by programmers when they need only a particular range of values to represent something. When the XNA team realized they needed to store information about a particular key on the keyboard, they could have used numbers. (For example, they could have decided that A was 65, B was 66, and so on.) However, they decided to create an enumerated type instead.

An enumerated type is one in which the programmer defines the range of possible values that variables of this type can have and creates names for each of these values. Possible keys on a keyboard include the letter keys A through Z, and the digit keys 0 through 9, as well as the left-hand and right-hand Shift keys, the Enter key, and the Esc key, so the `Keys` type has a value for each of these.

> **The Great Programmer Speaks: Enumerated Types Are Useful**   The Great Programmer is a big fan of enumerated types. She says that if you create a type that can have only certain values, it reduces the chances of your program doing silly things. As an example, she says that if you had a game that was either in Attract mode (nobody playing), Play mode (game in progress), or High Score mode (entering high score value), it makes very good sense to represent these states with a variable that can have only one of those three values. You could use an integer to store this and remember that 0, 1, and 2 mean the three different states, but this would not stop a novice programmer (or your younger brother) from putting "97" in there and causing the program to do strange things. It is much more sensible to create a special enumerated type to hold the state of the game, and you'll be doing this when you make a complete game.

The `Keys` enumeration does not include separate values for capital (uppercase) A and little (lowercase) a. It just represents the key itself. Your program will need to check if the A key and a Shift key are being pressed at the same time. If they are, the user is typing an uppercase A.

Working with Arrays, Objects, and References

The `GetPressedKeys` method returns an array of `Keys` values. Each element in the array describes a key that is presently pressed. The more keys that are pressed, the more elements there are in the array. Figure 9-1 shows how the array might look.

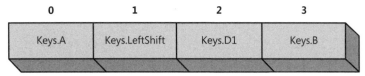

Figure 9-1   Keys array

From the figure, you can see that when the method was called, the A key, the left-hand Shift key, the digit 1, and the B key are all pressed down. This means that to determine which keys have been pressed on the keyboard, you'll need to work through the array of key information supplied by the `GetPressedKeys` method. However, before you write the code to do this, it's time to take a detour into how arrays and objects work together and to consider what the `GetPressedKeys` method actually gives you.

Values and References

Up until now, you've treated all objects equally. You've used `byte`, `string`, `Texture2D`, `double`, `Color`, `SpriteBatch`, and lots of other kinds of objects in your XNA programs and treated all of them in the same way. You know that different objects hold different amounts of data and that this data is held inside the object in *fields*. You also know that objects expose *properties* that you can use to access the values of the fields in the object and that objects also have *methods* that you can use to ask an object to do something for you. You can *declare* variables of these types, give them *identifiers*, and assign values to them using the = operator. Sometimes you need to use the keyword **new** to create instances (for example, for `SpriteBatch`), and sometimes you don't (for `byte`). Now is the time to improve your understanding of how objects are organized in memory. You'll need to consider the difference between *value* and *reference* types.

An array is a type that's managed by reference. It's very important that you understand how references work in C# programs. The Great Programmer reckons that you can't call yourself a proper programmer unless you understand how references work, and you'll need to consider this now. A *reference* is kind of variable that refers to something. It doesn't hold any data; rather, it refers to the object in memory that contains the data. If you wanted an array that could hold four `Keys` values, you would write the following:

```
Keys [] pressedKeys;
pressedKeys = new Keys[4];
```

The first statement creates an array reference named `pressedKeys`. The second statement makes an array that can hold four `Keys` values. These are two separate actions. When they are complete, you have an array reference that has been made to refer to a particular four-element array of `Keys` that is sitting in memory somewhere. At the moment, the reference `pressedKeys` is the only way that you can locate and use that four-element array.

Arrays as Offices

If you want to go back to the office example, you can think of an array as an office, as shown in Figure 9-2.

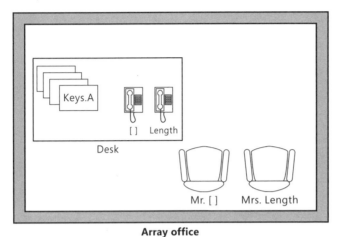

Array office

Figure 9-2 Keys array as an office

The office holds the usual desk with the properties on it and the telephones for the behaviors that the object can support. In the case of an array, there is a property called **Length** that's used to find out how many elements there are in the array. A *property* is a means by which an object can present a value to the outside world. When the **Length** phone rings, Mrs. Length gets up, counts the number of array elements on the property table, and tells the caller the result.

```
int keyCount = pressedKeys.Length;
```

This code shows how the **Length** property is used. If the **pressedKeys** reference refers to the array you created previously, the integer **keyCount** would be set to 4.

There's also another strange-looking property called [ ] in your array office. This property is how elements are accessed. Mr. [ ] provides access to the pile of elements on the table. He is given the subscript value and then counts down the pile of elements on the table to get to the one that you want. If you give the subscript 0, you get the top one, the subscript 1 gets you the one below that, and so on. Mr. [ ] can read values off the array elements and also can write new values at the appropriate place in the pile.

```
pressedKeys[0] = Keys.R;
```

This code shows how Mr. [ ] is used. It would cause him to put the value **Keys.R** in the element on the top of the pile.

You can think of a reference to an object as the phone number that you use to call to the people in that office. When a new instance of a class is created, it's as if you built an office, put in a desk and telephones, and hired a staff member for each behavior. Each telephone is identified with the phone number of the office, followed by an extension for the behavior in the object that you want to contact. So you could use `123435.Length` to get a hold of Mrs. Length in office 12345. Of course, in reality a reference is the place in memory where the object is stored rather than a telephone number, but the principle is the same. When you're given a reference, all you're told is how to get a hold of something.

```
pressedKeys = new Keys[4];
```

This code would create a new array and then set **pressedKeys** with the "telephone number" of that array. The only way that you can get a hold of this array is by using **pressedKeys** to locate it. If the variable **pressedKeys** is destroyed or overwritten, the object may as well not exist, as you have no way of getting in touch with it. This is the same as if you met someone wonderful at a party and failed to get his or her telephone number. If you can't get to an object, it might as well not be there.

Say Hello to the Garbage Collector

Within C#, there's a special mechanism for getting rid of objects that might as well not be there. The *garbage collector* process has the job of looking for objects that do not have anything referring to them and removing them from memory. Memory allocation is an important part of programming, and you need to be careful not to make too much work for the garbage collector. A novice programmer could write the following C# code:

```
Keys [] pressedKeys;
pressedKeys = new Keys[100];
pressedKeys = new Keys[200];
```

This is very stupid code. It's completely legal and would compile and run, but it's still very stupid, because the 100-element array that was created in the second statement is immediately made useless in the third, where **pressedKeys** is made to refer to another, larger array. This approach is like building a brand-new office and then destroying the only copy of the telephone number that could be used to contact it. The garbage collector would eventually notice that the array object had no references referring to it and would destroy it, but until this happened, a large chunk of memory would be unusable.

The Great Programmer makes sure that when she writes a program, it does not repeatedly create and destroy objects in this way; as a result, her software runs quickly and uses only the minimum amount of memory.

Using References and Values

You can see that reference variables are quite different from "ordinary" variables that simply hold values. It's important that you understand the difference. A reference variable holds the "telephone number" of an instance of an object. A value variable holds a particular value, like this:

```
int myAge;
myAge = 21;
```

These statements declare an `int` variable called `myAge` and set it to the rather optimistic (in my case) value of `21`. You can think of `myAge` as a piece of paper with space to write a single integer value on it. When a value is assigned to the variable, it's equivalent to writing a new number on the paper. If I assign the value in `myAge` to another `int` variable, the value on the paper is copied across.

```
int myAge;
myAge = 21;
int tempAge;
tempAge = myAge;
```

You now have a new `int` variable called `tempAge`. This will have the value 21 written on it because that's the value that was copied from the `myAge` variable. In other words, when you work with value types, you're copying values from one piece of paper to another. Changing the value written on one piece of paper will not change the value on another.

```
tempAge++; // this will not change the value in myAge
```

If the value in `tempAge` is increased by 1, `tempAge` will now hold the value 22, but `myAge` will still have the value 21.

However, consider what happens when the program performs assignments using references.

```
Keys [ ] pressedKeys;
pressedKeys = new Keys[100];
Keys oldKeys;
oldKeys = pressedKeys;
```

The variable `oldKeys` is a reference that can refer to an array of `Keys`. If I set `oldKeys` equal to `pressedKeys`, it means that it refers to the same object as `pressedKeys` does. In other words, it contains the same office phone number. Whether you use `oldKeys.Length()` or `pressedKeys.Length()`, you get the same Mrs. Length on the end of the line. So you can see that the following statements both set the element at the start of the same array:

```
oldKeys[0] = Keys.X;
pressedKeys[0] = Keys.Y;
```

First the element is set to X, and then it is set to Y. At the end of these two statements, `oldKeys[0]` and `pressedKeys[0]` both contain Y.

An object managed by reference doesn't have a name; rather, it's identified only in terms of the things that are referring to it. You should never say "the array called `oldKeys`"; you can say only "the array that `oldKeys` is currently referring to." During the lifetime of the `oldKeys` reference, it could be made to refer to many different arrays.

Why Do We Have References and Values?

You might be wondering why the designers of C# have bothered with value and reference types. All they have done so far is make programming more confusing in that assignment statements can assign either references or values.

```
x = y;
```

This statement could mean "make the reference **x** refer to the same thing that **y** refers to," or it could mean "take the value in **y** and copy it into **x**." Without knowing what type **x** and **y** are, you can't decide. However, references are very useful in programs. As an example, consider the **Texture2D** type. You've used this in your programs to store an image you might want to draw. The image might be very large, in which case a **Texture2D** instance would take up a lot of memory. Because of this, textures are managed by reference. If I want to give someone my texture, I'll pass them a reference to it. In a game, you often want to do this because you'll be using the same texture to draw lots of objects. In a space shooter game, each of the identical aliens that are attacking your spaceship could be drawn using the same texture. Value types on the other hand are small and copies can easily be passed between different parts of a program.

References and GetPressedKeys

Up until now, you've been using value types and reference types without worrying too much about the difference, but as you write more complicated games, you'll need to deal with both kinds. Later, you'll revisit the way that value and references are used when you design some data types of your own; for now, the important concept to remember is that an array is a type that is managed by reference, and that what you get back from **GetPressedKeys** is a reference to an array.

Displaying Keys

You'll start your message board off by writing a program that displays the keys that are presently being held down on a keyboard. The **Update** method will create a message string that the **Draw** method will put up on the screen for you. The code in the **Update** method must look through the array of pressed keys and add a description of each key to the message string as follows:

```
string messageString;
protected override void Update(GameTime gameTime)
{
   KeyboardState keyState = Keyboard.GetState();
   // Allows the game to exit by pressing the Esc key
   if (keyState.IsKeyDown(Keys.Escape))
   {
      this.Exit();
   }
   Keys[] pressedKeys;
   pressedKeys = keyState.GetPressedKeys();
   messageString = "";
   for (int i = 0; i < pressedKeys.Length; i++)
   {
      messageString = messageString + pressedKeys[i].ToString() + " " ;
   }
   base.Update(gameTime);
}
```

The first part of the method sets messageString to an empty string. Then the string representation for each Keys item in the array is added to the end of the message. You used the ToString method before when you converted dates and times into strings for your clock. This method provides a way for an object to provide a string of text that describes the information the object holds. When you call ToString on an instance of a Key, the ToString method should tell you what key it is. The string that is built in the Update method is displayed by the Draw method.

```
protected override void Draw(GameTime gameTime)
{
    graphics.GraphicsDevice.Clear(Color.CornflowerBlue);
    Vector2 messageVector = new Vector2(50, 100);
    gameSpriteBatch.Begin();
    gameSpriteBatch.DrawString(font, messageString, messageVector, Color.White);
    gameSpriteBatch.End();
    base.Draw(gameTime);
}
```

This Draw method simply draws the messageString on the screen. Figure 9-3 shows the output of the program if the Caps Lock key, the A key, and the left-hand Alt key are held down.

Figure 9-3   Drawing level-detected key presses on the screen

> **Sample Code: Key Viewer**   The KeyViewer project in the 01 KeyViewer directory in the resources for this chapter contains a program that uses the **Draw** and **Update** methods in this section to display the keys that are being pressed on the keyboard. Note that different hardware will be able to support different numbers of keys being held down at the same time, and this can vary depending on which keys are pressed simultaneously.

Detecting Key Presses

As you'll see with the KeyViewer program, the name of the key that is pressed is displayed as long as the key itself is held down. However, as we found with the gamepad, you want to register a key press only when you see a key change from up to down. You detect such changes by comparing the present state of the keyboard with the previous state. Figure 9-4 shows how this might work. It shows the **oldKeys** that were previously pressed and the **pressedKeys** that are presently pressed. Your program must decide which key has just been pressed.

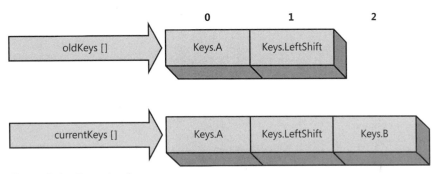

Figure 9-4   Detecting key presses

If you look at Figure 9-4, you can see that the key that must have just been pressed is the B key. The A key was already pressed, as was the left-hand Shift key. You need to find a sequence of operations that can work this out. The posh programming term for what we need at this point is an *algorithm*. This is nothing to do with music; it's simply a description of a means by which a problem can be solved.

When faced with a situation like this, I think that it's a bit like being a detective. A detective arrives at the scene of a crime, looks at the evidence, and then tries to build up a sequence of events that explains everything that has been found. A programmer has some information that comes in from which he or she must produce the desired output by a process that he or she needs to devise. If you have a problem like this, it's often useful to set out what you know and what you want to find out and then try to find a way of getting one from the other.

In this case, in the input side, you have a list of keys that were pressed before and a list of keys that are pressed now.

The output that you want is any keys that have been pressed since you last looked. If you think about it for a while, you can come up with a way to tell which keys have just been pressed.

"Any keys in the list of keys that are pressed now that are **not** in the list of keys that were pressed before are ones that have just been pressed."

You can test this by applying it to the keys in Figure 9-4. Both the A key and the left-hand Shift key are in the `oldKeys` array and the `pressedKeys` array. However, the B key is only in the `pressedKeys` array and so must have just been pressed down. At the moment, your solution does not give you any steps to follow; what you need to do now is convert it into a proper algorithm. Initially, you can write this in English; then you can convert it into C# code.

"Take each value in `pressedKeys` in turn and check to see if it occurs in `oldKeys`. If you don't find the value in `oldKeys`, that key must have been pressed since you last looked."

You know that to work your way through an array, you need to use a **for** loop of some kind. In this case, you'll need to put one **for** loop inside another, because you'll need to look through the `oldKeys` array for each of the values in `pressedKeys`. This is called "nesting" the **for** loops and is a very common programming technique.

```
// String we are going to display - initially an empty string
string messageString = "";
// the keys that were pressed before - initially an empty array
Keys[] oldKeys = new Keys[0];

protected override void Update(GameTime gameTime)
{
  KeyboardState keyState = Keyboard.GetState();
  // Allows the game to exit by pressing the Esc key
  if (keyState.IsKeyDown(Keys.Escape))
  {
    this.Exit();
  }

  // the keys that are currently pressed
  Keys[] pressedKeys;
  pressedKeys = keyState.GetPressedKeys();

  // work through each key that is presently pressed
  for (int i = 0; i < pressedKeys.Length; i++)
  {
    // set a flag to indicate we have not found the key
    bool foundIt = false;
    // work through each key that was previously pressed
    for (int j = 0; j < oldKeys.Length; j++)
    {
      if (pressedKeys[i] == oldKeys[j])
      {
        // we found the key in the previously pressed keys
        foundIt = true;
      }
    }
```

```
    if (foundIt == false)
    {
        // if we get here we didn't find the key in the old keys, so
        // add the key to the end of the message string
        messageString = messageString + pressedKeys[i].ToString();
    }
  }
// remember the currently pressed keys for next time
oldKeys = pressedKeys;
base.Update(gameTime);
}
```

This version of **Update** takes each key in the **pressedKeys** array and searches the **oldKeys** array to see whether that key is in there. If **Update** doesn't find the key, it adds a description of the key to the message string. I've added quite a few comments (the lines that start with //) that should make the code easier to understand. Note that I am using a **bool** variable called **foundIt** to record whether a key has been found when the old key array is searched. If this flag is not set during a search, that key value is not present in the old array and must be a new key. The message string itself is drawn in the same way as it was in the previous program.

> **Sample Code: First Message Display**   The MessageBoard project in the 02 First Message Display directory in the resources for this chapter contains a program that uses the **Update** method from this section to build and display a message from the keys that are pressed on the keyboard.

References and null

If you look closely at the code in **Update**, you will find that at the end of the method, the value of **oldKeys** is set to refer to the **pressedKeys** array so that the next time that **Update** is called, it will have some old keys to check against. However, the very first time that **Update** is called, there will be no old keys. This problem is solved by making **oldKeys** refer to an empty array when the variable is declared.

```
// the keys that were pressed before - initially an empty array
Keys[] oldKeys = new Keys[0];
```

The preceding declaration creates the **oldKeys** array reference and makes it refer to an array that contains zero elements. The program must do this because the **Update** method will use this reference to find the list of the keys that were pressed before. The first time that **Update** is called, it needs an array to look through (even if the array contains no elements), and so you need to create one.

> **Note**   If **oldKeys** was not set in this way, it would instead be an empty, or *null*, reference, which refers nowhere. Trying to follow a null reference is a bad thing for a program to do and would result in an error.

Using break to Improve Performance

The program that you've written works fine, but it's not as efficient as it could be. There's an additional feature of C# that you can use to improve it. The C# language provides a keyword called **break** that you can use to abandon the execution of a loop. When you're searching through oldKeys to see if it contains a key that is currently pressed, as soon as you find a match, there's no need look any further. You can use the **break** keyword to break out of the search loop, as shown in bold type here:

```
// work through each key in that was previously pressed
for (int j = 0; j < oldKeys.Length; j++)
{
  if (pressedKeys[i] == oldKeys[j])
  {
    // we found the key in the previously pressed keys
    foundIt = true;
    // no need to look any further
    break;
  }
}
```

If the program reaches the **break** instruction, the program abandons the loop and continues running at the statement after the loop.

Decoding Key Characters

You can now detect individual key presses, which is nice. However, at the moment, the text you get from the keys is not as useful as you might like. The letter keys seem to work okay, but keys such as Shift and the spacebar do not produce the output you want. Figure 9-5 shows what happens if you try to type "Hello World." When you press Shift to get the uppercase H, for example, Shift is registered as a key; the spacebar key doesn't work properly either, it displays "Space" instead of a space character.

What you need to do next is decode the keys into more useful strings. If you get the value **Keys.A**, you'd like to have "A" and so on. You could use a large number of **if** statements to do this, but C# provides a better way of doing this, called a **switch** statement:

```
string keyString = ""; // initially this is an empty string
switch (pressedKeys[i])
{
  // digits
  case Keys.D0:
    keyString = "0";
    break;
  case Keys.D1:
    keyString = "1";
    break;
  // rest of digits here
  case Keys.A:
    keyString = "A";
    break;
```

```
  case Keys.B:
    keyString = "B";
    break;
  // rest of alphabet here

  // punctuation characters
  case Keys.Space:
    keyString = " ";
    break;
  case Keys.OemPeriod:
    keyString = ".";
    break;
}
```

Figure 9-5   Decoding problems with typed text

The **switch** statement selects a particular **case** based on the value of a *control expression*. (You would plug this **switch** statement into the **if (foundIt == false)** statement block just before setting **messageString**, and change the **messageString** statement to use **keyString**.) In this case, the control expression is **pressedKeys[i]**, which is the value of the key you've just discovered was pressed. Depending on this value, the code sets a string called **keyString** to the appropriate text. Once the string has been set, the code uses the C# **break** keyword, causing the program to exit from the **switch** statement. You've seen **break** before when you used it to exit from a **for** loop. You can also use it to exit from a **switch** statement.

If the value in the control expression does not match any of the cases, the statement has no effect. The **switch** statement does not make anything possible that you couldn't do with a large number of **if** statements, but it does make programming easier in some situations. If you use the previous code to decode your keys, you'll have a usable text reader, but at the moment the code doesn't use the Shift keys properly, so every letter that is typed will be uppercase. However, it turns out that you can easily fix this by adding the following code after your **switch** statement:

```
if (keyState.IsKeyUp(Keys.LeftShift) && keyState.IsKeyUp(Keys.RightShift))
{
    keyString = keyString.ToLower();
}
```

I'm quite proud of this code. It tests the state of the two Shift keys on the keyboard. If both Shift keys are in the up position, the string that has been pressed is converted into the lowercase version of that text. This works because the string type provides a method called **ToLower** that provides a lowercase version of the string, which turns out to be exactly what you want. **ToLower** is clever in that it affects only characters that are letters, not other characters such as numbers and punctuation.

The string type provides a huge number of methods that can be used to get a hold of processed versions of the string. It provides one called **ToUpper**, which will produce a version of the string containing all uppercase letters; it also provides a method that can be used to chop out a certain number of characters from the string. You can use this to provide your user with simple text editing.

```
if (pressedKeys[i] == Keys.Back)
{
    if (messageString.Length > 0)
    {
        messageString = messageString.Remove(messageString.Length - 1, 1);
    }
}
else
{
    // Switch statement goes here
}
```

If the user presses the Back key, this code removes a key from the end of the **messageString** by using the **Remove** method, which removes characters from the end of the string. **Remove** is told the position to start removing from and the number of characters to remove, so I give it the length of the string minus 1 to remove the last character and ask for one character to be removed. The code also checks to see whether the length of the string is zero, because if the string is zero length, there's nothing to remove.

The final enhancement you need to add is the ability to take a new line in your string so that the user can create messages greater than one line in size. A string can contain special *control characters* that control the layout of the text. The most useful of these is the new-line character, which instructs whatever is processing the string to take a new line. It turns out that the

`DrawString` method you use to draw the text on the screen will take a new line when it sees this character in a message, so all you need to do is convert the Enter key (which users will press when they want a new line on the display) into a new-line character. The convention in C# strings is that a control character is preceded by the backslash character (\).

```
case Keys.Enter:
  keyString = "\n";
  break;
```

This case is added to your `switch` statement to convert the Enter key into a string that will cause `DrawString` to take a new line. C# provides other special formatting characters, but for now you'll use only the new-line character.

Sample Code: Message Board Program   The MessageBoard project in the 03 Full Message Display directory in the resources for this chapter contains a program that uses the previously mentioned code to implement a message display with a changing color background, 3D text, and a clock.

Figure 9-6 shows the fully featured message board in action. The clock is always drawn on the line beneath the text.

Figure 9-6   Message board with clock

You can experiment with the sample code for the Message Board program. You could try using different sizes of text to create different kinds of display.

Conclusion

This has been an interesting chapter. You now have a way for users to type text into your XNA program, which can be the basis of some interesting games, as you'll see later. You've also started to look at how data is stored and structured in C# programs and at the difference between value and reference types. You've used a new program structure—the `switch` statement—that lets a program select between a number of different options depending on the value of a particular expression. Finally, you've taken a look at the things you can do with strings.

Pop Quiz

And now the ever-popular pop quiz. The questions are different, but the possible answers are still the same, true or false.

1. In XNA, a keyboard can register only one key at a time.

2. The `Keys` type holds a string.

3. There are separate `Keys` values for uppercase A and lowercase a.

4. The `Keys` type is an enumerated type.

5. A reference gives the location of an object in memory.

6. It's not possible for two references to refer to the same object in memory.

7. The garbage collector runs only when a program has finished.

8. The `break` keyword causes your program to stop.

9. A `switch` statement is used to turn off the power to the computer.

10. The `string` class provides a method to produce an uppercase version of a `string` object.

11. It's not possible to add two strings together.

Part III
Games and Programming

In this part:

Using C# Methods to Solve Problems

- Use image manipulation to write a game you might like to play.

- Discover how to create and use your first C# methods.

- Take a look at test-driven development.

- Make some mistakes and discover how to fix them.

Introduction

Your programming skills are coming along. Your programs can store different kinds of numbers, do things with them, and even make decisions. You also know how to add image assets to your games and display them on the screen.

Now you'll create a game based on image manipulation. To make your life easier, you'll create some C# methods of your own and also take a look at a development technique called "test-driven development."

Playing with Images

In Chapter 4, "Displaying Images," you discovered how to load images into your programs. Now you can start to have some fun with them. Up until now, the image drawing that you have performed simply displays a texture on the screen in the same place each time the **Draw** method is called. Moving the picture around the screen and maybe even zooming in on it would be really nice. You might even find that these abilities give you an idea for a game.

Zooming In On an Image

When you wrote your image display program, you created a variable called `spriteRect` of type `Rectangle`. This rectangle was the destination of the draw action. The size of the rectangle was set to the full screen in the `Initialize` method.

```
protected override void Initialize()
{
   gameSpriteBatch = new SpriteBatch(graphics.GraphicsDevice);
   spriteRect = new Rectangle(
     0,   // X position of top left hand corner
     0,   // Y position of top left hand corner
     graphics.GraphicsDevice.Viewport.Width,    // rectangle width
     graphics.GraphicsDevice.Viewport.Height); // rectangle height

   base.Initialize();
}
```

When the **Draw** method ran, it drew the image texture in the `spriteRect` rectangle.

```
protected override void Draw(GameTime gameTime)
{
   graphics.GraphicsDevice.Clear(Color.CornflowerBlue);
   gameSpriteBatch.Begin();
   gameSpriteBatch.Draw(gameTexture, spriteRect, Color.White);
   gameSpriteBatch.End();

   base.Draw(gameTime);
}
```

Now you'll change the way that the picture is drawn by changing the values in `spriteRect` as the program runs. The Xbox contains some very clever hardware and software that will automatically resize the picture for you so that you can move and scale your picture very easily. You'll start by adding the following **Update** method to the display program:

```
protected override void Update(GameTime gameTime)
{
   // Allows the game to exit
   if (GamePad.GetState(PlayerIndex.One).Buttons.Back == ButtonState.Pressed)
      this.Exit();

   spriteRect.Height++;
   spriteRect.Width++;
   base.Update(gameTime);
}
```

Each time the **Update** method is called, the width and height fields of the rectangle are increased by 1. These fields are the data members inside the rectangle that represent the rectangle dimensions. You get hold of a field in an object by giving the identifier of the variable, a period character (.), and then the name of the field you wish to use. Remember that this is the rectangle that describes where you want Jake to be drawn, so changing the size of this rectangle will change the size of the image on the screen.

XNA does not care that you're drawing off the screen and simply shows you the part of the picture that will fit on the screen. Figure 10-1 shows what the screen looks like after a program using this `Update` method has been running for a few seconds.

Figure 10-1   Stretching Jake

If you leave the program running a very long time, it will end up zooming in on a particular blade of grass, but this example does show how you can change the way that images are placed on the screen.

> **Sample Code: Jake Zoom**   The sample project in the 01 JakeZoom directory in the resources for this chapter will draw a picture of Jake and then slowly zoom in on it.

Game Idea: Super Zoom Out

You can use this zoom ability to make a game. Rather than starting with a picture and then zooming in on it, you could start with a zoomed-in image and slowly pull back (zoom out) to reveal more and more of the picture. The first person to correctly identify the picture wins the game. This game is quite fun, particularly if the images are familiar to the players.

Creating a Zoom-Out

The starting point of the game should be an enormous drawing rectangle that you'll reduce in size as the game continues, causing more and more of the image to be visible.

Updating the Drawing Rectangle

To make this work, you need to change the way that you set up the **Rectangle**, which describes the part of the image that you'll draw.

```
protected override void Initialize()
{
  gameSpriteBatch = new SpriteBatch(graphics.GraphicsDevice);
  spriteRect = new Rectangle(0, 0, 6000, 4500);
  base.Initialize();
}
```

This code creates a rectangle that's 6,000 pixels wide and 4,500 pixels high, or 10 times the original image size and much bigger than the screen. Figure 10-2 shows the effect of using a rectangle like this. If you use this rectangle to control the draw process, the image will be too large to fit on the display, so the screen shows only the top left-hand corner.

Figure 10-2   Jake in "Zoom"

The game will then reduce the width and height of the rectangle each time **Update** is called:

```
protected override void Update(GameTime gameTime)
{
 // Allows the game to exit
 if (GamePad.GetState(PlayerIndex.One).Buttons.Back == ButtonState.Pressed)
    this.Exit();
```

```
    spriteRect.Height--;
    spriteRect.Width--;

    base.Update(gameTime);
}
```

The idea of this **Update** is that each time it's called, the width and height fields of the rectangle are reduced by 1, decreasing the amount of zoom and making more of the picture visible.

> **Sample Code: Jake Display Bad Zoom**   The sample project in the 02 JakeDisplay Bad Zoom Out directory in the resources for this chapter will display a zoomed-in image of Jake and then use the **Update** method from this section to zoom out.

If you run the program, you find that although the zoom-out idea is a good one, the zoom-out is not as you would like. Figure 10-3 shows what happens after you run this program for a while.

Figure 10-3   Zooming out Jake

More of the picture is visible, but it seems to have been stretched for some reason. To understand what's happening, you need to think first about what you set out to do and then what you did.

1. You wanted to display only part of the image on the Xbox screen. This would allow you to show only part of the image so that the player has to guess what the picture is.

2. To achieve this, you made the draw rectangle enormous by multiplying its width and height by 10 so that only part of the drawn image was visible on the screen.

3. You then created an **Update** method to reduce the width and height of this rectangle by 1 each time it is called so that the amount of image in the screen will increase progressively.

You notice, however, that as this program "zooms out" of the image, it no longer looks right. The problem is that each time you reduce the width and height, you're reducing them by the same amount (that is, both the width and the height get smaller by 1). Figure 10-4 shows what's happening. It shows the path followed by the bottom left-hand corner of the Jake image if you repeatedly reduce the width and height of the picture by 1 each time.

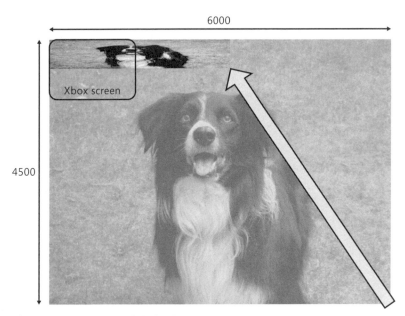

Figure 10-4   Zoom path behavior

The path does not follow the diagonal of the image; instead, it moves up too quickly and scrunches the height of the picture. This is happening because you're reducing the height and width by the same amount each time. Because the picture is not as high (4,500) as it is wide (6,000), the height is "used up" more quickly, leading to a scrunched picture.

You can fix the problem by reducing each value by a percentage each time rather than by a particular value. For example, if you wanted to reduce the picture size by 1 percent, you would take 45 (1 percent of 4,500) off the height and 60 (1 percent of 60,000) off the width. This sounds a bit complicated, so you ask the Great Programmer for advice.

> **The Great Programmer Speaks: Break Complicated Things Down**   The Great
> Programmer thinks that it's always a good idea to break more complicated tasks down into
> smaller chunks by using methods. She says there are three reasons you do this:
>
> It makes the programming simpler.
>
> Perhaps you can find someone else to do that task (or maybe a method already exists to
> do that).
>
> You might end up with methods that you can use in other parts of your program.
>
> In this case, you want to reduce the sizes by a particular percentage, so a good starting point
> would be a method that works out percentages.

Because the Great Programmer is never wrong, you now have to find out how to use methods
to help you solve your problem.

A Method to Calculate Percentages

As you've learned, a method is a block of code that does something for you. Each method has
an identifier that you use to refer to the method when you call it.

Putting a Method into Your Game Class

You've seen methods many times before. Mr. Draw and Mrs. Update are methods that were
written by the XNA team for you to use. Now you'll create a method of your own. This means
that you need to provide a name (identifier) for the method and a way that the method can tell
you a result. You also need to provide a list of instructions for the method to use when it's
asked to run. Figure 10-5 shows how this might work. You've given the method the name
getPercentage, and Mr. getPercentage now has a chair and a telephone in the Game1 office.

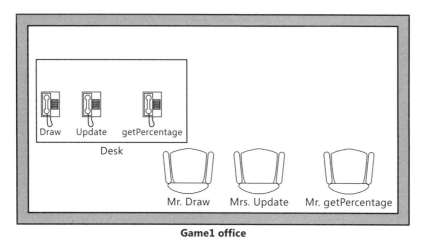

Figure 10-5   A new member of the Game1 class

When the **getPercentage** telephone rings, Mr. getPercentage will jump up and answer it. He'll be told the number and the percentage required. He will then need to work out the answer, write it down on a piece of paper, and have the value sent back to the caller. The details of what information is passed into the method (the telephone call) and the result it delivers (what's written on the piece of paper) are written in C# as the method *header*. The detailed information about what the method does is called the method *body*. Figure 10-6 shows the header and body for a method named **getPercentage**.

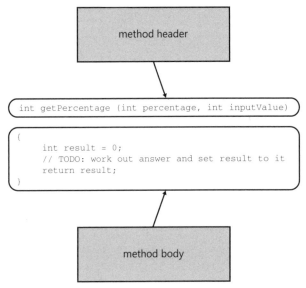

Figure 10-6   A getPercentage method header and body

This is not a very good **getPercentage** method in that it doesn't work out the result, but it does show how a C# method is made up of header and body.

As you've just learned, the *method header* gives the identifier for the method and what type of result it returns. It also gives the number and type of any parameters. A *parameter* is used to feed information into a method. It's how you told the **Clear** method which color to use when the screen was cleared way back in Chapter 1, "Computers, Xboxes, C#, XNA, and You." Once the compiler has the header of a method, it knows what the method "looks like" in that it can create the code to use the method. This description of a method is often called the *signature* of the method. The **getPercentage** method accepts two integer parameters and returns an integer result. When you create a method, you decide the type and number of the parameters that the method needs to do its job. Some methods have many parameters; others have none. The **Initialize** method does not accept any parameters; it's simply called to initialize the game program and does not need to be told anything.

The method header is followed by the method body. This method body is a block of statements that perform the task the method was created for. The body can be a very large number of statements or only one or two. If the method delivers a result (which your getPercentage method will need to do), the body must contain a statement that returns a value of the type specified in the method header. After the compiler has the body of the method, the compiler knows which statements need to be performed when the method is called. I've put a TODO into the place where the calculation needs to go. You haven't seen the **return** statement before, but it's composed of the keyword **return** followed by the value the method is to send back to the caller.

> **Note**   You might have noticed that Mr. getPercentage has an identifier that starts with a lowercase "g." This is not because I've made a mistake (as if), but because this method will have a slightly different (and more limited) status than **Update** and **Draw**, and I want to reflect this in the identifier it has.

Calling a Method

You've called methods many times in your programs. You use the **getPercentage** method like you would any other, but you need to make sure that you supply the right kinds of parameters.

```
height = height - getPercentage(1, height);
```

This line of code would use **getPercentage** to reduce the value of the variable called **height** by 1 percent. When a method call is made, the program performs a number of tasks in sequence:

1. It makes a note of where it is in the program so that it can come back to the right place when the method finishes.

2. It gets the values of any parameters and sets them up for the method to use.

3. It jumps into the method body and performs the statements in the method body.

4. At the end of the method body or when it reaches a **return** statement, it goes back and delivers whatever value was expected.

5. Then the program continues running at the statement following the method call.

> **Note**   You need to make sure that you call the method correctly. If you don't give two parameters, or one of them is not the correct type of data, the C# compiler shows you the errors and refuses to make a program that you can run.

Returning Nothing Using Void

The **getPercentage** method must return a value, but sometimes a method needs only to perform a task. The **Draw** and **Update** methods are like this. Though they're given parameters to work on, they don't return an answer for the caller to use. Methods that don't return a result are given the return type **void**. This tells the compiler that the method does not deliver any information to the caller.

```
protected override void Draw(GameTime gameTime)
{
    graphics.GraphicsDevice.Clear(Color.CornflowerBlue);

    // game draw behavior here
    base.Draw(gameTime);
}
```

Methods that don't return anything don't have to contain a **return** keyword to deliver a result. Instead, they return when the program reaches the end of the statements in the method body. Don't worry about the meaning of the **protected** and **override** keywords. If you want a method to return before the end of the method block, you can use the **return** keyword to cause a return at that point. If the method returns a value, the return must be followed by an expression that delivers a value of the required type.

It's up to you whether a method you create returns a value. Most of the methods that I write do return something. Sometimes they return a value that indicates whether the method has worked correctly.

Creating a getPercentage Method

At this point, you know how to create methods. Now you need to make one that will work for you. You started with an "empty" **getPercentage** method.

```
int getPercentage(int percentage, int inputValue)
{
    int result = 0;
    // TODO: work out answer and set result to it return result;
}
```

This code shows how the method will work, and this code will compile and run. However, because the method always returns 0, it won't do what you want it to. You need to add statements to the method body to get it to behave as you want.

Testing a Method

At this point, you've created a version of **getPercentage** that doesn't work properly, and this seems a bit silly. The Great Programmer tells you that it's quite sensible to create "broken" methods like this; you can use them to decide what the method looks like and then go back and fill in the statements later. You can also use them to write tests.

```
protected override void Draw(GameTime gameTime)
{
    if (getPercentage(10, 800) == 80)
    {
        graphics.GraphicsDevice.Clear(Color.Green);
    }
```

```
    else
    {
        graphics.GraphicsDevice.Clear(Color.Red);
    }
  base.Draw(gameTime);
}
```

This code is a test of the **getPercentage** method that turns the screen green if a call of the method works and red if it doesn't. Programmers usually use better ways to perform these tests, but this code shows the principle. This is a version of a professional development technique called *test-driven development*.

> **The Great Programmer Speaks: Test-Driven Development Is the Best Way to Write Programs**   The Great Programmer likes test-driven development even more than she likes shoe sales, which is to say, a lot. She says that creating tests and then writing program statements that will pass the tests is a very good way to develop software. But she warns that you should design your tests carefully.

Designing Tests for getPercentage

You could easily write a version of **getPercentage** that would pass the previously mentioned single test.

```
int getPercentage(int percentage, int inputValue)
{
    return 80;
}
```

This method would pass the one test that you've created but would not be a very good way to work out percentages. It does highlight a very important point, though: A test can prove only that a particular fault is not present. It can't prove that there are no faults. The test you wrote checks that your method could figure out that 10 percent of 800 is 80. Even the original method that always returned 0 would work whenever you tried to work out 0 percent of something or any percentage of 0. If someone says that his code is "fully tested," what he really means is that he can't think of a reason it shouldn't work, but these two ideas are not quite the same thing.

Testing computer programs is really difficult. If you want to test a design for a bridge over a river, you simply make a test bridge and put increasingly heavy things on it until it breaks. Then you know the heaviest thing that can go across that kind of bridge. Where computers are concerned, testing doesn't work like this. A computer program might work with one value and then fail with another slightly different one.

The good news, for most of you at least, is that your programs won't ever do anything that could be called "mission critical." However, if you end up writing programs for a living, make sure that you take testing very seriously. It's what separates the Great Programmers from the good programmers.

I've come up with some C# code that will give your method a reasonable workout. It is not a particularly comprehensive test, but it will do for now.

```
protected override void Draw(GameTime gameTime)
{
 if ((getPercentage(0, 0)     == 0)     &&    // 0 percent of 0
     (getPercentage(0, 100)   == 0)     &&    // 0 percent of 100
     (getPercentage(50, 100)  == 50)    &&    // 50 percent of 100
     (getPercentage(100, 50)  == 50)    &&    // 100 percent of 50
     (getPercentage(10, 100)  == 10))         // 10 percent of 100
 {
    graphics.GraphicsDevice.Clear(Color.Green);
 }
 else
 {
    graphics.GraphicsDevice.Clear(Color.Red);
 }
 base.Draw(gameTime);
}
```

Note that I'm using the AND (**&&**) operator to combine a bunch of conditions. You've seen the OR (**||**) condition before. I used to test if one thing *or* another was true. The **&&** condition lets me test to test if one thing *and* another is true. I want all the calls of **getPercentage** to work before I show the green screen. If any one of them fails, the **&&** condition will return false, and you'll get red a screen. This is not a very sensible way to manage large numbers of tests because if you get a red screen, you'll have difficulty working out which test has failed, but the principle is an important one. The objective now is to create a version of **getPercentage** that passes all the previously mentioned tests.

Creating the getPercentage Method Body

You now have a design for the method header and a set of tests for the method, so next you must create the method body. You could make it work like this:

1. Calculate the fraction of the amount that you want (this is the percentage divided by 100; in other words, 50 percent would give you 50/100, which is a half).

2. Multiply the incoming amount by this fraction to create the result.

The **getPercentage** method that uses this technique would look like the code shown here.

```
int getPercentage(int percentage, int inputValue)
{
   int fraction = percentage / 100;
   int result = fraction * inputValue;
   return result;
}
```

First you work out the fraction, then you do the multiplication. The / operator can be applied between two *operands* (things that operators work on) and will perform a division. The * operator is applied in the same way but performs multiplication.

Remember that when the method runs, the parameters `percentage` and `inputValue` are set to the values that they have in the call of the method.

```
int test;
test = getPercentage (10, 800);
```

The previous call would be performed with `percentage` set to 10 and `inputValue` set to 800.

```
int fraction = 10 / 100;
int result = fraction * 800;
```

If you plug the figures in and do the sums by hand, the result comes out fine. When you use this version of the method, you get a red screen, which is not good. Something is broken, and you need to fix it.

> **Sample Code: Percentage Test**   The sample project in the 03 Percentage Test directory in the resources for this chapter implements the previously mentioned **Update** method. You won't ever use this project as the basis of a game, but you will use it to investigate the problems that you're having with the **getPercentage** method.

Debugging C# Programs

By now, you've probably started to wonder if zooming is worth all this effort. You've done lots of work and found out about methods, parameters, tests, and other stuff, and you got a red screen for your trouble. The good news is that the techniques you're learning are how all programs are written. The process of failing to get a picture of Jake to zoom properly is teaching you a lot about how programs are constructed. But now you need to learn some more aspects of how C# programs work and how to debug them.

Debugging with Breakpoints

You know that your program isn't working because the screen goes red when it runs. That means that at least one of the tests is failing. However, at the moment, you don't know which of the conditions is wrong. It would be really nice if you could stop the program and take a look at the values to see what's going on when the screen goes red. Fortunately, using the magic of XNA Game Studio 2.0, you can do this by setting a breakpoint.

A *breakpoint* is a way of marking a particular statement in your program and saying to XNA Game Studio 2.0, "When you reach this statement, pause the program and let me take a look at stuff." Breakpoints make your game stop, so you'll use them not when you're playing the game but only for debugging. Breakpoints are easy to set; you simply open up the C# file in the XNA Game Studio 2.0 editor and click in the left margin in the position shown in Figure 10-7. XNA Game Studio 2.0 will highlight the line in brown, and a brown dot will appear next to the line. You want to stop the program when it has calculated a percentage, so the **return** statement is a good one to put the breakpoint on.

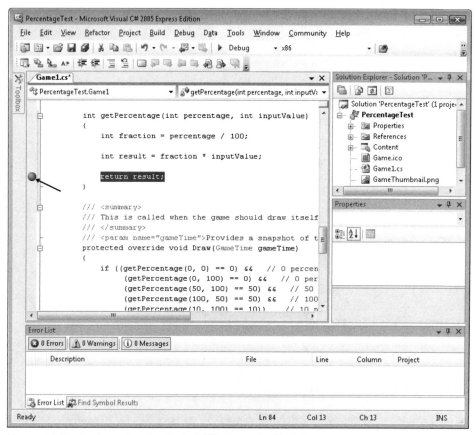

Figure 10-7   Setting a breakpoint in XNA Game Studio 2.0

You can set lots of breakpoints in a program. The program will stop at each breakpoint you've set for a statement. Real programmers call this "hitting a breakpoint," so I suppose we should, too.

Hitting a Breakpoint

If you now run the program, you'll see that when it gets to the line that you've marked as a breakpoint, it stops. This will work whether you're using a PC or a genuine Xbox for the development. This is impressive as a technical feat in that when you're using the Xbox, you're controlling the program remotely from XNA Game Studio 2.0, but I guess that today it's okay to take these things for granted. When your program hits the breakpoint, it will stop and give you the display shown in Figure 10-8.

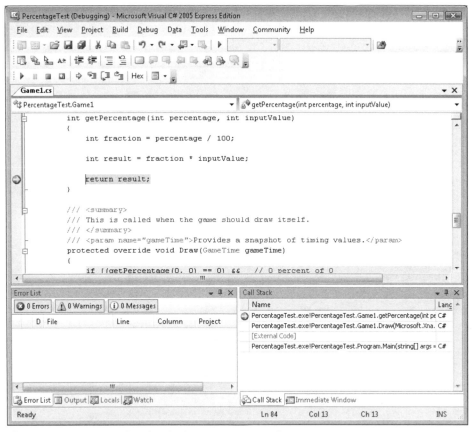

Figure 10-8   Hitting a breakpoint in XNA Game Studio 2.0

Viewing Variables

Now that the program has stopped, you can take a look at the values of the variables and see what's gone wrong. This is very easy to do; just rest the mouse pointer over the identifier of the variable in the code that you're interested in. A box will pop up and tell you the value in that variable, as shown in Figure 10-9, where I placed the cursor over the `fraction` variable.

```
        int getPercentage(int percentage, int inputValue)
        {
            int fraction = percentage / 100;
                        fraction  0
            int result = fraction * inputValue;

            return result;
        }
```

Figure 10-9   Viewing a variable value in XNA Game Studio 2.0

You can rest the cursor over any variable in the method to find out what it holds. If you do this the first time the breakpoint is hit, all the values for `fraction`, `inputValue`, and `percentage` will be 0. This is exactly what you'd expect. The very first call of `getPercentage` is as follows:

```
if ((getPercentage(0, 0) == 0) && // 0 percent of 0
```

For these input values, the method is working correctly in that 0 percent of 0 is 0. One of the later calls of `getPercentage` must be failing, so you need to run the program a bit further to find the problem. You can do this by clicking the green arrow in the program controls in the top left-hand corner, as shown in Figure 10-10.

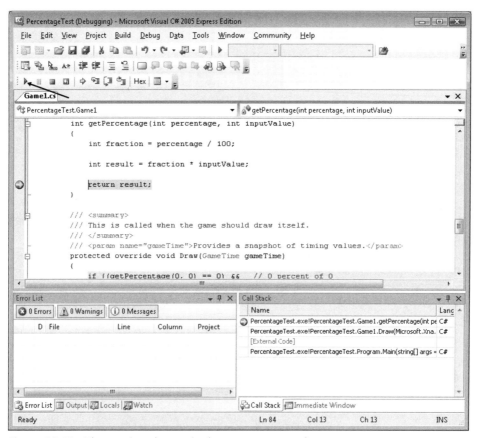

Figure 10-10   The continue button in the program controls

The program will run and hit the breakpoint again. This will be the second call of `getPercentage`, which has been asked to figure out 0 percent of 100. You can use the debugger to view the result value again, and when you do you'll find that it is 0, which is correct. So you need to continue the program again. This time, you stop the third call of `getPercentage`, where you're trying to work out 50 percent of 100. This should work out to be half of 100, or 50. But when you use the debugger, you find that the `result` being calculated has the value of 0, which is wrong. If you dig a little further, you find that the value of `fraction` is also 0. This looks like the problem. If `fraction` is 0, when you work out the calculation `fraction * inputValue`, you get 0, because anything multiplied by 0 is 0. So you need to take a close look at how you calculate the value of `fraction`:

```
int fraction = percentage / 100;
```

The problem has to do with the `int` type, which is used to hold integer values. An *integer* does not have any fractional part. When you try to work out `50 / 100`, which should be `0.5` or a half, there's no place in the variable `fraction` to put this. Integers are used to store values that do not have any fractional part. Using them to count pixels is reasonable because there's no such thing as half a pixel as far as the display is concerned. C# is quite happy to divide an integer by an integer, but it always produces an integer result when it does this, throwing away the fractional part.

However, for your program, you need to manipulate numbers that have that fractional bit; otherwise, the program won't work. Such numbers are called *real*, or *floating point*, numbers. Therefore, you need a new type of data storage that can hold this type of number.

Using Floating Point Numbers in C#

C# provides a variety of number storage options. For this task, you need to use the `float` type, which can hold floating point numbers. These are so called because they have a decimal point that can "float" up and down the number, depending on the value being held.

A floating point number would be capable of holding the `0.5` that you need to store. So you change the type of the fraction variable to `float` in your method.

```
int getPercentage(int percentage, int inputValue)
{
    float fraction = percentage / 100;
    int result = fraction * inputValue;

    return result;
}
```

However, when you try to build this method, things go horribly wrong. You now get an error message, as shown in Figure 10-11, because your program no longer compiles. The compiler has found something wrong with the code that you've written, and it can't produce an output program that will run.

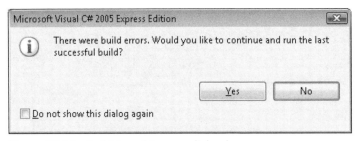

Figure 10-11   Build Error Message dialog box

This is quite often how programming is. You think you've found the answer to the problem, you put in the fix, and the problem promptly gets worse. The Great Programmer can tell many tales of bugs that she's found and fixed, and she has lots of experience with this kind of thing. She also has some good advice at this point.

> **The Great Programmer Speaks: Don't Let It Get to You**   When you get to a snag like this, don't panic. It's probably a good time to go off and get a cup of coffee, walk the dog, or do 20 push-ups or whatever you do to relax. The important point to remember is that you will find an answer to the problem, you will make it work, and you will understand what's going on.

People tell me things like "I spent five hours last night trying to fix a bug in a program" as if that is supposed to impress me. Not so. If you can't fix it after an hour or so, you should go and do something else. It doesn't matter what that thing is; just don't think too hard about the program problem while you do it. When you come back to the code, it's amazing how many times you can then fix the bug in an instant, as if the back of your brain has been chugging away on the problem—suddenly you have the answer.

The Compiler and C# Types

In this case, you're having problems because you don't know all about how C# works and what the compiler is worrying about. If you go back and look at your method now that you have the error, you'll see that XNA Game Studio 2.0 is trying to tell you something about the program. Some parts of the code are underlined in wavy blue lines. This indicates that the compiler is unhappy about some aspect of these statements. If you rest the cursor over the offending text, a message pops up that describes what the compiler thinks is wrong. Figure 10-12 shows what happens if you do this on your broken version of **getPercentage**.

```
int getPercentage(int percentage, int inputValue)
{
    float fraction = percentage / 100;

    int result = fraction * inputValue;
        Cannot implicitly convert type 'float' to 'int'. An explicit conversion exists (are you missing a cast?)
    return result;
}
```

Figure 10-12   Compilation errors in getPercentage

The compiler is saying "**Cannot implicitly convert type 'float' to 'int'. An explicit conversion exists (are you missing a cast?).**" This is a technically correct description of the problem, but the compiler might as well be saying "**Cannot put pizza in briefcase, but I can chop off a slice so it fits if you like**" for all that this means at the moment. To understand what's going on, you need to get into the mind of the compiler and determine what it's really worried about.

The compiler has the job of converting the C# that you've written into instructions that the computer can perform. Consider a C# statement that performs an addition.

```
greenIntensity++;
```

This statement increases by 1 the value of the variable `greenIntensity`. The compiler might produce a sequence of machine code statements a bit like this:

1. Fetch the value of `greenIntensity` from memory.

2. Add 1 to this value.

3. Store the result back in the `greenIntensity` memory location.

So you can think of a compiler as a translator, only rather than converting from English to French, it's converting from C# into machine instructions. At the same time, the compiler tries very hard to stop a programmer from doing stupid things. In this case, it doesn't want your program to lose data. If you try to put a floating point value (with a fractional part, say, the value 2.9) into a variable of integer type (which doesn't have support for the floating bit), you'll be in danger of losing information. The line of code that you're looking at does just this.

```
int result = fraction * inputValue;
```

From your knowledge of math, you know that that if you multiply an integer value (`inputValue`) by a floating point value (`fraction`), the result will be a floating point value. When you move that into the `result`, you're moving a floating point value into an integer, which will result in data loss. In programming terms, this is called *narrowing*. You're moving values from a data type with a wide range of values (floating point) into a type with a narrower range of values (integer). This is rather like trying to sail a high-masted sailboat under a low bridge—there's a danger that something might get chopped off in the process. You'd be heading for exactly the same trouble if you tried to put the value of an integer variable into a byte. The C# compiler has been designed to look for situations like this, in which data might be lost by mistake, and to refuse to perform the conversion automatically.

Compilers and Casting

When the compiler sees a statement that narrows a value, it produces an error "`Cannot implicitly convert type 'float' to 'int'`." It's saying that the compiler won't produce output steps that perform the conversion unless you explicitly ask it to. This is because it thinks you might have made a mistake when you combined these two types.

The next part of the error gives you some more help. "`An explicit conversion exists (are you missing a cast?)`." This means that the compiler can perform such a conversion, but you need to use a cast to request that the action be performed. With a *cast*, you ask the compiler to produce code that will convert a value from one type to another. You're saying, "We know what we are doing, so trust us on this and let the conversion take place." The cast you want looks like this:

```
int result = (int)(fraction * inputValue);
```

A cast is the name of the type you want (in brackets). It precedes the value to be cast, which in this situation is the entire sum, which I've also put in brackets. Now the compiler is quite happy to perform the narrowing, because you've said that it's okay to do so.

Note that not all casts will work. You can't convert from a **Color** to an **int** by using a cast because the compiler hasn't been told how to generate code to do this. For casting from floating point to integer, though, the compiler knows just what to do. It generates code to throw away the fraction and put the integer part into the destination. This means that if what you are casting were **0.999999**, the destination would be set to **0**, something you might need to watch out for later. So, after all that, you now have a new, improved version of the method.

```
int getPercentage(int percentage, int inputValue)
{
    float fraction = percentage / 100;
    int result = (int)(fraction * inputValue);
    return result;
}
```

This version of the method will compile, so you can run the program with your bug fix. Except you still get your red screen again—which seems very unfair.

Expression Types

At this point, you might be thinking that programming is not for you. Nothing seems to work. You started off trying to draw a picture on the screen. You got that working and decided to do some zooming only to find that you need to do some serious messing about to make the picture stay the same shape. And it still doesn't work. If you put in some breakpoints and do some more digging, you find that the problem occurs when you work out the fraction.

```
float fraction = percentage / 100;
```

Even though you're storing the result of the division in a floating point variable, for some reason the calculation is generating a result of **0** when you divide **50** by **100**. You can blame the compiler again for this one. The compiler has the job of converting operators like **/** (divide) into the instructions that perform the division. There are two kinds of division: one kind produces an integer result, and one kind produces a floating point result. If the compiler sees an expression that divides an integer by another integer, it will perform the integer division, even if the result is being put into a floating point variable.

There is actually method in this madness. You want your programs to run as fast as possible, and calculating the fractional portion of the result takes extra time, so it makes sense not to do the full division if you don't need to. However, you need to force the compiler to perform floating point division, and the way you do that is to turn one of the components of the calculation into a floating point value. You can do this by casting again.

```
float fraction = (float) percentage / 100;
```

This forces the compiler to regard the percentage variable as floating point so that it uses a floating point divide to get the correct result. This means that your **getPercentage** method now looks like this:

```
int getPercentage(int percentage, int inputValue)
{
    float fraction = (float) percentage / 100;
    int result = (int)(fraction * inputValue);
    return result;
}
```

If you put this into your program and run it, you'll find that you have a green screen, meaning that this version of the method seems to work with the tests that you've created. So at this point, you can feel very pleased with yourself. You show your code to the Great Programmer. She wrinkles her nose, sits down at the keyboard, and types this:

```
int getPercentage(int percentage, int inputValue)
{
    return (inputValue * percentage) / 100;
}
```

This works fine as well and is much simpler than your version, which is annoying. However, both methods work okay, and unless you're performing many thousands of calls to them, the user won't notice the difference. And anyway, you learned a lot writing your method, so there. The Great Programmer even has a point about this.

The Great Programmer Speaks: Don't Get Upset with Other Programmers   If you end up writing programs for a living, you'll come up against programmers who are better than you (who you copy) and worse than you (who you help). It's important not to get upset when another programmer suggests a better way of doing something, finds something wrong with your code, or says something stupid. My experience has been that I am wrong as often as I am right, and the nicer I am about these situations, the more people want to work with me. Try to work in an "egoless" way if you can; it makes everyone happier in the long run. That's not to say that you shouldn't argue your point when you think your ideas or opinions are the best way forward, but if the argument goes against you, accept this in good grace. In any project, what you're really working toward is a "happy ending." There are many ways you can get to the ending—just make sure that you get there happy.

Sample Code: Working Jake Zoom Program   The sample project in the 04 Working Jake Zoom directory in the resources for this chapter uses the **GetPercentage** method that the Great Programmer wrote for us. It steadily zooms out of a picture of Jake. It is by no means a perfect program, though, because the picture gets smaller than the screen size and eventually stops zooming.

Stopping the Zoom

You need to find a way to stop the zoom when the image is the same size as the screen. It turns out that this is quite easy. You only need to change the size of the sprite rectangle while it's wider than the screen. You've already seen that you can use the Width property of the device viewport to determine this value, so you simply need to add a condition as follows:

```
if (spriteRect.Width > graphics.GraphicsDevice.Viewport.Width)
{
   spriteRect.Width = spriteRect.Width - getPercentage(1, spriteRect.Width);
   spriteRect.Height = spriteRect.Height - getPercentage(1, spriteRect.Height);
}
```

The program will now stop zooming, reducing the height and width of the drawing rectangle at the appropriate time.

Zooming from the Center

The zoom that you have at the moment starts off as zoomed in on the top left-hand corner of the image. This is because when you create **spriteRect**, you set its position to (0, 0), which is the top left-hand corner of the screen. Figure 10-13 shows what's happening. The the top left-hand corner of the image is being displayed because the rectangle is positioned at the top left hand corner of the display area.

Figure 10-13   Zooming in on the top left-hand corner of the image

If you want to zoom in on the center of the image, you need to move the top left-hand corner of the draw rectangle upward and to the left, as shown in Figure 10-14, moving the display area into the middle of the image. Remember that XNA will draw only the part of the rectangle starting at coordinate position (0, 0) and extending to the width and height of the screen's display area.

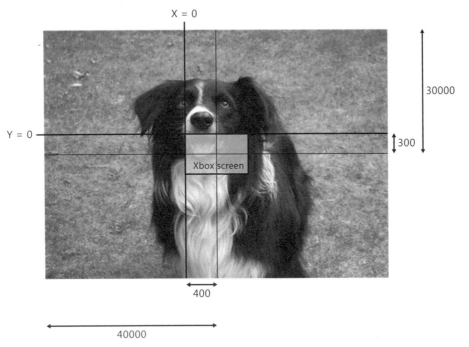

Figure 10-14   Zooming in on Jake's cheek

The thin lines on Figure 10-14 show both the center of the image of Jake and the center of the display area. To get the center of the image lined up exactly with the center of the display area, you must move the X (horizontal) position of the top left-hand corner of the rectangle 40,000 (half the image width) to the left and then 400 (half the screen width) to the right. You then need to do this for the Y (vertical) position.

```
spriteRect = new Rectangle(
    -(scaledWidth / 2) + (displayWidth / 2),
    -(scaledHeight / 2) + (displayHeight / 2),
    scaledWidth, scaledHeight);
```

To make this code clearer, I've created some extra variables that hold the width and height of the scaled image and the width and height of the display area. Note that you can make a number (or an expression) negative simply by putting a minus sign in front of it.

Now that you've put the viewing rectangle in the center of the screen, you need to move the draw position each time you scale the image. It turns out that if the width of the rectangle changes by X-amount, the position of the top left-hand corner must move to the right by half of X-amount to keep the rectangle centered with respect to the display area. The code to do this is as follows:

```
int widthChange = getPercentage(1, spriteRect.Width);
int heightChange = getPercentage(1,spriteRect.Height);
spriteRect.Width = spriteRect.Width - widthChange;
spriteRect.Height = spriteRect.Height - heightChange;
spriteRect.X = spriteRect.X + (widthChange / 2);
spriteRect.Y = spriteRect.Y + (heightChange / 2);
```

This code works out the change in width, updates the width and height of the rectangle, and then moves the X and Y positions of the rectangle to keep the drawing centered correctly. To get a good understanding of what's happening here, you can try some values and sketch some diagrams based on Figure 10-14. I often find it very useful to draw out what needs to happen on graph paper. (That's how I worked out what the previous code must do.)

> **Sample Code: Broken Jake Center Zoom Program**   The sample project in the 05 Broken Jake Center Zoom directory in the resources for this chapter uses the code given so far in this section to zoom out of the picture and keep the picture in the center of the display area. The name doesn't particularly inspire confidence, though, and when you run it, you'll find that it doesn't work properly.

The problem with this zoom program is that when the zoom finishes, the image is not lined up properly with the display. If you add some breakpoints and do some digging, you'll find that the X and Y draw positions, which should be 0 when you've fully zoomed out of the image, still hold negative values at the end of the zoom. The problem lies with the following two statements:

```
spriteRect.X = spriteRect.X + (widthChange / 2);
spriteRect.Y = spriteRect.Y + (heightChange / 2);
```

You know that you want to move these positions by half the change in the width and height. Unfortunately, you're dividing integers together. This means that you can get only an integer result; in other words, if the width change were 101, the change to the value of X would be 50, not 50.5. This calculation is repeated many times, and eventually this lack of precision leads to an answer that's incorrect. The only way to solve this problem is to change the data type you're using to hold all the values. Rather than using the integer values that are stored in the **spriteRect**, you need to create floating point variables and use them instead. Floating point values have a fractional part, meaning that they are better for representing a smooth transition from one coordinate to another.

```
float displayWidth;
float displayHeight;
float rectWidth;
float rectHeight;
float rectX;
float rectY;
```

These variables are set up by the `Initialize` method and used in all the calculations and are transferred into the `spriteRect` to position the drawing. (This code requires a floating point version of `getPercentage`.)

```
float widthChange = getPercentage(1, rectWidth);
rectWidth = rectWidth - widthChange;
rectX = rectX + (widthChange / 2);

float heightChange = getPercentage(1, rectHeight);
rectHeight = rectHeight - heightChange;
rectY = rectY + (heightChange / 2);

spriteRect.Width = (int)rectWidth;
spriteRect.Height = (int)rectHeight;
spriteRect.X = (int)rectX;
spriteRect.Y = (int)rectY;
```

> **Sample Code: Float Jake Center Zoom Program**   The sample project in the 06 Float Jake Center Zoom directory in the resources for this chapter uses floating point values to keep track of the size and position of the draw rectangle. Note that it also contains a floating point version of **getPercentage**.

It's not uncommon for games—and indeed other programs—to have problems with the precision of numeric calculations. The float and double data types provided by C# can hold numbers to very high levels of precision, but you need to remember that updates to the variables in games may take place many millions of times a second. Errors in values that build up over time, sometimes called cumulative errors, are something that programmers often need to address.

Conclusion

This has been another chapter in which you've been very busy. You began with a simple idea for a game and then got diverted into program design and structure. You made your first simple method, which worked on numbers that you gave it, and returned a result. You also took a look at the test-driven programming technique, which you can use to make sure the methods you create work correctly. Finally, you saw how to manage the draw position of an item on the screen and discovered why game programs need to use values stored to high levels of precision.

Pop Quiz

I'm feeling guilty about calling this a "pop quiz." After all, there's nothing about pop music in here at all.

1. You use an XNA `Rectangle` to draw a texture on the screen.

2. Only the creators of XNA are allowed to make methods.

3. Methods are created inside classes.

4. The body of a method is made up of C# statements.

5. Methods must return a result.

6. A method can contain only one return.

7. A method must have at least one parameter.

8. The C# compiler automatically fills in the value of any missing parameters when a method is called.

9. Test-driven development means that you do all the testing when the program is finished.

10. You can set breakpoints only when your program is not running.

11. The C# compiler will automatically convert a **float** value into an **int** value.

12. The C# compiler will let you move an integer into a double precision variable.

13. A cast requests that data be converted from one type into another.

14. You can cast a string into an integer.

Chapter 11

A Game as a C# Program

- Find out how XNA games are actually C# programs.

- Start to create a game from the contents of a grocery bag.

- Make your game display fits correctly on the screen.

- Get the first components of a game running.

Introduction

At the moment, you know quite a lot about how XNA works and how to use C# language constructions to control the facilities that XNA gives you. You have created games by investigating what you need to do inside the game class to get the desired effects on the screen. Now it's time to step back a little and consider how the XNA Framework and the C# language fit together and just what a C# program is. Understanding these ideas will help you understand how to construct games of your own and also how you can make programs other than games. If you like, you can think of this as "lifting the hood" on the C# process and looking at how the engine and transmission work underneath. You'll be considering what makes up a C# program and how it is actually started and given control.

To gain insights into how C# works, you'll create a brand new game from scratch using the contents of a grocery bag. You'll start by creating some simple game behaviors and then combine them until you get something that might be fun to play.

Game Idea: Bread and Cheese

Game ideas are tricky things. The way I see it, you can make a great game in two ways: You can wake up one morning with the idea perfectly formed in your head and then sit down and write the game program, or you can start off playing with a few pieces of program code and then tinker with them until you get something interesting.

You'll take the second approach for your game, using as your inspiration the contents of a grocery bag. The Great Programmer has been out getting some food and has come back with some bread, some cheese, and two tomatoes. She wonders if you might like to use these things in your game. She suggests that you get the cheese bouncing around the screen, maybe add the bread as a bat to hit the cheese around, and see where this takes you. For now, you decide to call the game `BreadAndCheese` and to find a use for the tomatoes later.

Creating Game Graphics

In a large-scale game development environment, the art department would create the graphics for you, but for your game, you are going to do all the work yourself. I created the graphics for the game (see Figure 11-1) by taking a well-lit picture of each item against a white background.

Figure 11-1   Your game objects

I then cut the central image out of the picture and pasted it onto a transparent background. To do this, I used a free graphics editing program called Paint .NET, which can be downloaded from *http://www.getpaint.net*. I then ate the cheese on the bread, and it was delicious. If you want to do something similar to create your game objects, you can very easily. You could use model cars, candy, toy soldiers, or anything else that's easy to photograph. When you take the pictures, ensure that the objects are as evenly lit as possible; ideally, take the pictures outside on a cloudy day. If you have friends who are good with a camera, you might ask them to give you a hand.

You'll add these images to the project in the same way that you added Jake to your first image-drawing program in Chapter 4, "Displaying Images." In the sample projects, the images have been stored in their own folder, in the same way that sound files were stored in Chapter 7, "Playing Sounds."

Projects, Resources, and Classes

You'll start by making a new game project by using XNA Game Studio 2.0 and call the project **BreadAndCheese**. Before you go any further, it's worth spending some time discovering how an XNA program fits together and actually gets to run. You can use this knowledge to tidy up your solution, which will help you better understand how C# programs are structured.

XNA Game Studio 2.0 Solutions and Projects

You know that when you make a new project, XNA Game Studio 2.0 creates a solution, a project, and some C# class files. Figure 11-2 shows how these appear in Solution Explorer. Some programmers call a solution a *workspace*, but I am going to use the word *solution* throughout this book.

Figure 11-2   The BreadAndCheese Solution and project

In Chapter 4, you learned that when you create a new project, you get new solution as well. An XNA Game Studio 2.0 solution can contain a number of projects. Each project brings together C# program source files and resources. In Chapter 7, in the section "Projects and Folders," you saw how you can create folders inside projects to hold resources that the project needs. Now you'll take a look at the program files that XNA Game Studio 2.0 has created for you.

You're already familiar with the Game1.cs file, which contains the program that provides all the game behaviors, including the **Update** and **Draw** methods. However, your program doesn't start running in this part of the source code. To discover where and how your program does start to run, you need to take a look in the Program.cs source file.

The Program.cs File

The Program.cs file is created automatically by XNA Game Studio 2.0 when you make a new game project. You don't have to change this file, but the Great Programmer (who is at the moment rather cross because I seem to have eaten all the cheese that she bought) reckons that you really should know how programs work if you're going to call yourself a programmer. If you take a look at the Program.cs file in XNA Game Studio 2.0, you'll find that it's quite small.

```
using System;
namespace BreadAndCheese
{
    static class Program
    {
      /// <summary>
      /// The main entry point for the application.
      /// </summary>
      static void Main(string[] args)
      {
        using (Game1 game = new Game1())
        {
           game.Run();
        }
      }
    }
}
```

The job of the C# code in this file is to create an instance of the game class and then start the game running. A C# program is started by the call to the program's **Main** method. You can see the **Main** method in the **Program** class shown in the preceding code, but you can also see some words that you have not seen before, and now is the time to consider what they mean.

Namespaces and Programs

At the top of the Program.cs file is the statement that tells the compiler to use the **System** namespace.

```
using System;
```

The word **using** has two meanings in C#, and it's used both ways in this code. In the first case, it's used as a compiler directive. A *compiler directive* is a message to the compiler and doesn't directly generate machine language instructions for the program that the compiler is creating. You use directives to tell the compiler what to do. In this case, you want to tell the compiler to use the **System** namespace.

A *namespace* is a space where names have meaning. You can think of it as a directory of services. The **System** namespace contains descriptions of lots of classes provided by .NET that you might want to use in your program. You've already used one class from the **System** namespace: the **DateTime** class, which is described there. You used **DateTime** to obtain the current time for the clock as described in Chapter 5, "Writing Text," in the section "Getting the Date and Time."

Whenever you use a name that the compiler hasn't seen before, it will look in all the namespaces that it has been told about to see whether it can find a resource that matches that name. If the name is found, the compiler will generate code that uses that resource. If the name is not found, the compiler will complain that it doesn't know about the item. As an example, consider what would happen if your program contained the following statement:

```
dateTime d;
```

The statement is intended to create a **DateTime** variable, but the name has not been typed correctly. When the program is compiled, this statement will produce a compilation error.

```
Error1   The type or namespace name 'dateTime' could not be found
(are you missing a using directive or an assembly reference?)
```

The compiler is complaining that it can't find anything called **dateTime**. It even suggests that you might need to add a **using** directive to identify the namespace that holds this item.

As far as programmers are concerned, a namespace is a way to make sure that when they invent an identifier for an object, that identifier is unique in their namespace and can't be confused with an identically named resource in any other namespace. In fact, the next line of Program.cs sets up a namespace for your solution.

```
namespace BreadAndCheese
{
    // Program class in here
}
```

XNA Game Studio 2.0 automatically creates a namespace to hold all your classes. The namespace is given the same name as the solution. If other C# programmers want to refer to the Game1 class that is in your namespace, they could insert **using BreadAndCheese** at the top of their program source files. If you use two namespaces that contain a class with identical names, the compiler will ask you to use the fully qualified form of the name, as in this example:

```
BreadAndCheese.Game1 myGame = new BreadAndCheese.Game1();
```

A *fully qualified* name includes the namespace that the name is part of, followed by the name of the class required.

A namespace can contain other namespaces so that programmers can build up a tree of namespaces that can be used to hold different categories of resources. The designers of XNA have created several namespaces that describe resources you've used in your programs. The **using** directives at the top of Game1.cs include the following:

```
using Microsoft.Xna.Framework;
using Microsoft.Xna.Framework.Audio;
using Microsoft.Xna.Framework.Content;
using Microsoft.Xna.Framework.Graphics;
using Microsoft.Xna.Framework.Input;
using Microsoft.Xna.Framework.Storage;
```

The features of XNA that you've used are described in appropriate namespaces; for example, the **Texture2D** class is described in the **Microsoft.XNA.Graphics** namespace.

> **Note**   It's important to remember that the namespace information is used by the compiler to get to the resources that are to be used. The resources themselves are loaded and used when the program runs, and your solution must have a reference to them. A solution contains a list of references that it is using. You can see this in Figure 11-2 just above the Content folder.

You'd create namespaces of your own if you wanted to use some classes in more than one solution. For example, you might create some classes that deal with game high scores. To do this, you might create a **HighScores** namespace that will store and display a high-score table.

Static Classes and Methods

The next line in Program.cs describes a class called **Program**.

```
static class Program
{
    // content of the class goes here
}
```

The class has been made **static**. You haven't seen the word *static* before, but it means "always there." In the programs you've written up until now, you've had to create instances of classes by using **new**. When a class is made **static**, there's always one and only one instance of that class present when the program is running. When a C# program starts up, before the code you've written is given control, any **static** classes are automatically created. So there's no need to ever create an instance of the **Program** class by using **new**, because **Program** is always there when your program starts.

The next line of the program declares a method called `Main` in the `Program` class.

```
static void Main(string[] args)
{
   // content of the Main method goes here
}
```

The `Main` method has also been made `static`, because it must exist before your program begins to run. When you run a program on a Windows PC or an Xbox, the operating system loads the program file into memory, creates all the `static` classes, and then finds and calls the `Main` method. One and only one of the classes in a program must contain a `Main` method so that the operating system knows where to start. Suppose you misspell the name of the method—for example, you write the following:

```
static void main(string[] args)
{
   // content of the Main method goes here
}
```

The compiler will produce an error message saying that the program cannot be started.

```
Program 'BreadAndCheese.exe' does not contain a static 'Main' method suitable
for an entry point
```

The compiler is trying to make an executable output (one that can be run as a program), and if the Main method isn't present, it literally doesn't know where to start the program.

Making Methods Static

Methods are made `static` so that they can be used without needing to have an instance of the class present. Static methods can be ones that are used to perform a particular task and are not part of a class instance. The `getPercentage` method that you created in Chapter 10, "Using C# Methods to Solve Problems," could be made `static` because it simply works out a calculation and returns the result.

Main Method Parameters

When the `Main` method is called to start the program, it's provided with a parameter called `args`, which is an array of strings. This parameter gives the `Main` method any arguments that have been supplied to the program when the program starts. An argument is a way of giving a program instructions when it runs. If a program is run from the command prompt (in other words, you type in a command to make the program run), you can provide arguments simply by typing them after the program command. For example, the Windows command `del` (for delete) is followed by a list of arguments that give the names of the files that are to be deleted.

```
del notes.txt oldImage.png
```

In this case, a program that implements the delete behavior would be provided with two strings, which are the names of two files to be deleted. Because XNA games are usually started from within Windows or by using the Xbox dashboard, you won't be providing arguments to the **Main** method, so you can ignore these parameters.

The C# Using Statement

The Program.cs file contains a second use of the keyword **using** (which is a bit confusing). Previously, you saw that **using** was a directive to the compiler meaning "look in here if you want to find out about something." Once you get inside the C# program itself, however, the keyword has a different meaning: "use this object and then dispose if it when you are finished." This second use is a way of explicitly telling the runtime system how long you need an object. You've seen that the garbage collector is continuously searching for objects that it can remove from memory. If you want to speed up this process and make sure that an object is disposed of as soon as the program has finished with it, an object should be used within a block of code following a **using** statement. As an example, consider how you'd use a class called **HugeObjectUsedForSums** in a program.

```
using (temp = new HugeObjectUsedForSums())
{
    // do things with temp to work out the answer
}
```

You need to make an instance of **HugeObjectUsedForSums** to perform some calculations, after which you want it removed as quickly as possible. The previous code will do this. As soon as the program leaves the block following the **using** statement, the system knows that **temp** is no longer required, and the resources it uses can be recovered.

The Main Method in an XNA Game

In an XNA game, the job of the **Main** method is to create an instance of the **Game1** class and then make it run.

```
static void Main(string[] args)
{
    using (Game1 game = new Game1())
    {
        game.Run();
    }
}
```

The designers of XNA wanted to make sure that the instance of the game class created to run the game is destroyed as soon as it's no longer needed, so they use the instance within a block of code after a creating it in a **using** statement.

The **Run** method runs your game. When **Run** is called, it calls the **Initialize** and **LoadContent** methods and then repeatedly calls the **Update** and **Draw** methods. When the game finishes, the **Run** method ends, the game class is destroyed, and the program finishes.

Renaming the Game1 Class

The Great Programmer doesn't like using the names that XNA Game Studio 2.0 creates. She suggests that rather than calling the game class **Game1**, you call it something else, perhaps **BreadAndCheeseGame**, to make it easier for other people to understand what your program does. At the moment, the **Game1** class is held in a file called Game1.cs. The C# language doesn't insist that the file and the class it holds have the same name, but it would seem sensible to make the two names match.

You can rename the Game1.cs file from within XNA Game Studio 2.0. One way to do this is to right-click the file name in Solution Explorer and select Rename from the menu that appears, as shown in Figure 11-3.

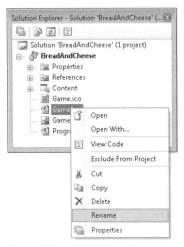

Figure 11-3   The Rename command for a source file

When you select Rename, you can type a new name, as shown in Figure 11-4.

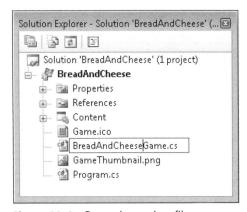

Figure 11-4   Renaming a class file

You need to make sure that you don't remove the ".cs" from the end of the file name. This is the file name extension and is how XNA Game Studio 2.0 and the rest of Windows know that the file contains a C# program. One really nice feature of XNA Game Studio 2.0 is that when you finish typing the new name and press Enter, the dialog box shown in Figure 11-5 appears.

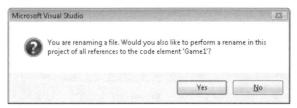

Figure 11-5   Renaming the class

XNA Game Studio 2.0 detects that you're renaming the file and offers to rename the class throughout all your files for you. To accept this useful offer, you simply click OK, and the **Game1** class is now renamed **BreadAndCheeseGame** in your source files. This renaming process is a lot more subtle than you might think. The class is renamed in the BreadAndCheeseGame.cs file and also where it's used in the Program.cs file.

The Great Programmer Speaks: Refactoring Is Good   Renaming components in source code as you've done in this section is called refactoring. *Refactoring* is changing the code you've written to make it better. If you find that a block of statements needs to be made into a method, you can use the refactoring support in XNA Game Studio 2.0 to do this for you. If you invent a better name for a variable than the one that you originally came up with, you can use XNA Game Studio 2.0 to change the name for you as well. Before we had tools like XNA Game Studio 2.0, changing the code in this way was very difficult to do, so programmers tended to be stuck with bad decisions made at the beginning of a project. Today, you can very easily make these changes. The Great Programmer is very keen on refactoring; she says that as you write a program, your understanding of the problem will improve, and you'll need to make these kinds of changes.

You can access the refactoring support in XNA Game Studio 2.0 by selecting the item you want to refactor and right-clicking the selection. You can then select Refactor from the menu that appears. Of course, you can rename only the items that you've created yourself; for example, it would not be sensible to try to rename the **Update** method.

Creating Game Objects

Now that you have a good understanding of your classes and how a game program fits together, you can start making objects that will be used in your game. You'll begin with the graphical items that will be drawn on the screen. To start, you'll draw the cheese and make it move, and then you'll implement the bread bat.

Sprites in Games

Graphical objects in a game are often called *sprites*. A sprite can be a very small image, such as a spaceship viewed from far away, a missile, or a piece of cheese. It can also be very large. The background of your screen will be a single sprite. Sprites have graphical content and a position on the screen. Your sprites will be drawn with a particular texture and have a position specified by a rectangle.

```
// Game World
Texture2D cheeseTexture;
Rectangle cheeseRectangle;
```

When the game starts, you load the texture from the image content, set the size of the draw rectangle, and draw the texture using techniques that you first saw in Chapter 4. Your finished game will contain a great many sprites.

Managing the Size of Game Sprites

Owners of Xbox consoles can choose from a variety of screen size and resolution settings. They can also select between standard and wide-screen screen shapes. Your game must work correctly with any of these sizes and give the player the same game-play experience with each. This means that your game will need to automatically set the size of the objects that you'll draw, depending on the display in use. The game must also adjust the speed at which the objects in the game move; otherwise, a game that works on a small TV might be unplayable on a large display.

You saw in Chapter 4 in the section "Filling the Screen" that you can get the dimensions of your screen from the display adapter viewport properties. However, getting hold of these is a rather laborious process, so you'll create two data fields in your game that will hold these values for you for to use. The best place to set these variables is in the `Initialize` method, which is called once when your game first starts running.

```
// Display settings
float displayWidth;
float displayHeight;
protected override void Initialize()
{
   displayWidth = graphics.GraphicsDevice.Viewport.Width;
   displayHeight = graphics.GraphicsDevice.Viewport.Height;
   base.Initialize();
}
```

Working with Floating Point Values and Integers

The previously mentioned `displayWidth` and `displayHeight` variables have been declared as floating point, although the display properties themselves are integers. This is because all your calculations involving the width and height of items need the fractional part that floating point variables give you.

However, all the properties of your display rectangle are integers, so you need to convert these floating point values into integers when you want to position the sprites. You know that you can use casting to convert from one type to another, but you also need to allow for the fact that casting always truncates; in other words, if the floating point input were 1.99999, that input would still be converted to 1, which would be inaccurate. You can make sure that the converted value is as accurate as possible by adding 0.5 to the floating point value before you truncate it so that 1.99999 would turn into 2.4999 and then be truncated down to 2. You can see this in action in the `scaleSprites` method later in this chapter.

Double Precision Floating Point Values

C# and XNA can use two different types to hold floating point values. One of these types is called **float** and holds a number with seven digits of precision. This means it could hold the mathematical constant pi as 3.14159274. The other type is called **double**. This second type uses twice as much memory to hold each value and is good for around 16 digits of accuracy, and could hold pi as 3.14159265358979. Very high levels of precision can be important in video games because values are being updated thousands of times a second, so errors will accumulate quickly. For the purpose of your game, you can use floating point. However, you need to remember that when you give a real number value (one with a decimal point) in the program text, the C# compiler will assume that it's a double precision value. So the following statement would cause a compilation error:

```
float pi = 3.14159;
```

The error is caused because 3.14159 is compiled as a double precision value, and you know that the C# compiler hates it when you perform an action that might result in a loss of data (which is what would happen if you put a double value into a float variable). There are two ways around this: you can cast the double value to floating point, or you can change the value in the program to be a floating point value, as shown here:

```
float pi = 3.14159f;
```

Putting the letter "f" after a floating point tells the compiler that you're writing a floating point value, not a double precision value.

Drawing and Aspect Ratios

When an image is drawn, you need to be careful to preserve its aspect ratio. The *aspect ratio* of an image is the ratio of the width to the height. For your cheese, this is just about 1 because the texture is square, but for your bread, it's quite different. Figure 11-6 shows the effect of getting the aspect ratio wrong when you draw the bread bat.

The bread has an aspect ratio of around 4 to 1, in other words, it is around four times as wide as it is high. The program can get the aspect ratio of the original image from the dimensions of the texture.

Correct Aspect Ratio

Distorted Aspect Ratio

Figure 11-6   The effect of aspect ratio on drawing

```
float aspectRatio = (float) cheeseTexture.Width / cheeseTexture.Height;
```

The program can now use the aspect ratio to calculate the correct height of a sprite given the width that we want it to have.

> **Note**   The variable **aspectRatio** is being declared and used in the program to hold a value which is going to be used in one particular part of the code. This is called a local variable as it is only used in one place in the code and has no need to be visible anywhere else.

Sprite Sizing

Next, you need to decide how large you'll make the cheese sprite. This depends on the game you're creating. Do you want to have a big cheese or a little cheese? In some games, the objects change size as the game progresses so that you can start with large sprites and then reduce their size and increase their speed to make the game more challenging. You think that having the cheese take up around a twentieth of the screen width would work well, but you're not sure. You ask the Great Programmer for advice because it was her cheese that you used for the game.

> **The Great Programmer Speaks: Flexibility Should Be Designed into Your Programs**   The Great Programmer has no idea what size cheese makes a good game. She suggests that you have no idea either. Therefore, you need to make sure that when you create the game, you make it as easy as possible to change the size of the cheese and all the other game sprites. Your program could use variables to represent the scale values so that rather than using the literal value of one-twentieth (0.05) to represent your desire to have the width of the cheese be a twentieth of the screen, you use a variable called **cheeseWidthFactor**. Then you can easily change the value everywhere it's used just by changing the value of **cheeseWidthFactor**. Your program could also use methods. If you create a method called **scaleSprites**, you can then call it to perform the scaling. If you decide that you need to change the size of the sprites during the game, you simply need to call this method.

With these points in mind, you create a method called **scaleSprites** and some variables to hold the width factors. You'll call the **scaleSprites** method from **LoadGraphicsContent** when the cheese texture has been loaded. It sets the size of the draw rectangle to match the display you're using.

```
void scaleSprites()
{
    cheeseRectangle.Width = (int)((displayWidth * cheeseWidthFactor) + 0.5f);
    float aspectRatio = (float) cheeseTexture.Width/cheeseTexture.Height;
    cheeseRectangle.Height = (int)((cheeseRectangle.Width/aspectRatio) + 0.5f);
    cheeseX = 0;
    cheeseY = 0;
    cheeseXSpeed = displayWidth/cheeseTicksToCrossScreen;
    cheeseYSpeed = cheeseXSpeed;
}
```

This **scaleSprites** method performs the required calculations. Note that you need to use casting to convert the floating point results into integers that can be used to set up the **cheeseRectangle**.

Moving Sprites

Now that you have your cheese sprite, you need to make it move. You'll use two floating point variables to hold the draw positions and two more floating point variables to hold the speed at which the cheese is moving.

```
float cheeseX;
float cheeseXSpeed;
float cheeseY;
float cheeseYSpeed;
```

Each time that **Update** is called in your game, you'll update the X and Y properties of **cheeseRectangle**, causing the cheese to be drawn in a different position and so appear to move.

```
protected override void Update(GameTime gameTime)
{
    // Allows the game to exit
    if (GamePad.GetState(PlayerIndex.One).Buttons.Back == ButtonState.Pressed)
        this.Exit();

    cheeseX = cheeseX + cheeseXSpeed;
    cheeseY = cheeseY + cheeseYSpeed;
    cheeseRectangle.X = (int)(cheeseX + 0.5f);
    cheeseRectangle.Y = (int)(cheeseY + 0.5f);
    base.Update(gameTime);
}
```

Each time this **Update** is called, it adds the speed values to the current position of your cheese, causing the cheese to appear to move across the screen. It's important that the cheese appears to move at the same speed on every kind of game display, so you need to calculate appropriate values for **cheeseXSpeed** and **cheeseYSpeed**. You know that the **Update** method is called 60 times a second. If **cheeseXSpeed** were set to a sixtieth of the screen width, this would mean that the cheese would take around a second to cross the screen. If you want your cheese to take around 2 seconds to cross the screen, the position of the cheese must change by a hundred-and-twentieth of the screen width each time. At this point, you remember what the Great Programmer said. She said that you should make important values into variables so that they are easy to change. With that in mind, you modify the **scaleSprites** method to calculate speed values as well as sizes.

```
float cheeseWidthFactor = 0.05f;
float cheeseTicksToCrossScreen = 200.0f;
void scaleSprites()
{
    cheeseRectangle.Width = (int)((displayWidth * cheeseWidthFactor) + 0.5f);
    float aspectRatio = (float) cheeseTexture.Width / cheeseTexture.Height;
    cheeseRectangle.Height = (int)((cheeseRectangle.Width / aspectRatio) + 0.5f);

    cheeseX = 0;
    cheeseY = 0;
    cheeseXSpeed = displayWidth/cheeseTicksToCrossScreen;
    cheeseYSpeed = cheeseXSpeed;
}
```

The interval between calls of **Update** is sometimes called a *tick*. The variable **cheeseTick-sToCrossScreen** sets the number of ticks that the cheese will take to move across the screen. The larger this number, the slower the cheese moves. It turns out that 200 ticks is a reasonable number. Note that the value of **cheeseYSpeed** has been made the same as **cheeseXSpeed**. This means that the cheese will move at 45 degrees down and across the screen rather than along the diagonal of the screen.

> **Sample Code: Moving Cheese**   The sample project in the 01 Moving Cheese directory in the resources for this chapter draws a piece of cheese that flies down the screen and vanishes off the bottom.

Bouncing the Cheese

What you really want to do is have the cheese bounce around the screen, so you need to reverse the direction of the cheese movement when the cheese reaches the edge of the screen. This is what happens when things bounce: to reverse a direction of movement, you simply need to multiply the speed value by −1. You can use the size of the screen and the size of your draw rectangle to determine when you've reached an edge.

```
if (cheeseX + cheeseRectangle.Width >= displayWidth)
{
    cheeseXSpeed = cheeseXSpeed * -1;
}
```

```
if (cheeseX <= 0)
{
    cheeseXSpeed = cheeseXSpeed * -1;
}
```

This code performs two tests. The first one checks to see whether the cheese has gone off the right side of the display. If the X position plus the width of the cheese is greater than the width of the display, it's time for the cheese to change direction. If the X position is less than or equal to 0, the cheese must change direction again. You need to perform the same tests for the Y movement so that you can get your cheese to bounce properly.

> **Sample Code: Bouncing Cheese** The sample project in the 02 Bouncing Cheese directory in the resources for this chapter draws a piece of cheese that bounces around the screen.

Dealing with Display Overscan

The sample program you've created so far (and contained in the 02 Bouncing Cheese directory in the resources for this chapter) will run correctly on the Xbox or a desktop PC. However, some Xbox owners will find a game based on this code rather hard to play. If they're using an older display device or a TV screen, they'll complain that the cheese goes off the screen at the edges. This is because TV displays use what is called *overscan*. Figure 11-7 shows the problem. The cheese has managed to almost completely disappear from the TV picture.

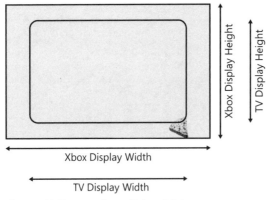

Figure 11-7   Drawing off the visible screen

The problem arises because a TV does not show the entire Xbox display; it shows only a central region. Glass TV tubes cannot be made to precisely align with the edge of the picture they are showing, so TV signals have an area of overscan in which program makers must be careful not to put important parts of a scene. If you let your game objects go into the overscan area, players are in danger of not being able to see them, which would be very bad for game play.

The amount of overscan (in other words, the amount of the display that you lose) varies from one display to another. It's usually expressed as a percentage, perhaps 10 percent or 20 percent. The bigger the number, the greater the amount of lost screen. You need to calculate the range of the available screen coordinates that you can use to place items on display if you want them to be visible. You can do this when you set up the scaling values, and you can use a floating point version of your **getPercentage** method from Chapter 10, "Using C# Methods to Solve Problems," to help you.

```
// Display settings
float displayWidth;
float displayHeight;
float overScanPercentage = 10.0f;
float minDisplayX;
float maxDisplayX;
float minDisplayY;
float maxDisplayY;

float getPercentage(float percentage, float inputValue)
{
    return (inputValue * percentage) / 100;
}

private void setupScreen ()
{
    displayWidth = graphics.GraphicsDevice.Viewport.Width;
    displayHeight = graphics.GraphicsDevice.Viewport.Height;
    float xOverscanMargin = getPercentage(overScanPercentage, displayWidth) / 2.0f;
    float yOverscanMargin = getPercentage(overScanPercentage, displayHeight) / 2.0f;
    minDisplayX = xOverscanMargin;
    minDisplayY = yOverscanMargin;
    maxDisplayX = displayWidth - xOverscanMargin;
    maxDisplayY = displayHeight - yOverscanMargin;
}
```

The **setupScreen** method is called by the **Initialize** method when the game starts running. It calculates the width and height values based on a particular overscan percentage. It does this by figuring out the margins required around the screen and then creating maximum and minimum values for the X and Y coordinates. It also provides the game with minimum and maximum values that can be used to place the cheese on the screen at the start of the game and also in the code that bounces the cheese.

```
if (cheeseX + cheeseRectangle.Width >= maxDisplayX)
{
 cheeseXSpeed = cheeseXSpeed * -1;
}
if (cheeseX <= minDisplayX)
{
 cheeseXSpeed = cheeseXSpeed * -1;
}
```

This code uses the new boundary values to ensure that the cheese never leaves the visible part of the screen.

> **Sample Code: Bouncing Cheese**   The sample project in the 03 Overscan Bouncing Cheese directory in the resources for this chapter draws a piece of cheese that bounces around the screen and stays within a 10 percent overscan boundary.

You now have some bouncing cheese that will provide the same gaming experience on an Xbox or a desktop PC, and you can take any image of yours and make it bounce around the screen. In the next chapter, you'll add the bread bat and start hitting the cheese about with it.

Conclusion

In this chapter, you learned a lot. For the first time, you took a look at how a game application is structured. You saw how the application is spread over more than one class and how the Program.cs file gets the game running. You also learned the meaning of some more C# keywords. Now you know how one program can be given information provided from another by means of the **using** compiler directive. You saw how the **static** keyword can make methods and classes that are part of your application without you needing to create them, and you took a look at the **Main** method, which is how C# programs are started. You completed your delve into how C# programs work with a look at the **using** keyword. Then you moved on to creating your game and found out how to ensure that games work correctly on different types, sizes, and resolutions of the display device. Finally, you created a sprite and got it moving around the visible portion of the display.

Pop Quiz

If you're thinking that you're due for another pop quiz about now, you're right.

1. Images for use in games must be bought from a special XNA image bank.

2. An XNA Game Studio 2.0 project contains a solution.

3. You need to create your own Program.cs file to run your programs.

4. The Program.cs source file does not contain your game program.

5. Namespaces are used in a program to locate resources.

6. The **main** method is called to start the program.

7. If something is made **static**, it means it can't be moved around in memory.

8. The C# **using** statement is provided to help the garbage collector work more effectively.

9. The cast from floating point to integer value automatically rounds up values with a fractional value greater than .5.

Chapter 12
Games, Objects, and State

- Discover a better way to structure your programs.

- Add some bread that you'll use to bash the cheese around.

- Give yourself some targets to hit the cheese at.

Introduction

You have the basis of a little game at the moment. You know how to place objects on the screen and manage their movement. You also know how to make sure that the games you create will work with different display sizes and resolutions. In this chapter, you'll develop the game play further, add some more sprites, and create a game that has proper game-play.

Adding Bread to Your Game

You can continue working on the sample code "03 Overscan Bouncing Cheese" that you were using in Chapter 11, "A Game as a C# Program." You need to add some bread to your game. The bread will be the bat that the player will use to hit the cheese around the screen. You think that tomatoes might make good targets, but first you need to get the bread working.

In the game, you need to store all the same information about the bread as you do about the cheese: the bread will have a position, a texture, and a speed. The only difference will be in the **Update** behavior. Whereas the cheese travels in a particular direction each time it's updated and bounces off the edges of the playfield, the bread will be controlled by one of the thumbsticks on gamepad 1. So you could go ahead and create all the class member variables for the bread and cheese like this:

```
Texture2D cheeseTexture;
Rectangle cheeseRectangle;
float cheeseX;
```

```
float cheeseXSpeed;
float cheeseY;
float cheeseYSpeed;
float cheeseWidthFactor = 0.05f;
float cheeseTicksToCrossScreen = 200.0f;

Texture2D breadTexture;
Rectangle breadRectangle;
float breadX;
float breadXSpeed;
float breadY;
float breadYSpeed;
float breadWidthFactor = 0.05f;
float breadTicksToCrossScreen = 200.0f;
```

This code has a copy of all the cheese variables but renamed for bread. However, from a programming point of view, this is not really the best way to organize the variables. The Great Programmer would certainly not approve. She doesn't like it when you have lots of separate variables all relating to one thing. She reckons that all the information about a particular item should be grouped together in one place. There should be a "cheese group" and a "bread group."

You've seen this "grouping together" in XNA ever since you started writing programs. For example, you know that XNA holds **Color** information in the form of a structure with fields that represent the red, green, and blue intensity of a particular color. For your bread and cheese, you'd like to group all this information together in the same way.

Using a Structure to Hold Sprite Information

C# provides a kind of object called a *structure* to allow programmers to group things together. Structures are like classes in that they can contain methods and data, but they are managed by value. You found out about values and references in Chapter 9, "Reading Text Input," in the section "Working with Arrays, Objects, and References." The fact that structures are managed by value makes them ideal for holding small lumps of data that you want to treat as a whole. You can design a structure that holds all the information about a sprite on the screen.

```
struct GameSpriteStruct
{
    public Texture2D SpriteTexture;
    public Rectangle SpriteRectangle;
    public float X;
    public float Y;
    public float XSpeed;
    public float YSpeed;
    public float WidthFactor;
    public float TicksToCrossScreen;
}
```

Each of the items in the structure is a field. If you compare the fields of the structure **GameSpriteStruct** with the variables you used in the original bouncing cheese program, you'll find that the structure holds all the information you need for a sprite. It holds the texture, the rectangle in which to draw the sprite, the current position of the sprite, the speed at which the sprite moves, and the size and speed settings. Once you've created this structure, you can declare variables of this type for use in your game.

```
GameSpriteStruct cheese;
GameSpriteStruct bread;
```

When you declare a `GameSpriteStruct` variable, you get a structure that contains all the fields grouped together in it. You can then use the fields in the structure as follows:

```
cheese.SpriteTexture = Content.Load<Texture2D>("Images\\Cheese");
bread.SpriteTexture = Content.Load<Texture2D>("Images\\Bread");
```

These statements would set the textures for the bread and cheese to ones loaded from images placed in your project. You can get hold of any of the fields in your structure by following the name of the structure variable with a period (.) and then the name of the field. This works because you've made the fields *public*. If you look back to the declaration of `GameSpriteStruct`, you'll see that each field has the C# key word `public` in front of it. Words placed in front of fields like this are called *modifiers*. There are a number of different modifiers in C#; `public` is an "access modifier" in that it determines the level of access to a field. Fields marked as `public` can be used by code outside the class or structure. You can make fields `private` so that code outside the class or structure can't read or write the value in the field. For now, though, `public` fields are fine because they are easy to use and you don't have any particular need for security. Now that you have your bread and cheese structures, you can set the values in them.

```
void scaleSprites()
{
    cheese.TicksToCrossScreen = 200.0f;
    cheese.WidthFactor = 0.05f;

    cheese.SpriteRectangle.Width = (int)((displayWidth * cheese.WidthFactor) + 0.5f);
    float aspectRatio = (float)cheese.SpriteTexture.Width / cheese.SpriteTexture.Height;
    cheese.SpriteRectangle.Height =
        (int)((cheese.SpriteRectangle.Width / aspectRatio) + 0.5f);
    cheese.X = minDisplayX;
    cheese.Y = minDisplayY;
    cheese.XSpeed = displayWidth / cheese.TicksToCrossScreen;
    cheese.YSpeed = cheese.XSpeed;

    bread.WidthFactor = 0.15f;
    bread.TicksToCrossScreen = 120.0f;

    bread.SpriteRectangle.Width = (int)((displayWidth * bread.WidthFactor) + 0.5f);
    aspectRatio = (float)bread.SpriteTexture.Width / bread.SpriteTexture.Height;
    bread.SpriteRectangle.Height = (int)((bread.SpriteRectangle.Width / aspectRatio) + 0.5f);
    bread.X = displayWidth / 2;
    bread.Y = displayHeight / 2;
    bread.XSpeed = displayWidth / bread.TicksToCrossScreen;
    bread.YSpeed = bread.XSpeed;
}
```

This version of `scaleSprites` sets the width, height, speed, and initial position of the bread and the cheese sprites. It makes the bread take up slightly more of the width of the screen and allows it to move a bit faster than the cheese. The **ScaleSprites** method also sets the initial position of the bread as the middle of the screen and places the cheese at the top left hand corner of the display area.

Using the Gamepad Thumbsticks to Control Movement

You've decided that the player will control the bread and use it as a bat to hit the cheese. To make the bread move, you need to add some statements to the **Update** method. This turns out to be very easy. The Xbox gamepad has two thumbsticks that can be used to control games. These generate floating point values that you can use to direct the movement of the bread bat. Figure 12-1 shows the range of values the thumbstick produces. If the thumbstick is pushed all the way to the left, it will generate −1.0 for the **X** value. If it's pushed halfway to the left, it will generate −0.5. If the thumbstick is positioned in the center, the **X** and **Y** values are zero.

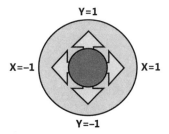

Figure 12-1   Thumbstick values

You've used the **GamePadState** structure before to read the state of buttons on a gamepad. This structure also provides a **ThumbSticks** property that contains two vectors (one for each thumbstick) that allow your program to read the current thumbstick values.

To get the amount of movement of the bread, you simply need to take the values from the thumbsticks and multiply them by the speed values for your bread sprite. The farther the thumbsticks are moved, the bigger the values and the faster the bread will move across the screen.

```
GamePadState gamePad1 = GamePad.GetState(PlayerIndex.One);
// Allows the game to exit
if (gamePad1.Buttons.Back == ButtonState.Pressed)
    this.Exit();

// Move the bread

bread.X = bread.X + (bread.XSpeed * gamePad1.ThumbSticks.Left.X);
bread.Y = bread.Y - (bread.YSpeed * gamePad1.ThumbSticks.Left.Y);
bread.SpriteRectangle.X = (int)bread.X;
bread.SpriteRectangle.Y = (int)bread.Y;
```

This code is placed in the **Update** method and updates the position of the bread rectangle according to the setting of the thumbsticks. Note that the code must subtract the speed value from the **Y** coordinate. This is because the **Y** coordinate goes down the screen, with 0 at the top. If the speed value was added to to the **Y** coordinate, the bread would go down the screen when the thumbstick is moved up, making it harder to control. This version of the bread movement does not restrict the bread to the screen, so it is possible for the player to move the bread right off the screen.

> **Sample Code: Bread and Cheese**   The sample project in the 01 Bread and Cheese directory in the resources for this chapter draws cheese bouncing around the screen and a bread bat that you can move around the screen with the left thumbstick. It works very well, and the feeling of control that you get is very impressive for such a simple program. The bread doesn't yet interact with the cheese; you'll add that later.

Improving Programs Using Methods

The Great Programmer has just been around and has taken a look at your code. She purses her lips when she sees something she doesn't like, and she's doing that now. The bit of code she doesn't like is the **scaleSprites** method, where you set up the bread and cheese sprites.

```
void scaleSprites()
{
   cheese.TicksToCrossScreen = 200.0f;
   cheese.WidthFactor = 0.05f;

   cheese.SpriteRectangle.Width = (int)((displayWidth * cheese.WidthFactor) + 0.5f);
   float aspectRatio = (float)cheese.SpriteTexture.Width / cheese.SpriteTexture.Height;
   cheese.SpriteRectangle.Height =
       (int)((cheese.SpriteRectangle.Width / aspectRatio) + 0.5f);
   cheese.X = minDisplayX;
   cheese.Y = minDisplayY;
   cheese.XSpeed = displayWidth / cheese.TicksToCrossScreen;
   cheese.YSpeed = cheese.XSpeed;

   bread.WidthFactor = 0.15f;
   bread.TicksToCrossScreen = 120.0f;

   bread.SpriteRectangle.Width = (int)((displayWidth * bread.WidthFactor) + 0.5f);
   aspectRatio = (float)bread.SpriteTexture.Width / bread.SpriteTexture.Height;
   bread.SpriteRectangle.Height = (int)((bread.SpriteRectangle.Width / aspectRatio) + 0.5f);
   bread.X = displayWidth / 2;
   bread.Y = displayHeight / 2;
   bread.XSpeed = displayWidth / bread.TicksToCrossScreen;
   bread.YSpeed = bread.XSpeed;
}
```

For a start, she reckons that the name is no longer correct. The method doesn't only scale the sprites; it also sets their initial position on the screen and their speed of movement. So you promise to go through and change the name of the method. You can do this using the refactoring technique you learned in Chapter 11. The next issue she doesn't like to see is the same piece of code repeated. Rather than perform exactly the same sequence of statements for the bread as for the cheese, she suggests that you make a method called **setupSprite** that sets up a sprite. You then call this for every sprite you want to set up. You know that you'll have tomato sprites later, so this seems like a sensible plan that'll save time. You can pass the **setupSprite** method parameters that give it all the information it needs to work on, so you begin to write the method.

```
void setupSprite(
    GameSpriteStruct sprite,
    float widthFactor,
    float ticksToCrossScreen,
    float initialX,
    float initialY)
{
    sprite.WidthFactor = widthFactor;
    sprite.TicksToCrossScreen = ticksToCrossScreen;
    sprite.SpriteRectangle.Width = (int)((displayWidth * widthFactor) + 0.5f);
    float aspectRatio = (float)sprite.SpriteTexture.Width / sprite.SpriteTexture.Height;
    sprite.SpriteRectangle.Height =
        (int)((sprite.SpriteRectangle.Width / aspectRatio) + 0.5f);
    sprite.X = initialX;
    sprite.Y = initialY;
    sprite.XSpeed = displayWidth / ticksToCrossScreen;
    sprite.YSpeed = sprite.XSpeed;
}
```

The method is given the sprite to set up along with the width factor, the time taken to cross the screen, and the initial start position of the sprite. You can then set up the cheese and bread by calling the method twice.

```
void setupSprites()
{
    setupSprite(cheese, 0.05f, 200.0f, minDisplayX, minDisplayY);
    setupSprite(bread, 0.15f, 120.0f, displayWidth / 2, displayHeight / 2);
}
```

This looks much neater, and you're really pleased with the code that you've written. You feed all your setup values into the method call, and it calculates the content of the **gameSpriteStruct** that needs to be set up. The only problem is that it doesn't work. The method call doesn't seem to have any effect on the bread or cheese sprite values.

Value and Reference Parameters

It turns out that your program doesn't work because the parameters in your method are passed by *value*. A parameter is the means by which you can pass information into a method.

When a method is called, the value given in the call is copied into the parameter. This means that when code in a method assigns a value to the parameter, the copy is changed but not the original. In other words, the statement `sprite.X = initialX;` will change the value of a copy of the `GameSpriteStruct` that was supplied as a parameter. When a method ends, all the parameter copies are discarded, and the updated values are lost.

Passing value parameters into method calls is fine when you want to tell a method something but is less useful when you want the method to change the parameter. To make the method useful, you need to find a way of pointing the method at the variable you want it to change. It turns out that you have a way to do this, and you've seen it before. The device you'll use is called a reference. If you give the method a reference to the thing you want it to change, the method can follow the reference and make changes to your bread and cheese objects rather than to the copies. In Chapter 9 in the section "Working with Arrays, Objects, and References," you discovered that some variables are managed by value and some by reference. C# structures are managed by value, which is why the value of the cheese and bread sprites gets copied when the method is called. To tell C# to manage a particular parameter as a reference, you need to change the header of the method.

```
void setupSprite(
   ref GameSpriteStruct sprite,
   float widthFactor,
   float ticksToCrossScreen,
   float initialX,
   float initialY)
{
   // method goes here
}
```

The **ref** modifier before the `GameSpriteStruct` parameter in the method header tells the compiler to pass a reference to the parameter's location in memory rather than copy a value stored in that memory location. You also need to use the **ref** modifier when you make a call to the method.

```
setupSprite(ref cheese, 0.05f, 200.0f, minDisplayX, minDisplayY);
setupSprite(ref bread, 0.15f, 120.0f, displayWidth / 2, displayHeight / 2);
```

Now when `setupSprite` runs, it will be given the values of the rest of the parameters it needs to work with and a reference to the `GameSpriteStruct` object that needs to be changed. You don't need to change any code in the body of the method itself; the compiler will make sure that the machine instructions it produces follow the reference and update the correct values in memory rather than update a copy of the values.

> **Sample Code: Bread and Cheese with Setup Method**   The sample project in the 02 Bread and Cheese with Setup Method directory in the resources for this chapter uses a **setupSprite** method to set up the sprites.

Handling Collisions

You have a bread bat and some cheese, and you can move the bread around the game and chase the cheese, but nothing happens when you hit the cheese with the bread. You now need to add the interaction between these two sprites. The first thing the game needs to do is detect when the bread and the cheese collide. The best way to do this is to use the rectangles that define the size and position of the two sprites on the screen. When these two rectangles intersect (that is, both of them cover the same part of the screen), a collision has taken place. Figure 12-2 shows how this works.

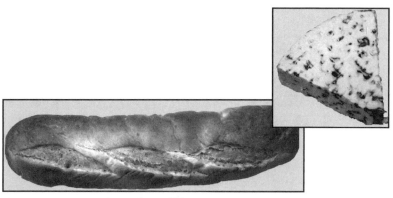

Figure 12-2   Detecting sprite collisions

What you need is a method that you can use to detect when a collision happens. Researching code to accomplish specific tasks is the kind of thing the Internet is very good for, and after a bit of digging, you find a method that will do what you want.

```
bool intersectsWith(Rectangle r1, Rectangle r2)
{
   return !( r2.Left > r1.Right || r2.Right < r1.Left
          || r2.Top > r1.Bottom
          || r2.Bottom < r1.Top );
}
```

This method is given two rectangles as parameters and returns **true** if they intersect. This is clever code. Figure 12-3 shows how it works. The **Rectangle** class provides properties that give the position of the left, right, top, and bottom edges of the region that the **Rectangle** bounds. If the left-hand edge of **r1** is beyond the right-hand edge of **r2** (as it is in this case), it's impossible for the rectangles to intersect.

There are four ways that rectangles can't intersect: one rectangle can be above, below, to the left, or to the right of the other. If you look at the conditions in **intersectsWith**, you can see how it tests each of these possibilities to decide whether the two rectangles intersect. If any one of them is true, they can't overlap, so the results of the tests are combined using the OR operator to produce a condition that evaluates to **true** if the rectangles don't intersect. You want a method that returns **true** when the rectangles do intersect, so the method uses the logical NOT (**!**) operator to invert the result before sending it back.

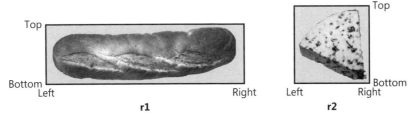

Figure 12-3   Testing for Rectangle intersection

Note   If the top and bottom conditions in this method seem wrong, remember that for XNA, the Y coordinate goes down the screen; in other words, above and below are inverted.

Making the Cheese Bounce off the Bat

Now that you can detect when the cheese and the bread collide, you need to make the cheese "bounce" off the bat. Because the bread is horizontal, it makes sense to bounce the cheese up and down the screen so that whenever the cheese hits the bat, it will reverse its movement in the Y direction. The code to achieve this is very simple; you do the same thing with the Y speed as you do when the cheese hits the top or bottom of the game region.

```
if (intersectsWith(bread.SpriteRectangle,cheese.SpriteRectangle))
{
    cheese.YSpeed = cheese.YSpeed * -1;
}
```

This code can be placed at the end of the **Update** method to cause the cheese to bounce off the bat.

Sample Code: Cheese and Bread Bat   The sample project in the 03 Cheese and Bread Bat directory in the resources for this chapter lets players hit the cheese up and down the screen with the bread bat.

Strange Bounce Behavior

When you run the game, you find that it works well, and you can guide the cheese around the screen successfully. However, you make the mistake of letting your younger brother have a go, and he's soon complaining that there's a bug in your game. Sometimes the cheese gets "stuck" on the bread. You ask him to show you what happens, and it turns out that he's right. It seems to happen when the bread is moving when it hits the cheese. The cheese travels along the bread, vibrating up and down as it moves. After some thought, you work out what's causing the problem. Figure 12-4 shows what's happening.

When the cheese rectangle and the bread rectangle intersect, the program reverses the direction of movement of the cheese. Normally, this means that the next time the position of the

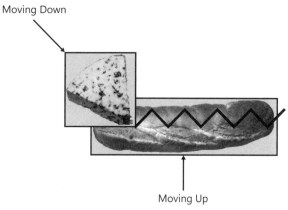

Moving Down

Moving Up

Figure 12-4   Cheese that gets stuck on the bread

cheese is updated, the cheese will move away from the bread, and the rectangles will no longer intersect. However, if the cheese is moving down and the bread is moving up when they collide, the cheese will go so far "in" to the bread that, even after the cheese has been updated, the bread and cheese rectangles still intersect. If this is the case, the **Update** method will reverse the vertical direction of movement of the cheese, causing the cheese to move back into the bread. This will continue as the cheese moves along the bread, following the path shown in Figure 12-4, until it finally escapes off the end. There are a number of ways you can solve this problem:

1.   When the cheese collides with the bread, the program could stop detecting collisions for a while until the cheese has hopefully moved clear of the bread. To implement this, you need to add a variable that counts a certain number of ticks after the collision and not allow collisions until after the specified number of ticks.

2.   The program could move the cheese away from the bread after a collision so that the two sprite rectangles no longer intersect at the next update. To implement this, you need to know which direction the cheese is moving so that you can move it that way.

3.   You could change the rules of the game and tell the player about this special trick shot where a skillful player can send the cheese in a particular direction by making it stick to the bat in this way. This would require no additional programming at all.

The important thing to remember is that because you own the game universe, including what you say the game is supposed to do, you can change the rules to suit what your program does. The Great Programmer doesn't have this freedom; usually she's paid a large sum of money to make a solution that does what the customer wants. However, quite a few games have turned out the way they did because of the way the programmer made them work or because of a bug that turned out to make the game more fun. In this case, you decide to use the third approach and tell your younger brother that the game is meant to work like that, and he has found a secret feature.

Strange Edge Behavior

Your younger brother is now very pleased with himself and with you. He is pleased with you for making a game that rewards clever play and pleased with himself for finding this new trick in the game. However, this doesn't last long because he soon comes back and tells you that he's found a proper bug in the game. He can make the cheese go right off the screen and not come back. You ask him to show you, and sure enough, if he uses the bread to chase the cheese right to the top of the screen, he can send the cheese right off the screen. This is definitely a bug, and you can't pass it off as a feature.

Debugging a Running Program

One of the great things about XNA Game Studio 2.0 is that you can stop the game and take a look at what's happening. Once you've persuaded your younger brother to make the problem happen, you can put a breakpoint into the program and stop it so that you can look at the values of the variables. You can do this even as the program is running, either on the Xbox or on a desktop PC. You've used breakpoints before in Chapter 10, "Using C# Methods to Solve Problems," in the section "A Method to Calculate Percentages" where you were debugging the `getPercentage` method. Now you'll use them again to find out how your cheese is escaping from the screen.

You can put a breakpoint in the `Update` method by clicking next to the line at which you want it to stop. XNA Game Studio 2.0 indicates that a breakpoint has been set by highlighting the line, as shown in Figure 12-5.

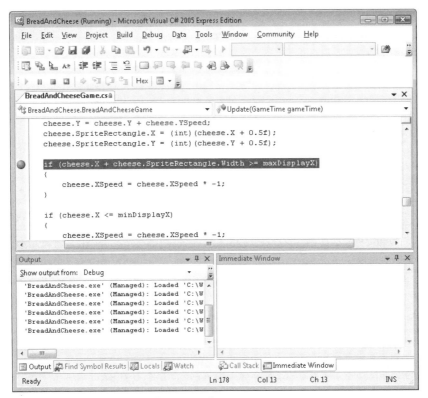

Figure 12-5   Adding a breakpoint to the program

The next time the program reaches this statement, it will stop, and XNA Game Studio 2.0 will enter debugging mode. You can then take a look at the values of the variables to see what's going wrong. You did this in Chapter 10 as well. You add the breakpoint, and the program stops at that line. When you take a look at the values in the cheese sprite, you find that the X coordinate value is fine but the Y coordinate is −50, which is wrong. The cheese Y coordinate should never get as low as this because the direction of the cheese movement should reverse when it reaches an edge. You take another look at the code responsible for the reversal, and it looks sensible.

```
if (cheese.Y <= minDisplayY)
{
    cheese.YSpeed = cheese.YSpeed * -1;
}
```

If the cheese Y value becomes less than the allowable minimum, the direction of movement is reversed to bring it back onto the screen. The program does this by multiplying the speed of the cheese by −1, which made perfect sense when you wrote it. You take a look at the cheese Y speed and find that it is 4. This means that next time the cheese is updated, the Y position of the cheese will be changed to −46 (which is still much lower than it's supposed to be). The result is that the same condition will be triggered again, reversing the direction of the Y speed and sending the Y position of the cheese back to −50. So the cheese remains forever off the screen, dancing backward and forward just out of view. The problem happens because the bread collision testing is performed after the cheese bounces when it hits the edge of the screen, so if the cheese repeatedly bounces off the bread when it's on the edge of the screen, it can vanish like this.

There are a number of ways you can fix the bug. You can stop the bread from going too close to the edges so that it can't harass the cheese like this, or you can fix the bounce problem of the cheese. You can't really say that this behavior is a feature, although you could create a completely different game where the aim was to push all the objects off the screen, perhaps something called "Herd the Cheese" or "Sweep the Table." However, you decide to fix the problem.

The problem lies with the use of multiplication by −1 to change the direction of movement. If the next update brings the cheese back into the required range, then all's well, but if by some mischance it doesn't, you get the dancing behavior that you've just uncovered.

The best way to fix this is to explicitly set the direction of movement of the cheese to the one in which you need it to go. Rather than bouncing, where you simply reverse the sign of the speed value, you should say "if the cheese Y position is less than the limit, then make the movement positive so that the cheese will always be brought back onto the screen." Even if the cheese Y position remains less than the limit next time, the movement will still be correct and result in the cheese heading in the right direction.

This fix turns out to be easy. You can use a method called **Abs**, which is provided by .NET. The **Abs** method is held in the **Math** class and returns the absolute value or magnitude of a number. The absolute value of a number is simply its value, positive or negative. For example, the absolute value of −4 is 4. The **Math** class provides a number of **static** methods (which are always available) for use in your programs. The `Math` class is in the `System` namespace, so you can use it without having to add any `using` directives to your program. The code to deal with the `Y` position of the cheese ends up looking like this:

```
if (cheese.Y + cheese.SpriteRectangle.Height >= maxDisplayY)
{
    cheese.YSpeed = Math.Abs(cheese.YSpeed) * -1;
}
if (cheese.Y <= minDisplayY)
{
    cheese.YSpeed = Math.Abs(cheese.YSpeed) ;
}
```

If the cheese is too high, you make it move downward. If the cheese is too low, you make it move upward. Now, there's no way the cheese can get stuck off the screen.

Unfortunately it is still possible to move the bat off the screen, To solve this, you will have to add code to limit the movement of the bread.

> **Sample Code: Absolute Cheese Bouncing**   The sample project in the 04 Absolute Cheese Bouncing directory in the resources for this chapter has the updated cheese bounce behavior so that the cheese cannot be forced off the screen.

Adding Tomato Targets

Your younger brother has become adept at balancing the cheese on the bat, but he wants something to aim at, so now's the time to provide some targets. You decide to use tomatoes for this, so you need to add them to your program. You want to have lots of tomatoes, so you'll need to create an array of `GameSpriteStruct` instances to hold all these.

```
Texture2D tomatoTexture;
GameSpriteStruct[] tomatoes;
int numberOfTomatoes = 20;
```

These are the fields that you have to create to hold tomato information. Note that while I've created an array reference called **tomatoes**, I haven't yet created the array itself. You'll load the tomato texture from your image into a single **Texture2D** object which will be loaded with the rest of the content for the game.

```
protected override void LoadContent()
{
    // Create a new SpriteBatch, which can be used to draw textures.
    spriteBatch = new SpriteBatch(GraphicsDevice);

    cheese.SpriteTexture = Content.Load<Texture2D>("Images\\Cheese");
    bread.SpriteTexture = Content.Load<Texture2D>("Images\\Bread");
    tomatoTexture = Content.Load<Texture2D>("Images\\Tomato");
    setupSprites();
}
```

Textures are classes, and are managed by reference, not value, so each of your tomatoes will contain a reference to the same tomato texture.

```
void setupSprites()
{
   setupSprite(ref cheese, 0.05f, 200.0f, minDisplayX, minDisplayY);
   setupSprite(ref bread, 0.15f, 120.0f, displayWidth / 2, displayHeight / 2);
   tomatoes = new GameSpriteStruct[numberOfTomatoes];

   float tomatoSpacing = (maxDisplayX - minDisplayX) / numberOfTomatoes;

   for (int i = 0; i < numberOfTomatoes; i++)
   {
      tomatoes[i].SpriteTexture = tomatoTexture;
      setupSprite(
         ref tomatoes[i],
         0.05f, // 20 tomatoes across the screen
         1000,  // 1000 ticks to move across the screen
         minDisplayX + (i * tomatoSpacing), minDisplayY);
   }
}
```

The **setupSprites** method creates the tomatoes array and contains a **for** loop that works through each of the tomato sprites and sets their size and position. Your first version of the game has the tomatoes evenly spaced in a line along the top of the screen. To make this work, the method uses a local variable called **tomatoSpacing** that's set to the width of the display divided by the number of tomatoes that you're using in the game. Note that you're following the advice of the Great Programmer in that it will be very easy to change the number of tomatoes in the game; you need to change the value of only one variable.

At the moment, you won't be making the tomatoes move, so the **Update** method only needs to copy the X and Y positions of the tomato into the rectangle for that sprite.

```
for (int i = 0; i < numberOfTomatoes; i++)
{
   tomatoes[i].SpriteRectangle.X = (int)tomatoes[i].X;
   tomatoes[i].SpriteRectangle.Y = (int)tomatoes[i].Y;
}
```

The last thing you need to do is add the code to draw all the tomatoes. This is placed in the **Draw** method.

```
protected override void Draw(GameTime gameTime)
{
   graphics.GraphicsDevice.Clear(Color.CornflowerBlue);

   spriteBatch.Begin();
   spriteBatch.Draw(cheese.SpriteTexture, cheese.SpriteRectangle, Color.White);
   spriteBatch.Draw(bread.SpriteTexture, bread.SpriteRectangle, Color.White);
```

```
for (int i = 0; i < numberOfTomatoes; i++)
{
    spriteBatch.Draw(tomatoes[i].SpriteTexture, tomatoes[i].SpriteRectangle, Color.White);
}
spriteBatch.End();

base.Draw(gameTime);
}
```

The `Draw` method contains another **for** loop that draws each of the tomatoes in turn. Figure 12-6 shows the display produced with your 20 tomatoes along the top.

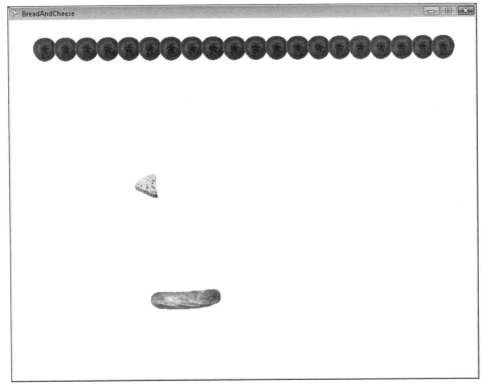

Figure 12-6   Bread, cheese, and 20 tomatoes

Sample Code: Adding Tomatoes   The sample project in the 05 Adding Tomatoes directory in the resources for this chapter draws 20 tomatoes along the top of the screen.

Tomato Collisions

The idea of the game is that when the cheese hits a tomato, the tomato will vanish. This means that you need a way of making the tomatoes disappear. You can't make them vanish, but you can decide not to draw them.

Controlling Sprite Visibility

The game must have some way of deciding when a particular sprite shouldn't be drawn. This turns out to be easy; you need only add an extra field to the GameSpriteStruct structure.

```
struct GameSpriteStruct
{
    public Texture2D SpriteTexture;
    public Rectangle SpriteRectangle;
    public float X;
    public float Y;
    public float XSpeed;
    public float YSpeed;
    public float WidthFactor;
    public float TicksToCrossScreen;
    public bool Visible;
}
```

The Visible field is set to true if the sprite is to be drawn on the screen.

Setting the Initial Visibility state

The initial value of Visible can be set by the setupSprite method, which is now given an additional parameter that is used to set the initial visibility of the sprite.

```
void setupSprite(
    ref GameSpriteStruct sprite,
    float widthFactor,
    float ticksToCrossScreen,
    float initialX,
    float initialY,
    bool initialVisibility)
{
    // original setup code here
    sprite.Visible = initialVisibility;
}
```

Initially, Visible is set to true for all the tomatoes, the cheese, and the bread in the setupSprites method.

```
void setupSprites()
{
    setupSprite(ref cheese, 0.05f, 200.0f, 200, 100, true);
    setupSprite(ref bread, 0.15f, 120.0f, displayWidth / 2, displayHeight / 2, true);

    tomatoes = new GameSpriteStruct[numberOfTomatoes];

    float tomatoSpacing = (maxDisplayX - minDisplayX) / numberOfTomatoes;
```

```
    for (int i = 0; i < numberOfTomatoes; i++)
    {
        tomatoes[i].SpriteTexture = tomatoTexture;
        setupSprite(
        ref tomatoes[i],
        0.05f, // 20 tomatos across the screen
        1000,  // 1000 ticks to move across the screen
        minDisplayX + (i * tomatoSpacing), minDisplayY,
        true // initially visible);
    }
}
```

This `setupSprites` method also sets the initial position of the cheese a bit further into the screen so that it does not initially collide with any tomatoes.

Using the Visibility field when drawing

You use the value of the `Visible` field when you draw the sprites in the `Draw` method.

```
for (int i = 0; i < numberOfTomatoes; i++)
{
   if (tomatoes[i].Visible)
   {
       spriteBatch.Draw(tomatoes[i].SpriteTexture, tomatoes[i].SpriteRectangle, Color.White);
   }
}
```

Only tomatoes that have the `Visible` field set to `true` are drawn on the screen. To make a tomato vanish, you simply set its `Visible` property to `false`. You do this in the `Update` method.

```
for (int i = 0; i < numberOfTomatoes; i++)
{
   if (tomatoes[i].Visible)
   {
       if (intersectsWith(cheese.SpriteRectangle, tomatoes[i].SpriteRectangle))
       {
           tomatoes[i].Visible = false;
           cheese.YSpeed = cheese.YSpeed * -1;
           break;
       }
   }
   tomatoes[i].SpriteRectangle.X = (int)tomatoes[i].X;
   tomatoes[i].SpriteRectangle.Y = (int)tomatoes[i].Y;
}
```

The `for` loop looks through all the tomatoes and tests to see whether any of the tomato rectangles intersect with the cheese. If it finds an intersection, it sets the `Visible` property of the tomato to `false` and then reverses the direction of the cheese movement to make it "bounce" off the tomato it has just destroyed. Once it has removed one tomato, it stops looking for any more because the **break** statement causes the **for** loop to end at that point. This is important, because otherwise the cheese might collide with and destroy more than one tomato at a time, making the game too easy.

> **Sample Code: Tomato Killer**   The sample project in the 06 Tomato Killer directory lets a player steer the cheese around the screen and use it to destroy tomatoes.

Conclusion

You're now starting to make games that look like "proper" ones. You're building your understanding of how C# lets you structure the data in your programs so that it's easier to work with. You also discovered how to use references so that methods can change the content of variables passed as parameters, and you found another use for the XNA Game Studio 2.0 debugger.

Pop Quiz

Here's the twelfth pop quiz. You know the procedure by now.

1. Structures are held in fields.

2. Structures let programmers group things together in their programs.

3. Structures are managed by reference.

4. Making a member of a class public stops code in other classes from using that item.

5. The absolute value of a number is always negative.

6. Parameters to a C# method by default are passed by copying their value into the method.

7. You can't put a breakpoint in a running program.

8. The **Abs** method is **static**, so you don't need an instance of the **Math** class to use it.

9. You can't change the name of a method once you've created it.

Chapter 13

Creating Gameplay

- Finish off the game play in your game.

- Add some features to make the game more exciting.

- Discover how to improve the structure of the game program itself.

- Find out how to use state machines to add a title screen to the game.

Introduction

You can now create programs with all the behaviors required to create a "proper" game. You know how to place objects on the screen and manage their movement. You also know how to make sure that the games you create will work on different display sizes. You can also display text and produce sounds. In this chapter, you'll develop the game play further, add some more sprites, and create a game that has proper gameplay states.

Making a Finished Game

You now have the basis of a single-player tomato killer game. The game play is simple—you use the bread to steer the cheese around at the tomatoes—but even your younger brother, who is easy to amuse, will quickly find the game boring. Thus, you need to add some more game-play elements: scores, survival, and progression.

Adding Scores to a Game

Even a simple game can be made addictive by adding a score component. It gets even more interesting when you add a high score so that the player always has something to beat. The game score is another integer variable that's set to 0 when the game starts and increases each time a tomato is killed. You've decided that tomatoes are worth 10 points, so each time the cheese crashes into a tomato, the score goes up by 10. The code that manages the cheese and tomato collisions is in the **Update** method.

```
if (intersectsWith(cheese.SpriteRectangle, tomatoes[i].SpriteRectangle))
{
    cheese.YSpeed = cheese.YSpeed * -1;
    score = score + 10;
    tomatoes[i].Visible = false;
    break;
}
```

You could make the game even more interesting by making the value of the tomatoes change over time so that the longer the player takes to destroy them, the less they're worth, but for now, you'll simply give the player 10 points for every tomato destroyed.

Drawing Text in the Game

Now that you have a score value to display, you need some code to write it on the screen so that the player can see the score increasing. The best way to do this is to create a general purpose method for drawing text. You can then use the method to draw text whenever you need to display a message. The method needs to be given the text to be displayed, the position of the text, and the color of the text.

```
void drawText(string text, Color textColor, float x, float y)
{
    int layer;
    Vector2 textVector = new Vector2(x, y);

    // Draw the shadow
    Color backColor = new Color(0, 0, 0, 20);
    for (layer = 0; layer < 10; layer++)
    {
        spriteBatch.DrawString(font, text, textVector, backColor);
        textVector.X++;
        textVector.Y++;
    }

    // Draw the solid part of the characters
    backColor = new Color(190, 190, 190);
    for (layer = 0; layer < 5; layer++)
    {
        spriteBatch.DrawString(font, text, textVector, backColor);
        textVector.X++;
        textVector.Y++;
    }

    // Draw the top of the characters
    spriteBatch.DrawString(font, text, textVector, textColor);
}
```

The **drawText** method is the same code you used to draw the clock in Chapter 5, "Writing Text." However, it's been packaged up as a method that you can use whenever you want to put text onto the screen. It is supplied with the string to be displayed, the color of the text, and the position on the screen at which to draw it. The font to be used must be loaded by the **LoadContent** method. To draw the score on the screen, you need to call the **drawText** method within the **Draw** method.

```
protected override void Draw(GameTime gameTime)
{

    graphics.GraphicsDevice.Clear(Color.CornflowerBlue);
    spriteBatch.Begin();
    spriteBatch.Draw(cheese.SpriteTexture, cheese.SpriteRectangle, Color.White);
    spriteBatch.Draw(bread.SpriteTexture, bread.SpriteRectangle, Color.White);
    for (int i = 0; i < numberOfTomatoes; i++)
    {
        if (tomatoes[i].Visible)
        {
            spriteBatch.Draw(tomatoes[i].SpriteTexture, tomatoes[i].SpriteRectangle,
              Color.White);
        }
    }

    drawText("Score : " + score.ToString(), Color.White, minDisplayX, maxDisplayY - 50);
    spriteBatch.End();

    base.Draw(gameTime);
}
```

This **Draw** method draws all the game objects and then puts the score on last, so the score values will be shown "on top" of all the other game items. You can call the **drawText** method several times if you want to draw multiple messages.

Adding Survival

At the moment, the player is under no particular pressure during the game. If the player makes a mistake, it doesn't cost him or her anything. You need to add some bad news to the game. Later, you could add deadly peppers and a hunting banana, but for now, you'll cause the player to lose a life if the cheese hits the bottom of the screen. The life counter is just another variable in the game. There seems to be a tradition in computer games that you always start with three lives and that each time something bad happens, you lose a life. When you have no lives left, your game ends. The **Update** method contains the code that checks for the cheese hitting the bottom of the screen; you need only add some code that updates the life counter when this happens. The lives counter must be reduced only when the player has some lives left, so the program must test for this.

```
if (cheese.Y + cheese.SpriteRectangle.Height >= maxDisplayY)
{
    cheese.YSpeed = Math.Abs(cheese.YSpeed) * -1;
    if (lives > 0)
    {
        lives = lives - 1;
    }
}
```

Next, you need to stop the game from continuing when the number of lives reaches 0. The best way to do this is to exit from the **Update** method after you've moved the cheese but before you update the bread and look for tomatoes to collide with. This code takes advantage of the C# feature that lets a program return from a method at any point during the method.

```
protected override void Update(GameTime gameTime)
{
    ...
    // code to move the cheese and update the life counter
    ...
    if (lives <= 0)
    {
        return;
    }

    ...
    // Code to update the bread position
    // Code to check for the cheese hitting the tomatoes
    ...
}
```

The effect of this is that when all the lives are used up, the cheese will continue bouncing around the screen, but the score will not change, and the player will be unable to control the bread.

Adding Progression

Once the player has killed all the tomatoes, your game becomes very boring in that there's nothing left to do. Many games are built around the idea of successive levels, with each one being progressively more difficult than the last. The task of the player is to survive as long as possible, building up the highest score possible before all the lives are used up. One way you can achieve progression is by redrawing the tomatoes each time all of them have been destroyed. To make the game more difficult, you can redraw them lower down the screen so that the player has less time to react with each passing level.

To achieve this, you need to detect when all the tomatoes have been destroyed. One way to do this is to use a flag that's set when a tomato is found, as shown in the following code:

```
bool noTomatoes = true;

for (int i = 0; i < numberOfTomatoes; i++)
{
    if (tomatoes[i].Visible)
    {
        noTomatoes = false;
        if (intersectsWith(cheese.SpriteRectangle, tomatoes[i].SpriteRectangle))
        {
            cheese.YSpeed = cheese.YSpeed * -1;
            score = score + 10;
            tomatoes[i].Visible = false;
            break;
        }
    }
}
```

```
        tomatoes[i].SpriteRectangle.X = (int)tomatoes[i].X;
        tomatoes[i].SpriteRectangle.Y = (int)tomatoes[i].Y;
    }

if (noTomatoes)
{
    resetTomatoDisplay();
}
```

The **noTomatoes** flag is set to false if a visible tomato is found in the list. If the loop completes and **noTomatoes** is still true, the program must call the **resetTomatoDisplay** method to put the tomatoes back on the screen again. The method moves the tomato draw height down the screen and then uses a loop to update the draw height of each tomato and make the tomato visible again.

```
float tomatoStepFactor = 0.1f;

void resetTomatoDisplay()
{
    tomatoHeight = tomatoHeight + (displayHeight * tomatoStepFactor);
    if (tomatoHeight > tomatoHeightLimit)
    {
        tomatoHeight = minDisplayY;
    }
    for (int i = 0; i < numberOfTomatoes; i++)
    {
        tomatoes[i].Visible = true;
        tomatoes[i].Y = tomatoHeight;
    }
}
```

The **resetTomatoDisplay** method cannot move the tomatoes down the screen indefinitely; otherwise, they would eventually fall off the bottom of the display. To prevent this, the method imposes a limit on how far down the screen tomatoes can be drawn. Once this limit is reached, the tomatoes are moved back to the top of the screen again. The limit value is set when the game starts, in the method that sets up the tomatoes.

```
void setupTomatoes()
{
    tomatoHeight = minDisplayY;
    tomatoHeightLimit = minDisplayY + ((maxDisplayY - minDisplayY) / 2);
    tomatoes = new GameSpriteStruct[numberOfTomatoes];
    float tomatoSpacing = (maxDisplayX - minDisplayX) / numberOfTomatoes;

    for (int i = 0; i < numberOfTomatoes; i++)
    {
        tomatoes[i].SpriteTexture = tomatoTexture;
        setupSprite(
          ref tomatoes[i],
          0.05f, // 20 tomatoes across the screen
          1000, // 1000 ticks to move across the screen
          minDisplayX + (i * tomatoSpacing), tomatoHeight,
          true // initially visible);
    }
}
```

> **Sample Code: Bread and Cheese Game** The sample project in the 01 Bread and Cheese Game directory in the resources for this chapter is a fully working version of the game. Use the bread bat to hit the cheese at the tomato targets. When you've destroyed a complete row, the tomatoes are all redrawn. If you let the cheese hit the bottom of the screen, the life counter is reduced. Once all three lives have been used up, you will be unable to control the bread, and the score will not update.

> **Note** There are some gameplay issues with this design that your younger brother might notice, particularly the way that, after a level is redrawn, the cheese often collides instantly with one of the tomatoes and gets above the tomato row, bouncing about and making a huge score. Another issue is that the vertical direction but not the horizontal direction of the cheese changes regardless of whether the cheese hits the top, bottom, or side of a tomato. If you decide that these issues are significant, you can fix them in a number of ways. I'll leave it to you to sort it out.

Improving Code Design

In Chapter 11, "A Game as a C# Program," in the section "Renaming the Game1 Class," you changed the name of the class to one that better reflects the game being created. Now you'll consider other ways that your programs can be better structured. At the moment, you haven't given much thought to the structure of the game program itself. When you've needed extra code, you've just added it where it seemed to do the job. However, this is not very good design practice.

It's much easier if code is structured into well-defined areas. If you think about it, all the cheese, bread, and tomato game elements are used in the same way. The game program performs a number of fundamental actions with these elements during a game:

1. The game elements are set up at the beginning of the game.

2. The game elements are updated during the game.

3. The game elements are drawn during the game.

At the moment, these actions are performed in a piecemeal fashion in the game methods that perform these tasks. However, it makes very good sense to bring the code for each element together so that it's all easier to manage. Rather than having bits of behavior for all the elements in the **Update** method, you can change the **Update** method so that it instead calls a method for each game element type. (You'll need to change **gamePad1** to be a global variable.)

```
protected override void Update(GameTime gameTime)
{
    gamePad1 = GamePad.GetState(PlayerIndex.One);
    if (gamePad1.Buttons.Back == ButtonState.Pressed)
    this.Exit();
    updateCheese();
```

```
    if (lives <= 0)
    {
        return;
    }

    updateBread();
    updateTomatoes();
    base.Update(gameTime);
}
```

The same pattern could be used in the **Setup** and **Draw** methods. Note that these changes won't make the game program run more quickly (in fact, the method calls will slow things down very slightly), but it will make things much easier for the programmer, as shown later. You might remember that the process of tidying up a program like this is known as refactoring. Visual Studio provides some useful refactoring features to help you organize your program and perform the refactoring itself.

Refactoring by Creating Methods from Code

The refactoring support in Visual Studio makes creating a method from a block of statements easy. First, you highlight the statements that are to be placed in the new method. Then, you right-click the block of code to bring up the Context menu and select Refactor from that menu. You select Extract Method from the Refactor menu, as shown in Figure 13-1.

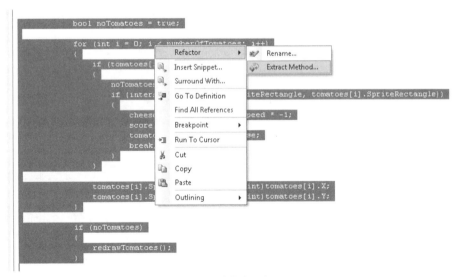

Figure 13-1   Opening the Extract Method dialog box

The Extract Method dialog box will appear, as shown in Figure 13-2. Enter the name of the method to be created and click OK.

Visual Studio will create a method with the name you've entered, place the selected code into the method, and place a call to the method where the code used to be. You could have performed all this yourself, but the automation does make the process much easier.

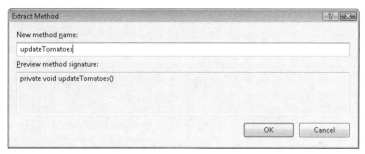

Figure 13-2   Creating a method

> **Note**   If the statements that you have extracted use variables that are local to the block of code from which the statements were taken, you'll find that extracting a method will stop your program from compiling correctly. You'll need to fix the problem by declaring parameters for the new method and passing the variables as arguments.

Refactoring by Changing Identifiers

Frequently, you'll need to change the identifiers as you develop your program because the purpose of the variables and methods changes as you gain a better understanding of the problem you're solving. At the start of the development, you created a method called **scaleSprites**, which you then changed to **setupSprites** because it set up all the sprite settings, not just the sprite scaling, for the elements in the game. However, this method now has other responsibilities—it must also set the score and life counters. If the purpose of a method changes, as this one has, you should again make sure that the method name is changed to reflect the method's current purpose. In this case, you'll change the name of the method to **setupGame**. The refactoring support in Visual Studio makes this name change easy. To rename an identifier, right-click the identifier you want to rename and select the appropriate refactoring command, as shown in Figure 13-3.

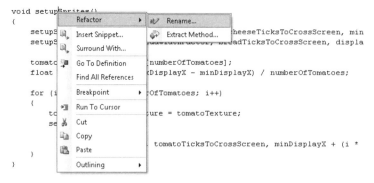

Figure 13-3   Selecting the rename operation

The Rename dialog box will now appear, as shown in Figure 13-4. You can type in the new name of the method and select options to control the renaming process. If you've created comments or text strings that refer to the method, you can ask Visual Studio to update these, too.

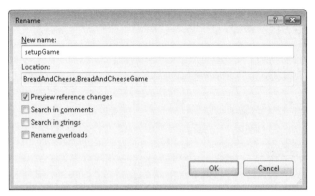

Figure 13-4   Renaming a method

By default, the Preview Reference Changes check box is selected so that you'll be given a chance to see the names that are about to be changed, as shown in Figure 13-5. You can control which changes are to be made by selecting the check box next to each change.

Figure 13-5   Previewing name changes

When you click OK, the changes that you requested are applied, and the program source code is updated. When renaming items, you must be careful not to break your program. Figure 13-6 shows the warning that Visual Studio displays if it detects that you're about to rename something that's used in other parts of the program.

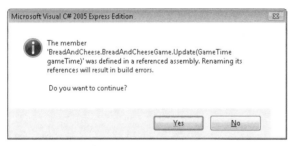

Figure 13-6   Invalid name changes

If you ignore this warning and perform the changes anyway, it's very likely that you'll prevent your program from compiling. The good news here, though, is that you can always use the Visual Studio Undo command to remove the changes that you've made. Figure 13-7 shows where the command is on the Edit menu; you can also invoke it by pressing the left looping arrow on the toolbar or by using the key combination Ctrl+Z or Alt+Backspace.

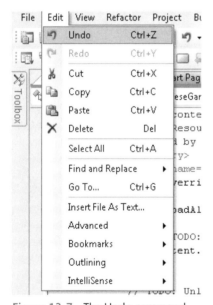

Figure 13-7   The Undo command

Creating Code Regions

Another way to make program listings easier to understand is to use regions. A *region* is an area of the code that you can expand or contract. For example, you can expand or contract the view of your code by clicking the plus (+) or minus (−) signs at the top of a method. You can also create regions that can be expanded or contracted by enclosing related code in **#region** compiler directives, as shown in Figure 13-8. Figure 13-8 shows a region around the contracted methods that were created to manage the tomatoes in the game.

```
#region Tomato code and data

Texture2D tomatoTexture;
GameSpriteStruct[] tomatoes;
int numberOfTomatoes = 20;
float tomatoHeight;
float tomatoStepFactor = 0.1f;
float tomatoHeightLimit;

private void loadTomatoContent()...

void setupTomatoes()...

void resetTomatoDisplay()...


void updateTomatoes()...

void drawTomatoes()...

#endregion
```

Figure 13-8   Creating code regions

Regions can be placed inside regions to make it easier for other programmers to find their way around your programs.

Creating Useful Comments

You've seen that Visual Studio provides Intellisense when you're writing a program. When you're typing a statement that contains a method call, the structure of the method call is described to you automatically. Some of this information is obtained from specially formatted comments that have been added to the method itself. You first saw comments in Chapter 2, "Programs, Data, and Pretty Colors." They provide a way for you to leave notes in your program that are ignored by the compiler. If you write comments in a particular format, they can be used by the compiler to provide Intellisense to other programmers. As an example, consider the **drawText** method. Each of the parameters has a particular purpose, and you can add comments to describe these.

```
/// <summary>
/// Draws text on the screen
/// </summary>
/// <param name="text">text to write</param>
/// <param name="textColor">color of text</param>
/// <param name="x">left hand edge of text</param>
/// <param name="y">top of text</param>
```

```
void drawText(string text, Color textColor, float x, float y)
{
    // Draw statements
}
```

The comments are formatted in a manner that provides the Visual Studio editor with Intellisense information. So now when you create a call of the method, the extra information is displayed. Figure 13-9 shows how the information is displayed when a call of **drawText** is being made.

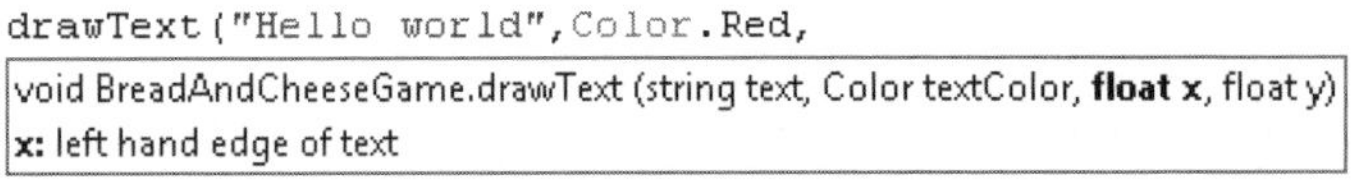

```
drawText("Hello world",Color.Red,
```
> void BreadAndCheeseGame.drawText (string text, Color textColor, **float x**, float y)
> **x:** left hand edge of text

Figure 13-9   Using Intellisense comments

The structure of the Intellisense comments has to be exactly right; otherwise, no help is displayed. You can create these comments manually, or you can use Visual Studio to create a template for you to fill in. To obtain the template, you type three forward slash (/) characters in succession in the editor immediately above the item to which you wish to add the comment.

> **The Great Programmer Speaks: A Great Program Is a Work of Art**   The Great Programmer reckons that, just as there is artistry in the design of a bridge or other great engineering work, well-written code is also a thing of beauty. Code that uses properly chosen identifiers and appropriate methods, and that is broken down into regions, is regarded by her as being as worthy of admiration as any other work of art. She always tries to make sure that her code looks good.

> **Sample Code: Refactored Bread and Cheese Game**   The sample project in the 02 Refactored Bread and Cheese Game directory in the resources for this chapter is a refactored version of the game. From the player's point of view, it's exactly the same game. However, if you look at the source code of this program, you'll find that the code has been organized into a set of methods and separated into regions. You should find it much easier to locate particular items of code in the source file.

Adding a Background

At the moment, the game is played on the blue background that is provided by XNA. This is okay, but it doesn't look very special. To improve the look, you could add a texture that's drawn behind the game by following the same pattern that was used for the other graphics items. The set of background methods shown in the following code match those that are provided for the bread, cheese, and tomatoes. The background texture itself has been scaled so that it fills the entire screen. You need only put calls to the following methods into the appropriate game methods to have a game with an attractive background image.

```
#region Background code and data

GameSpriteStruct background;

private void loadBackgroundContent()
{
   background.SpriteTexture = Content.Load<Texture2D>("Images\\Background");
}

private void setupBackground()
{
   setupSprite(ref background,
     1,       // full width of screen
     1000,    // large number of ticks to cross screen
     0,0,     // top left hand corner
     true);   // visible
}

private void updateBackground()
{
}

private void drawBackground()
{
   spriteBatch.Draw(background.SpriteTexture, background.SpriteRectangle, Color.White);
}

#endregion
```

Note that the call to **drawBackground** replaces the call to **GraphicsDevice.Clear** in the **Draw** method, and the call must go between the **spriteBatch.Begin** and **spriteBatch.End** calls. Also note that there's an **updateBackround** method, but at the moment this is empty. Later, you might want to make the background flutter in the breeze or change color as the player approaches the high score. This technique of leaving the method blank makes adding code to modify the game program much easier.

> **Sample Code: Bread and Cheese with Background**   The sample project in the 03 Bread and Cheese with Background directory in the resources for this chapter is a version of the game with a rather snazzy tablecloth in the background.

This technique also makes it easier to swap one element for another. If other programmers wanted to create a different type of background, you could tell them what methods they would need to provide, and then their code could plug directly into the game code.

Adding a Title Screen

At the moment, the game starts when you run the program and then finishes when the last life has been used up by the player. This is not how real games work. If you ever watch a real game, you'll notice that it has an "attract" mode where it shows a screen intended to entice the player into playing the game. You'll create a simple version of this by adding a title screen.

This screen will be displayed when the game is not active. You will create a title GameSpriteStruct and all the associated methods in the same way as you created a background in the previous section.

Figure 13-10   A tasteful title screen

Games and State

To make the title screen appear correctly, the program must manage the *state* of the game. The best way to do this is to create an enumerated type that has values to represent the states that the game can occupy. You first saw enumerated types in Chapter 9, "Reading Text Input." Each of the possible keys that the keyboard can generate is represented by a value of the enumerated type **Keys**. You'll create an enumerated type to hold the state of the game. This type will have only two values: one representing a state when the title screen is displayed, and the other representing a state when the game is being played. Once the type has been created, you can make a variable of that type to hold the state of the game, setting it initially to the title screen state.

```
enum GameState
{
    titleScreen,
    playingGame
}
GameState state = GameState.titleScreen;
```

If the program can occupy only two states, you might think that this approach is overkill. You could have just used a Boolean type, perhaps called `gameActive`, because Boolean types have only two values. However, suppose you decide later to add other game states, perhaps one in which the high-score table is displayed. Such an enhancement will be easier to implement if you use an enumerated type instead of a Boolean type, because you will simply need to add a new value to the enumerated type to represent this state.

Using the State Values

The state variable in the game will control what happens in the **Draw** and **Update** methods. When the game is in the title screen state, the title screen needs to be drawn. When the game is in the **playingGame** state, the background, cheese, bread, and tomatoes need to be drawn.

```
protected override void Draw(GameTime gameTime)
{
    spriteBatch.Begin();

    switch (state)
    {
        case GameState.titleScreen:
          drawTitle();
          break;
        case GameState.playingGame:
          drawBackground();
          drawCheese();
          drawBread();
          drawTomatoes();
          drawScore();
          break;
    }

    spriteBatch.End();

    base.Draw(gameTime);
}
```

The **Update** method in the game contains a similar switch construction that's used to select the appropriate behavior.

```
protected override void Update(GameTime gameTime)
{
    gamePad1 = GamePad.GetState(PlayerIndex.One);

    if (gamePad1.Buttons.Back == ButtonState.Pressed)
        this.Exit();

    switch (state)
    {
        case GameState.titleScreen:
          updateTitle();
          break;
```

```
    case GameState.playingGame:
      updateCheese();
      updateBread();
      updateTomatoes();
      updateScore();
      break;
  }

  base.Update(gameTime);
}
```

Building a State Machine

Now that you've identified the states that the game will occupy, you need to consider what will cause the game program to move from one state to another. In professional programming, you use a state diagram to express this, as shown in Figure 13-11.

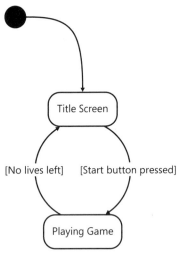

Figure 13-11   Game state diagram

A state diagram shows the entry point (a black filled-in blob) and then arrows that show transition from one state to another. Some of the arrows have "guard conditions" on them that identify what must happen for the transition to take place. The diagram in Figure 13-11 shows that when the game starts, it moves into the "Title Screen" state, and then, if the Start button is pressed, the game moves into the "Playing Game" state. Once the player has no lives left, the game program moves back onto the title screen.

State diagrams are very useful for showing how a program will behave and telling the programmer that at certain points, the program must behave in a certain way. For example, the diagram in Figure 13-11 shows that testing the start key when the player is playing the game is unnecessary. Developers often use state diagrams when developing games in which game items have a range of possible states.

Once you've identified the states, you need to create some methods that will manage the transition from one state to another. You need one method to start the game and one that's called when the game is over. The methods must set up all the variables as required and then change the state of the game.

```
#region Game state management

void startGame()
{
    score = 0;
    lives = 3;
    startTomatoes();
    // make all the tomatoes visible at the top
    state = GameState.playingGame;
}

void gameOver()
{
    if (score > highScore)
    {
        highScore = score;
    }
    state = GameState.titleScreen;
}

#endregion
```

The `startGame` method clears the score, sets the number of lives left to 3, and begins the game. The `gameOver` method updates the high score if it's been beaten and then puts the game back to the `titleScreen` state. Now all you need to do is call these methods at the appropriate times to change the states in the game state machine. When the player presses the Start button, the game must call the `startGame` method. The test for this should be placed in the `updateTitle` method, which updates the title screen.

```
if (gamePad1.Buttons.Start == ButtonState.Pressed)
{
    startGame();
}
```

A game ends when the cheese reaches the bottom of the screen and the last life is used up. The test for this should be placed in the `cheeseUpdate` method.

```
if (cheese.Y + cheese.SpriteRectangle.Height >= maxDisplayY)
{
    cheese.YSpeed = Math.Abs(cheese.YSpeed) * -1;
    lives = lives - 1;
    if (lives == 0)
    {
        gameOver();
    }
}
```

> **Sample Code: Bread and Cheese with Title Screen**   The sample project in the 04 Bread and Cheese with Title Screen directory in the resources for this chapter is a version of the game that operates using a state machine to provide a title screen.

Many games show different displays during their "attract mode." It's easy to get your game to do this by making the program change from one state to another over time. The game code can do this by counting the number of times that `titleUpdate` has been called and then moving to another state when the counter reaches a particular value.

> **The Great Programmer Speaks: State Machines Are a Great Way to Write Programs**   The Great Programmer uses state machines a lot in her code. They let her programs "remember" where they are so that they can respond correctly when an event happens. She starts off by working out what states her program must occupy and identifying the events that cause the states to change. Once she has done this and drawn her state diagram, she can go ahead and write the code.

Conclusion

At last, you've created what might be regarded as a finished game. It has some rough edges and is rather simple to play, but it should keep your younger brother quiet for an hour or so. You've seen how the way a program is structured and laid out in the source file can have a huge impact on how easily you are able to work with the code. You've also discovered some fundamentals of game program behavior by finding out how a state machine can be used to manage the operation of a game.

Pop Quiz

Will the thirteenth pop quiz be luck for you? Answer the questions and find out.

1. A program will return from a method only when it reaches the end of that method block.

2. Refactoring is where you change the type of the variables.

3. Method names can't be changed once a program has been written.

4. Each code region in a program is stored in a separate source file.

5. Intellisense information is retrieved from code regions.

6. A state machine can have only two possible states.

Chapter 14

Making Complete Games

In this chapter:

■ See how we can use C# and XNA to make some very silly games.

Introduction

Because this is the last chapter in the book, I asked around to find out what should be in it. The Great Programmer thinks that at this point you should go on to explore classes, interfaces, encapsulation, properties, public and private methods, delegates, and inheritance. Your younger brother just wants more games to play.

To properly cover all the things that the Great Programmer wants me to mention would require at least another book, and I really want your younger brother to understand that there's more to programming than just playing games, so I've decided on a compromise. You are going to look at some very silly (but great fun) games and pull out of them some of the more advanced programming techniques that you might want to explore. This is not going to be a detailed text on all the wonderful things that you can do with C# and XNA, but it should provide plenty of sample code and silly ideas to get you started. Each of the games discussed here is fully formed and completely playable. Before you read the program descriptions, I strongly advise you to play the games for a while so that you have an understanding of what the programs actually do.

Note These games do not use all the state-of-the-art programming techniques that the Great Programmer knows about. They are intended to be easy to understand. If you can think of a better way to make the games work than the ones that I've used, then congratulations, you are on your way to becoming a proper programmer. If you find them hard to understand, then you should consider how the game actually plays and then try to relate that to what the code does.

Hide The Gamepad

Hide the Gamepad is a very silly game with very simple but silly rules for two or more players. You need two wireless gamepads for this game. At the start of the game one player, "the searcher," leaves the room. While the searcher is outside, the other players hide gamepad 1 somewhere in the room. Then they call back in the searcher and press a button on gamepad 2 to select how long the searcher has to find the gamepad. The times range from 5 minutes down to 2. Once the time limit has been selected, the clock starts, and the searcher must search the room to find the missing gamepad. Other players are allowed to shout hints, such as "warmer" or "colder," if they wish.

The game counts down on the screen how much time is left. During the last minute, the hidden gamepad will start to vibrate, quietly at first, to make it easier to find. If the searcher finds the gamepad and presses the Y button on it, the searcher has won, and the screen displays how much time the searcher had left till the end of the game. If the searcher doesn't make it in time, the screen displays an end-of-game image, and the searcher has lost. The players then choose another searcher, and the game continues. The ultimate winner is the player who had the most time left at the end of his or her search. Figure 14-1 shows a tense moment in the game.

Figure 14-1   Not long now!

> **Sample Code: Hide the Gamepad Game**   The sample project in the 01 Hide the Gamepad directory in the resources for this chapter is a fully working version of the game.

Hide the Gamepad as a State Machine

The game itself runs as a *state machine*. You saw these in Chapter 13, "Creating Gameplay," in the section "Building a State Machine." Figure 14-2 shows the states that the game can occupy and the events that cause a change from one state to another.

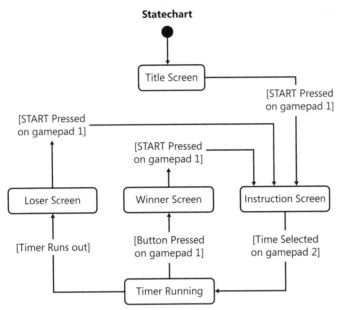

Figure 14-2   Hide the Gamepad as a state machine

As an example, if the game is in the "Game Active" state and the timer runs out, the state of the game changes to "Game Lost." The actual states are represented by an enumerated type called **GameState** that has a value for each of the states. The program contains a variable of type **GameState** that holds the state of the game at any instant.

```
enum GameState
{
    TitleScreen,
    InstructionScreen,
    GameActive,
    GameWon,
    GameLost
}
GameState state = GameState.TitleScreen;
```

From the point of view of the state diagram in Figure 14-2, the **state** variable can hold a value representing any state that the game can occupy. When the game starts off, the initial state is displaying the title screen. The **Update** and **Draw** methods contain switch constructions controlled by this **state** variable. The **Draw** method displays appropriate textures for each state, and if the game is active, it also displays the timer value.

Creating a Timer

You have seen how the .NET Framework provides date and time services for programs, but for this game, I decided to keep things very simple and create my own timer. The timer is made up of three integers:

```
int countdownTimerMins;
int countdownTimerSecs;
int countdownTimerTicks;
```

These hold the number of minutes, seconds, and "ticks" left before the game ends. A "tick" in this game is a sixtieth of a second. The **Update** method in an XNA game is called 60 times a second. The program measures the passage of time by reducing the value in countdownTimerTicks each time **Update** is called. When all 60 ticks in a second have been used up, the program resets the tick counter and reduces the number of seconds left by 1. When all the seconds have been used up, the program resets the second counter and reduces the minute counter. When all the minutes have been used up, the program plays a "Game Lost" sound and changes the state of the game to **GameState.GameLost**. Each time a second goes by, the sound cue "tick" is played. In the last minute, when **countdownTimerMins** is zero, the "loudTick" sound cue is used instead, allowing the sound to change toward the end and create extra excitement.

```
countdownTimerTicks = countdownTimerTicks - 1;
if (countdownTimerTicks < 0)
{
   // A second has gone by
   // reset the tick counter
   countdownTimerTicks = 59;

   // Play a sound - use a different sound in the last minute
   if (countdownTimerMins > 0)
   {
      sounds.PlayCue("tick");
   }
   else
   {
      sounds.PlayCue("loudTick");
   }
   countdownTimerSecs = countdownTimerSecs - 1;
   if (countdownTimerSecs < 0)
   {
      // A minute has gone by
      countdownTimerSecs = 59;
      countdownTimerMins = countdownTimerMins - 1;
      if (countdownTimerMins < 0)
      {
         // We have run out of time
         sounds.PlayCue("lose");
         GamePad.SetVibration(PlayerIndex.One, 0, 0);
         state = GameState.GameLost;
      }
   }
}
```

In the last minute of the game, the gamepad also starts to vibrate with increasing strength. The screen also changes to flash a warning message when the gamepad vibrates.

```
if (countdownTimerMins == 0 )
{
   if (countdownTimerTicks < 30)
   {
      GamePad.SetVibration(PlayerIndex.One, 0, 0);
      playtexture = gameTexture;
   }
   else
   {
      GamePad.SetVibration(PlayerIndex.One,
         (60 - countdownTimerSecs) / 60f,
         (60 - countdownTimerSecs) / 60f);
      playtexture = warningTexture;
   }
}
```

The gamepad does not vibrate for the first half of each second, when the tick value is less than 30. In the second half of each second, it vibrates at an amount that increases as the number of seconds left gets smaller.

Game Improvements

As it stands, the game is quite fun. You might like to improve it by allowing a player to help the search by pressing a button on gamepad 2 to make gamepad 1 vibrate. To do this, you can use the code from the secret message program in Chapter 3, "Getting Player Input."

Pelmanism

This is not actually a silly game at all. It is very popular as a memory game where the player has to match pairs of cards. Your mom might like this game, and there's a good chance that she might have heard of it.

Play starts by dealing a number of card pairs face down on the table. At each turn, a player turns over two of the cards on the table, and if both of them have the same image on their reverse, they are removed. If the images are different, the cards are placed back face down in the same position, and the player has another go. Play repeats until all the cards have been matched and removed. The aim of the game is to remember where particular images are so that you can find them again when the matching card turns up. Figure 14-3 shows a game in progress; the player has just matched two cards that will be removed. The darker squares show cards that have already been matched.

To make the game more exciting, there's a timer in the bottom left-hand corner that measures how long the player takes to clear the screen. Each time the game is played, the cards are shuffled into a random arrangement. The game is operated by a state machine that's very similar to the one used in Hide the Gamepad but has slightly different states to manage the various actions that the user performs.

Figure 14-3 A Pelmanism game in progress

> **Sample Code: Pelmanism** The sample project in the 02 Pelmanism directory in the resources for this chapter is a fully working version of the game.

Game Cards

Each of the cards on the screen is represented by a structure that holds the texture to be drawn on it and the position of that card on the screen. A card can be in one of a number of possible states that are represented by another enumerated type.

```
enum CardState
{
    ShowingBack,
    ShowingFront,
    Matched
}
```

A card can be showing the back of the card, showing the front of the card, or matched with another card. In other respects, the cards are a lot like the sprites in the "Bread and Cheese" game you created in Chapter 12, "Games, Objects and State."

```
struct gameCard
{
    public Texture2D DrawTexture;
    public CardState State;
    public Rectangle DrawRectangle;
}
```

The actual playing area is held as a two-dimensional array of **gameCard** values. You have seen arrays before, in the section "Adding Tomato Targets" in Chapter 12, but we have not used two-dimensional ones before. I have decided to place 42 cards on the playfield, arranged in a grid which will be 7 cards across and 6 cards down. The best way to do this is to use a two dimensional array of this size. An array lets the program hold a large number of data items. In Chapter 12, you wanted to hold only one row of tomatoes, but here you need to hold a grid, or table, of cards. A two-dimensional array is very easy to create; you simply need to tell the C# compiler that you'll be using two subscripts to locate elements:

```
private gameCard[,] cards;
```

The comma in the declaration says that there will be two subscripts used to locate elements. For a three-dimensional array, you would add another comma. Note that in the tradition of arrays, the statement has not created an array instance; the actual array is constructed when the **new** statement is used to make it. Figure 14-4 shows how the game array is used. The top left-hand corner is element 0,0, and the bottom right one is 6,5. These subscripts look a lot like graph coordinates, and you can regard them in the same way if you like.

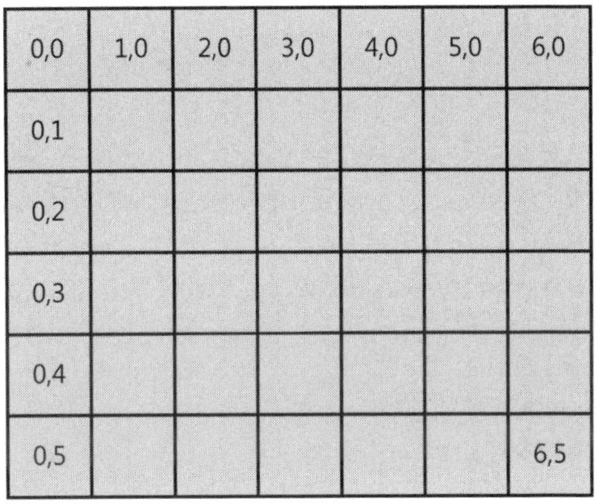

0,0	1,0	2,0	3,0	4,0	5,0	6,0
0,1						
0,2						
0,3						
0,4						
0,5						6,5

Figure 14-4   The game array

The **setupCards** method creates an array of cards and sets the rectangles in each to map onto the correct areas of the screen. It uses two nested **for** loops to work through the rows and columns in the array, creating an appropriately sized and positioned rectangle for each.

```
// product must be an even number
private int cardsAcross = 7;
private int cardsDown = 6;

private void setupCards()
{
    cards = new gameCard[cardsAcross, cardsDown];
    float xPos = 0;
    float yPos = 0;
    float xStep = (float)displayWidth / cardsAcross;
    float yStep = (float)displayHeight / cardsDown;
```

```
for (int i = 0; i < cardsAcross; i++)
{
    yPos = 0;
    for (int j = 0; j < cardsDown; j++)
    {
        cards[i, j].DrawRectangle.X = minDisplayX + (int)(xPos + 0.5f);
        cards[i, j].DrawRectangle.Y = minDisplayY + (int)(yPos + 0.5f);
        cards[i, j].DrawRectangle.Width = (int)(xStep + 0.5f);
        cards[i, j].DrawRectangle.Height = (int)(yStep + 0.5f);
        yPos = yPos + yStep;
    }
    xPos = xPos + xStep;
}
}
```

Note that the playing area must contain an even number of cards; otherwise, there will be nothing for the last remaining card to match with. While you're developing the code, you might want to change the values of **cardsAcross** and **cardsDown** to 2. That makes it much easier to test the behavior of the game; rather than having to match 42 cards when testing, you need only match four. Later, you'll see some other tricks that you can use to make testing the game easier. The **setupCards** method is called only once, at the start of the game.

Adding Textures

Now that you have your cards, you need to find some textures for them. I did this by getting hold of 50 pictures from my photo collection and resizing them to 400 × 325 pixels. There's no need for these pictures to be too large, as an image with these dimensions takes up around 40 kilobytes of storage. The textures are stored in files with the names **tile0**, **tile1**, and so on, up to **tile49**. This makes it easy to use a loop to construct the name of each resource and read all the textures into a one-dimensional array.

```
private int noOfTextures = 50;

private Texture2D[] textures;

private void loadTextures()
{
    textures = new Texture2D[noOfTextures];
    for (int i = 0; i < noOfTextures; i++)
    {
        string textureName = "images\\tile" + i.ToString();
        textures[i] = Content.Load<Texture2D>(textureName);
    }
}
```

The **loadTextures** method is called once when all the other graphical resources are being loaded into the game. The **noOfTextures** variable is set to 50, the present number of textures, but this could be changed in a later version of the program if you add more pictures.

Setting Up The Game

At this stage you have all the ingredients that are needed to create the gameplay. You know how each card will be represented, you know how all the cards are going to be stored in the game, and you have fifty picture textures to be used as the images on the cards. If you were playing the game by hand you would now have to shuffle the cards and place them face down on the table. That is what the program must do next. The program will do the job in three stages:

1. Select the pictures to be used on the cards

2. Create the pairs of cards that are to be matched.

3. Shuffle the pairs around.

Note that this is not quite how a human player might set the game up, and there might be slightly more efficient methods than the ones that I am suggesting, but these are quite easy to understand and they do work.

Selecting Picture Textures

Each time the game is played, the program needs to generate a set of cards that has been randomly set up with pairs of textures. The present version displays 42 cards. This means that 21 textures are needed for each game. The program loads 50 textures and so when a game starts it must choose 21 different textures from the 50 available. As you will see in a moment, it is easy to generate a random number to select a particular picture number, however it is more difficult to make sure that a particular picture number has not already been used. To get around this the program does not pick random textures, instead it "shuffles" the array of textures and then takes the textures out of the array in order, just like you would shuffle a deck of playing cards before dealing them.

This is exactly the same problem as dealing playing cards from a deck, so you can use this solution to deal playing cards as well.

Shuffling by Swapping

To shuffle the textures, the program will repeatedly pick two random locations in the array and swap them. By doing this many times, it creates a random arrangement of textures. At this point, you have to solve another problem. You need to know how to get the random location numbers.

Random Numbers

Computers are carefully designed to do exactly the same thing when given the same sequence of instructions. A computer that did not do this would be called a "broken" one. From a programming perspective, getting truly random behavior is difficult. Fortunately, these problems have been solved, and the .NET Framework provides a way of getting "pseudorandom" numbers very easily.

Pseudorandom Numbers

A source of pseudorandom numbers is not completely random, but it is random enough to be useful. It uses the previous random number to generate the next one and so produces a sequence of numbers that appear random.

The sequence starts with a particular "seed" value. The process will always produce the same sequence from the same seed. This is why it's called "pseudorandom" rather than "completely random." The .NET Framework uses a seed that's obtained from the precise time that the program runs, so that the game program will get a different random sequence each time the game is played.

```
Random rand = new Random();

// jumble up the list of textures
for (int i = 0; i < noOfTextures * 5; i++)
{
    int p1 = rand.Next(noOfTextures);
    int p2 = rand.Next(noOfTextures);
    Texture2D swap = textures[p1];
    textures[p1] = textures[p2];
    textures[p2] = swap;
}
```

The **Random** class contains a method called **Next**, which gives the next random number in the sequence. The **Next** method provides a parameter to specify the upper limit of the random number required. For the shuffle, this is the size of the texture array. Two variables, **p1** and **p2**, are set to random values and then used to locate texture items to be swapped.

When a **Random** instance is created as in the code above, it will pick a seed based on the current time. However, you can also construct a **Random** instance with a particular seed value as follows:

```
Random rand = new Random(1);
```

This produces random numbers using 1 as the seed value. Each time the **Next** method is called, it will return the next number in that sequence. This can be very useful in debugging in that if the random number is seeded with a particular value, it will produce the same sequence each time, meaning that the shuffled deck will end up in the same order. You can then make a note of the matches and find them in successive tests because they will always be in the same place. Your younger brother might like to use this as a way of cheating at the game in that he could learn where the cards are on the basis of a particular sequence.

Creating Pairs of Cards

Now that you have a random sequence of pictures, the game must assign these to the cards to be placed in front of the player. The game uses a similar technique to the way that the textures were selected in that it sets all of them up in order and then shuffles them to random positions later. The code works down each column of cards in turn, assigning a texture to each card and setting the card state to face down. It keeps a counter so that two cards are assigned each texture. You could change the limit of the counter to create "pelmanism-ultra," where the player has to find three or more matching cards.

```
// assign the textures to the cards and turn the cards face down
int texturePos = 0;
int imageCount = 0;
for (int i = 0; i < cardsAcross; i++)
{
   for (int j = 0; j < cardsDown; j++)
   {
      cards[i, j].DrawTexture = textures[texturePos];
      cards[i, j].State = CardState.ShowingBack;
      // we are putting two copies of each texture on the table
      imageCount++;
      if (imageCount == 2)
      {
         imageCount = 0;
         texturePos++;
      }
   }
}
```

Once this code has completed, the program has assigned a texture to a pair of cards, but they are both adjacent. To make the game ready to play the card textures have to be shuffled around.

> **Note**   In the preceding block of code I have used the operator ++ to increase the values of **i**, **j**, imageCount, and **texturePos**, whereas previously I have used statements such as:
>
> countdownTimerMins = countdownTimerMins − 1.
>
> There is no particular reason why I have changed my style, howwever, you must be prepared to see programs that perform these actions in different ways.

Shuffling the Card Pairs

Once the cards have been assigned textures, the game must shuffle their textures around. This is performed by code that should look very familiar in that it uses the same technique used to shuffle the array of textures. Two random positions are identified, and the textures on the cards are swapped between them. This action is repeated a large number of times.

```
// now shuffle around the pictures on the cards
for (int i = 0; i < 5 * cardsAcross * cardsDown; i++)
{
    int r1 = rand.Next(cardsAcross);
    int c1 = rand.Next(cardsDown);
    int r2 = rand.Next(cardsAcross);
    int c2 = rand.Next(cardsDown);
    Texture2D swapTexture = cards[r1, c1].DrawTexture;
    cards[r1, c1].DrawTexture = cards[r2, c2].DrawTexture;
    cards[r2, c2].DrawTexture = swapTexture;
}
```

Once this has been done, the textures have been moved to random positions, and the game is ready to play. Figure 14-5 shows a face-up view of all the card pictures.

Figure 14-5   All the cards face up

Seeing Figure 14-5 actually gave me an idea for another game where the player must identify the one image that does not have a matching card. This would be quite easy to implement and would be fun to play. I've not written this version of the game, but you might like to.

Playing the Game

The game keeps track of the currently selected card and draws a "cursor" at that position. The player uses the dpad on the gamepad to move the cursor around. This means that the game must respond to individual presses on the pad, which as you've seen before, is a problem because the XNA methods that read the gamepad return only the state of the buttons. If the cursor were moved each time the game program detected that the left side of the dpad was held down, this would result in the cursor position changing repeatedly.

You had the same problem when you were reading about the keyboard in Chapter 6, "Creating a Multi-Player Game." The game needs to detect when the key has just been pressed down rather than the down state of the key. To achieve this, a method is used to detect new key presses and to make them available for the game code. If a button is pressed down and the state of the button has changed since the buttons were last tested, a flag is set to indicate this. The **updateButtons** method is called to update flags that are then used in the game. Of course you would need to add variables and code for any other button presses you need to check during in your **Update** method.

```
private bool aPressed = false;
private bool bPressed = false;
private bool leftPressed = false;
private bool rightPressed = false;

private GamePadState oldGamepadState;

private void updateButtons()
{
   GamePadState pad = GamePad.GetState(PlayerIndex.One);
   aPressed = (pad.Buttons.A == ButtonState.Pressed &&
               pad.Buttons.A != oldGamepadState.Buttons.A);
   bPressed = (pad.Buttons.B == ButtonState.Pressed &&
               pad.Buttons.B != oldGamepadState.Buttons.B);
   leftPressed = (pad.DPad.Left == ButtonState.Pressed &&
                  pad.DPad.Left != oldGamepadState.DPad.Left);
   rightPressed = (pad.DPad.Right == ButtonState.Pressed &&
                   pad.DPad.Right != oldGamepadState.DPad.Right);
   oldGamepadState = pad;
}
```

The method works by assigning the result of a boolean expression (the button is down AND the old button state is different from the current button state) to boolean variables that are then used in the game. At the end of the method, the current state of the gamepad is recorded for the next time the method is called. The **updateButtons** method is called at the start of the **Update** method to set up the button and dpad flags. These are then tested to manage movement around the cards.

Moving the Cursor

The program uses two variables to hold the row and column position of the cursor, and these are updated when the dpad is pressed. If the player moves the cursor off one edge of the playfield, it is repositioned at the opposite edge.

```
if (rightPressed)
{
   sounds.PlayCue("click");
   cursorRow++;
```

```
    if (cursorRow >= cardsAcross)
    {
        cursorRow = 0;
    }
}
```

This code is repeated for each of the dpad directions. The cursor itself is a texture which is loaded when the game starts and is drawn using a transparent color so that it is displayed over the top of the selected card.

```
private Texture2D cursorTexture;
private Color cursorColor;

...

// Cursor texture and color set in loadTextures
cursorTexture = Content.Load<Texture2D>("images\\cursor");
cursorColor = new Color(255, 255, 255, 100);

...

// Cursor drawn in the Draw method
spriteBatch.Draw(cursorTexture, cards[cursorRow, cursorCol].DrawRectangle, cursorColor);
```

Selecting the First Card

When players have found the card they want to select as the first of the pair, they press the A button on the gamepad. The game uses the variables **cursorRow** and **cursorCol** to keep track of the cursor and uses these to locate the card to be selected. Only cards which have not been matched can be selected. Once the first card has been selected, the state of the game is changed to **SelectingSecondCard**, and the card selection process is repeated.

```
if (aPressed)
{
    // If this card has been matched already
    // it cannot be selected
    if (cards[cursorRow, cursorCol].State == CardState.Matched)
    {
        break;
    }

    sounds.PlayCue("click");
    // Record the position of the first card
    firstCardRow = cursorRow;
    firstCardCol = cursorCol;
    // Make the front of the card visible now
    cards[cursorRow, cursorCol].State = CardState.ShowingFront;
    // Now the game is selecting the second card
    state = GameState.SelectingSecondCard;
}
```

Detecting a Match

When players have selected the position of the second card, they press A again to ask the game to compare the textures on the two cards selected. A match is detected if the both card items contain a reference to the same texture, as shown in Figure 14-6.

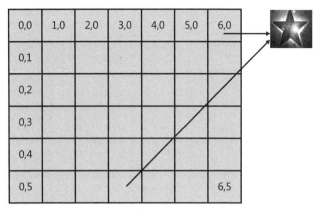

Figure 14-6   Matching textures

This works because textures are stored in classes and managed by reference. The game has only one copy of the texture, and it's managed in terms of references to that single copy. When two instances contain a reference to the same object, as the ones in locations (3,5) and (6,0) do in Figure 14-6, this is counted as a match.

```
if (aPressed)
{
    // If the card has been matched already it can't
    // be matched now
    if (cards[cursorRow, cursorCol].State == CardState.Matched)
    {
        break;
    }

    // If the cursor is on the first card it should not
    // be matched
    if (cursorRow == firstCardRow && cursorCol == firstCardCol)
    {
        break;
    }

    secondCardRow = cursorRow;
    secondCardCol = cursorCol;

    // If the cards match, play the winning sound
    // Will change their matched state once they
    // have been displayed for a while.
    if (cards[firstCardRow, firstCardCol].DrawTexture ==
        cards[secondCardRow, secondCardCol].DrawTexture)
    {
        sounds.PlayCue("match");
    }
```

```
    else
    {
        sounds.PlayCue("matchFail");
    }
    // Make the second card visible
    cards[secondCardRow, secondCardCol].State = CardState.ShowingFront;
    // Going to display the cards for a short while
    stateTimer = 0;
    // Show the pair of cards for a while
    state = GameState.ShowingPair;
}
```

Displaying the Selected Pair

When a pair of cards have been selected they must be displayed for a short while. This must happen whether or not they have matched. The game does this by using a timer variable called **stateTimer**. This is set to 0 when the game enters the **ShowingPair** state. Each time **Update** is called the behavior for **ShowingPair** will increase this timer until it reaches a limit. I have used the value 45, so that the pair are shown for three quarters of a second. When the display has finished, the game must update the state of the two selected cards and decide whether the game is finished.

```
stateTimer++;
if (stateTimer == viewLength)
{
    if (cards[firstCardRow, firstCardCol].DrawTexture ==
        cards[secondCardRow, secondCardCol].DrawTexture)
    {
      // Cards matched - see if the game is over
      cardsLeft--;
      if (cardsLeft == 0)
      {
          endTime = DateTime.Now;
          state = GameState.GameOver;
          sounds.PlayCue("matchFail");
          break;
      }
      cards[firstCardRow, firstCardCol].State = CardState.Matched;
      cards[secondCardRow, secondCardCol].State = CardState.Matched;
    }
    else
    {
        cards[firstCardRow, firstCardCol].State = CardState.ShowingBack;
        cards[secondCardRow, secondCardCol].State = CardState.ShowingBack;
    }
    state = GameState.SelectingFirstCard;
}
```

When a match is found, the number of matches left to be found is reduced, and if this is the last pair, the state of the game is changed to **GameOver** so that the appropriate screen is displayed. The game also records the time at which the game ended so that it can compute and display the time taken to solve the puzzle.

Pell Mell Pelmanism

The game of Pelmanism is a single player game. Having made it work, I wondered what it would be like for several players to play it at the same time. If the players were using real cards on a table, they would have to take turns, otherwise this would be impossible, as there would be no easy way to track of which player had turned over which card. However, a program can keep track of any number of cards and players, so I decided to convert Pelmanism to a multiplayer game. The Pell Mell version provides the same gameplay but for up to four players at once. The cards are dealt and displayed in exactly the same way as for the single player mode. Once the game starts, players can join the game by pressing the yellow Y button on their gamepad. Each player has his or her own cursor and moves it with the gamepad to select and match cards. The game keeps track of the number of pairs that each player has matched, and the winner is the player who matches the most pairs in one game. Players need to be careful because when they select a card it becomes visible for all other players, who can then try to match it first. It is not turn based but rather a complete free-for-all. This leads to really frantic gameplay, as the players select and pair cards as quickly as they can.

> **Sample Code: Pell Mell Pelmanism**   The sample project in the 03 Pell Mell Pelmanism directory in the resources for this chapter is a fully working version of the game.

Making Pelmanism a Multiplayer game

Making Pelmanism a multiplayer game requires additional classes and state machines to be added. Each player is represented by a class that holds all their information.

```
class PellPlayer
{
    public PlayerIndex Index;
    public Texture2D CursorTexture;
    public Color CursorColor;
    public PadButtons PlayerButtons = new PadButtons();
    public GamePadState OldGamePadState;
    public PellPlayerState PlayerState;
    public string PlayerClickCue;
    public string PlayerWinCue;
    public string PlayerLoseCue;
    public int Row;
    public int Col;
    public int SelectedRow;
    public int SelectedCol;
    public int StateTimer;
    public int Score;
...
}
```

All the members of the class have been made **public** so that other classes can use them. C# also lets you make data members **private** so that they cannot be changed by code that is not part of the class. This is useful if you're writing a program to manage bank accounts or store confidential data, but for the purpose of this game, there's no need for such security.

The **PellPlayer** class contains a state variable, **PlayerState**, which is initially set to the value **NotPlaying**. The players in the game are managed in an array of **PellPlayer** instances, one for each player. Note that there are members for the sound cues that are used when the player wins or loses; this makes it possible for players to customize their game experience.

Players can join in at any time by pressing the Y button on their gamepad. This causes the state of their player instance to change to **SelectingFirstCard** and their game cursor to be displayed. During **Update**, the game calls the methods that manage all the player states.

```
protected override void Update(GameTime gameTime)
{
    updateAllButtons();

    // Allows the game to exit
    if (players[0].PlayerButtons.BackPressed)
        this.Exit();

    switch (state)
    {
        case GameState.TitleScreen:
            doUpdateTitleState();
            break;

        case GameState.InstructionScreen:
            doUpdateInstuctionState();
            break;

        case GameState.PlayingGame:
            doUpdatePlayingGame();
            break;

        case GameState.GameOver:
            doUpdateGameOver();
            break;
    }
    base.Update(gameTime);
}
```

The methods that update each of the game states have been taken out of the **Update** method to make the code easier to understand. The **Draw** method has a similar structure.

Game Creation

Hide the Gamepad and Pelmanism are quite different games, but when it comes to implementing the programs, they have many similarities. Both make use of a number of state machines to control what's happening in the game at any given instant. Each of the games contains data that reflects the state of the game world and that's used by the `Draw` method to produce a display. The game world data is updated each time the `Update` method is called.

Conclusion

In this chapter you've seen how the techniques you developed in the previous chapters can be used to produce fully formed games. You've seen that at the core of each game is a state machine that controls how the game responds to events. You've also found that one game development can easily lead to another as you generate new ideas from exploring a game you've created.

Very Silly Games

Even the simplest of ideas can be explored in a way that generates fun. So take what I've provided, mess around with it, and use it as the basis for silly games of your own. You have a very powerful platform, a lot of flexibility, and gamepads that can lead to some really interesting developments, even without considering the high-powered graphics and processing power that XNA provides . Many of the games that people play for fun, particularly in groups, are extremely simple to play and very amenable to a computer-based interpretation. So think of silly things that you like to do and make some games based around them. The way I see it, you'll have fun both ways, enjoying the challenge of writing the code and enjoying seeing people having fun with your creations.

The Great Programmer says that programming is "The Science of the Happy Ending" in that, at the end of a development, users should have something that does what they want and maybe even that they like working with. She says that there's nothing quite like seeing a bunch of people enjoying using a system that your code is making work, and I'm inclined to agree with her on that.

This slim volume will not teach you everything there is to know about C# and XNA, but I hope it will get you started on the road to enjoying programming and producing games that you and others can enjoy playing.

verysillygames.com

As you can see, I think there's definitely a place in the world for very silly gameplay, so all the game ideas used as examples in this book have been packaged up as fully playable games that can be downloaded from the Web site *http://www.verysillygames.com*. If you have silly games of your own that you would like to post on this site, please contact *newgames@verysillygames.com* and let me know.

Appendix A
Pop Quiz Answers

Chapter 1: Pop Quiz Answers

1. False. If you enjoy solving problems and working with people, that will make you a great programmer.

2. False. You can write XNA game programs and run them on your PC if you don't have an Xbox.

3. False. XNA is a framework for writing games. It is written in a programming language and is used by programs, but it is not a programming language.

4. Indeed it is.

5. False. The C# compiler produces a file containing a sequence of machine instructions that the computer can follow when the program runs. Once you have the instructions, you don't need the compiler anymore.

6. False. C# is a programming language. XNA is the framework.

7. Indeed you do. But you don't need to be a club member to write games for the PC.

8. False. The compiler converts your source code into lower-level instructions for the computer to follow. But once the compiler has done this, you can just run the program that the compiler has produced.

9. Nope. The screen is initially blue.

10. Actually, you can do this, and it works very well (especially for games on a PC that require a joystick).

Chapter 2: Pop Quiz Answers

1. False. A program is a sequence of statements. A variable is the way that you represent values that you want our program to work on.

2. False. You can call the file what you like; when coding in C#, it must have the language extension (the bit after the dot) of .cs. XNA Game Studio 2.0 puts the game program into a file called Game1.cs by default, which is a good start.

3. True. You need to think of a name that represents the value that the identifier is going to hold or the action the method is going to do for you.

4. True. A method contains a sequence of statements. It also has an identifier as a name. Your program can "call" the method by name, and when the method is called, it will perform the statements in the method. You don't have to write every method yourself; instead, you can call methods provided by other programmers.

5.   False. The `Draw` method is not in charge of updating the game. Instead, it is supposed to perform the drawing. The method that performs the update is called, not surprisingly, `Update`.

6.   False. A block of statements is a number of statements that have been enclosed in curly brackets. C# can treat an entire block as a whole.

7.   False. A comment is put into the program by the programmer as a kind of "note to myself." The compiler will completely ignore any comments.

8.   False. A byte can hold only a number in the range 0 to 255. When creating a color, each of the primary colors (red, green, and blue) has a byte value that represents the intensity it has in that color. So a `Color` must be held as at least 3 bytes.

9.   True. The C# compiler is very keen to make sure that you don't combine variables in an incorrect way. Trying to place a `Color` into a `byte` would not work because it would not fit. Therefore, the compiler will refuse to compile a program that does this.

10. False. You create the identifiers. If you need to keep track of the highest score in the game, you may well create the identifier `HighScore`, which you use to identify the variable where you store the high score.

11. True. This is exactly what a variable does. You create a variable every time you need to store something in your program. Each variable has a different identifier and has a particular type.

12. False. The Boolean type does have just two possible values, but they are `true` and `false`, not 0 and 1.

13. False. The word that starts a conditional statement is `if`.

14. False. You don't need to add an `else` part to an `if` condition unless your program needs it.

15. True. A recipe tells you how to combine and process ingredients to cook something. An algorithm gives a sequence of actions that you can perform to achieve something.

16. False. A single equals character is used to assign a value to a variable.

17. True. The methods provide the class with things it can do (behaviors) and a place to hold information (data).

18. False. `PlayGame` sounds like a good identifier for a method (that is, a thing that does an action of some kind), but it is not a good name for a class. Classes have names like `Sprite, Session, Game, Invoice,` or `Car`. A class represents a whole thing that you want to create and interact with, not just a single action.

19. True. `Explode` is a word that implies that an action is being performed; perhaps you are going to make one of your game objects perform an explosion behavior. Method names should be "doing" words, like verbs.

20. False. A byte holds 8 bits organized in one lump. Each of the bits can be either true or false, which means that a byte can actually occupy 256 different states.

21. False. ++ works on a single numeric operand and makes the value in the thing it works on one bigger. You use it to increase the intensity of the color values in your program. It has a complementary − − operator.

22. False. This is false for two reasons. One is that the compiler does not have control when your program runs. It just prepares the program for execution. So there is no way that it can react to things that are going to happen when the program runs. The second reason is that when some numbers overflow (for example, if you try to overfill the **byte** type), the processor doesn't always notice. You have to make sure that the values in your programs always stay within the range of the variables that you create to hold them.

23. True. In programs you often need to represent things that can be either true or false. These allow you to decide whether you do something (true) or not (false).

Chapter 3: Pop Quiz Answers

1. False. A method does something. A desk is just a holder for values. It is more sensible to regard a method as a person in the office who can do something when the method is called.

2. False. The compiler will convert your C# source code into machine language instructions for the computer or Xbox, but it is not around when your program is running. The class instances are created when the program runs.

3. False. You need to add the **else** part only if you want to perform some other statement or block of statements if the condition is not true.

4. False. The parameter feeds information into a method.

5. False. It is performed only if the condition controlling the **if** statement is false when the program runs.

6. False (aren't we having a lot of false answers this time?). The gamepad is represented by a special XNA structure that holds all the gamepad settings. The structure is called **GamePadState**.

7. False. This method will give your program a **GamePadState** structure. You can use the **GamePadState** structure to find out what the button state is.

8. True (at last). This is exactly what a block is.

9. True. The logical expression (**true || false**) will work out to true, as would (**true || true**) and (**false || true**). In fact, the only condition involving explicit values and the logical OR operator that works out false is (**false || false**).

10. False. I feel terrible about this one. The condition is fine, but it does not test the value of **greenIntensity**.

11. False. We may have to do this ourselves when the game is stopped.

Chapter 4: Pop Quiz Answers

1. False. The compiler is the program that converts C# source code into machine instructions for the computer. Images are held by the XNA Content Manager, which ensures that they are incorporated into your program once it has been compiled successfully.

2. True. A texture is a special type of data that can hold images. The examples in this chapter use the `Texture2D` data type to hold an image because the examples are for textures that are to be displayed as flat.

3. False. The method to load content is called Load, but it does not display the image on the screen.

4. This might be true, but it is not relevant to XNA graphics. A sprite is a texture and a position. It represents something in the game you want to draw at a particular position. In your programs, you've used a `Texture2D` to hold the image to be drawn and a `Rectangle` to express where the image is to be put on the screen.

5. True. The clue is in the name. You can use `SpriteBatch` to perform a number of drawing operations, and then, when it actually does the drawing, it can organize all the draw operations in the most resource-efficient way.

6. True-ish. The `Initialize` method is simply a placeholder where you can put C# code that will run when the game is being initialized. If you need to get control at this point in the game process, you can add code to this method. Otherwise, you can leave it empty.

7. True. It also has a `Height` field for the height and `X` and `Y` fields that describe where on the screen it is to be positioned.

8. False. It can store many image resources. Each of them is given a name and can be loaded when required.

Chapter 5: Pop Quiz Answers

1. False. The font information is concerned with the shape of the characters. You decide the color of the text only when you use the font to draw the text on your output device.

2. False. You can incorporate as many fonts as you like in an XNA game. You just need to remember that each additional font will use up space in the memory and make the game program larger.

3. False. The Content Manager is told which fonts are required. It then reads the font information and makes it part of your game in a way that makes it possible for you to use it.

4. True. This is exactly what a resource is. The resource itself is fetched only when the program is being created.

5. False. Nice thought, though. XML stands for Extensible Markup Language. XML is widely used in computing to allow two different programs to share information. An XML file contains the names of settings/values (for example, <size>) and the values that these should have (for example, 100).

6. True. A vector is given as coordinates that identify a point, such as (200, 300). You get the direction and distance of movement by considering how you would travel from the origin (0, 0) to that point. In the case of (200, 300), you would be moving across and down the screen if you were drawing in 2D.

7. False. The first program you write should display "Hello World."

8. False. While the Xbox can be programmed to update the clock by using a network connection, the hardware itself holds a battery-backed-up clock that will keep track of time for the Xbox device.

9. False. Both the PC and the Xbox have special software to "localize" them to a particular area. One aspect of localization is how the date and the time are displayed, so the same program code might display the date and time differently on machines in different countries.

10. True. That is exactly what it does. Inside the structure itself are fields that hold the day, month, year, hour, minute, and second that the particular value of `DateTime` represents.

11. False. As an example the `DateTime` structure provides a property called Now. This delivers a `DateTime` instance that is set to the current time. Properties are used by objects as a way for the outside world to interact with the data that they hold.

12. True. That is what `ToString()` is for. Exactly what you get when you call `ToString` depends on what the object holds and what the programmer who created the type of object has decided that `ToString()` should return. In the case of the `DateTime` object, the `ToString()` method returns the date.

13. False. A programmer can make it run forever, either intentionally or by mistake. However, how long the **for** loop runs depends on your requirements. In this chapter, you've used it to repeatedly draw items a particular number of times.

14. False. The first time around the loop, the value of `layer` would be 0, the second time it would be 1, the third time it would be 2, and the fourth time it would be 3. At the end of the fourth time around the loop, the value of `layer` would be increased to 4. Since this is not less than 4, the condition would no longer be true, and the loop would end after four times around.

15. False (nasty ones these). The value left in `layer` when the loop has stopped is the value that caused the condition to fail. The value 10 would not cause the condition to fail, as `layer` would be equal to 10. The value of `layer` that causes the loop to end would be 11 since that is not less than or equal to 10.

16. True. The test is always performed before the code controlled by the **for** loop is obeyed. The first time the test is performed, the value of `layer` is 4. Since 4 is not less than 0, the test fails, and the loop never runs.

17. True. Sort of. Since you're making the value of **layer** 1 bigger each time and it starts at 4, the condition (layer > 0) will always be true, so you would expect the loop to repeat forever. But this is not quite the case, given what you know about variable types. If **layer** was a byte, you know that the range of a byte is from 0 to 255. This means that once the value of **layer** reached 255, it would wrap around to 0, and the loop would stop. Note that this kind of mistake would result in the program acting strangely and would be hard to fix.

18. True. They can. This is where the idea of a color as a paint can or colored light breaks down. You'd be happy drawing red text on the screen by using the red color. However, you can also use red text through which the background can be seen by using a red color value with a transparency value. Furthermore, since you know that you can draw images in a particular color, this means that you can draw transparent images by drawing them with a transparent color.

Chapter 6: Pop Quiz Answers

1. False. Any of the buttons on a gamepad can be used with edge detection.

2. True. The program can notice that a signal has changed only if it has "old" and "current" values that it can compare. If these two values are the same, there has been no change, but if they are different, it means that the signal has changed.

3. False. The whole point of an edge-trigged input is that you detect when the button goes down. They are used for flicking switches, changing gears in a car, or for your button press counting game. The only way that you can detect an edge is to compare the state now with the state it had last time you looked. If the two are different, it means that something has changed and that an edge has occurred.

4. False. The clue is in the name. The compilation process, where your program is converted into executable statements, is where conditional compilation takes place. By the time the program runs, the statements have been either included in the program or ignored.

5. False. The preprocessor, as the name implies, looks at the C# code going into the compiler. If it's given commands to ignore sections of the program, these are not passed into the compiler for conversion into machine instructions in the finished program.

Chapter 7: Pop Quiz Answers

1. False. It runs as a totally separate PC application, making files that are picked up by XNA Game Studio 2.0 when a game is built.

2. False. The XACT program will load only WAV files. However, XACT can compress the sound files before they are sent on to the target device.

3. False. A sound bank holds sounds. A sound is made up of a number of tracks, each of which refers to a sound sample in a wave bank.

4.   True. XNA Game Studio 2.0 will create folders that can hold information relating to a particular part of a task; however, these are actually directories in the file system (although they are sometimes referred to in the operating system as folders as well).

5.   False. You need only one instance of the audio engine to play all the sounds in your game. The best place to make this is during the initialization of the game.

6.   True. That is exactly what a cue does. It also contains methods that can be called to control the playback of the sound.

Chapter 8: Pop Quiz Answers

1.   False. The code would create a variable called `scores` that can refer to arrays of integers, but it does not create the array itself. The program must actually construct the array in order to use it: `int [] scores = new int [4];` would do this. To make the array bigger, change the 4 to a different value. You can even use a variable to set the size of an array so that a program can automatically allocate the correct amount of storage for its needs.

2.   This is both true and false. You can create an array of any type, so you can have arrays of integers, arrays of strings, and pretty much arrays of anything you like. However, once an array has been created, it has a particular type and keeps that type forever; for example, an array of integers can hold only integer values.

3.   True. When you create an array, you make an instance of an array object. You can tell this because making the array (i.e., the bit where you set up how many elements the array has in it) uses the key word new. The identifier you give the array is a reference that refers to the array object.

4.   False. In some languages, this is true (for example, Microsoft Visual Basic), but in C# the convention is that the first element in the array is zero. If you think of a subscript as giving the distance down the array you need to travel to get to the element, then it is reasonable to have a subscript value of zero. It is unfortunate that different languages handle this differently, but there's nothing you can do about it.

5.   Very false. The system running your programs cares a great deal about this. If you try to get hold of an array element that is not there, your program will be stopped.

Chapter 9: Pop Quiz Answers

1.   False. Exactly how many keys can be pressed at once depends on the keyboard hardware, but multiple keys can be registered.

2.   False. The `Keys` type holds information that describes a particular key on the keyboard. For every key on the keyboard (including the Shift, Ctrl, and Alt keys), a corresponding `Keys` value matches it.

3.   False. The `Keys` type has values just for physical keys on the keyboard. The only way that you can determine whether an uppercase letter has been typed is by checking the state of the Shift keys when the key press is detected.

4. True. Each value of a variable of type **Keys** describes one physical key on the keyboard. There are as many **Keys** values as there are keys on the keyboard. An enumerated type allows programmers to create their own types that have just the values that are required by their application.

5. False. A reference provides a way that a program can find and use an object. However, you should not regard a reference as letting your programs find out where in memory something is stored. The way that C# works, you're not allowed to know where the objects in your program are actually located. In this respect, a "telephone number" analogy works best in that a telephone number provides a way you can contact someone but does not tell you where he or she physically is. You can think of a variable that refers to an object in memory as holding the "telephone number" of that object.

6. False. It's very common in C# programs for a particular object to have multiple references referring to it. This is the best way that a large resource (for example, a particular texture or sound) can be shared in a program.

7. False. In C#, Garbage collection takes place the entire time a program is active. The garbage collection process runs alongside your program to make sure that the maximum amount of memory is available at all times.

8. False. You've used the **break** key word in two situations: when you wanted to exit from a **for** loop, and when you wanted to exit from a case in a **switch** statement. It does not stop the program; instead, it says, "I've done all I want here, and I want to escape from this construction."

9. False. The idea of a program turning the computer off is interesting but is not what the **switch** statement is used for. It's used to select an option from a number of different possible ones, depending on the value of a control.

10. True. Note that this does not cause the contents of the string itself to change; instead, you should regard methods like **ToUpper** and **ToLower** as different views of the string, similar to how you can get a **DateTime** instance to give you a string that contains only the time information.

11. False. You can add strings together, but the effect is to put one string on the end of the other, which is called string concatenation. C# uses the same operator, +, for adding numbers and for concatenating strings, but the meaning of the action changes depending on what it is applied to. A + between two integers would add them together. A + between two strings causes them to be strung together to make a longer string.

Chapter 10: Pop Quiz Answers

1. False. The **Rectangle** will tell the draw process the position and size of the drawing area, but it will not do the drawing itself.

2. False. Although the XNA programmers have made methods for you to use, nothing is stopping you from creating methods of your own.

3. True. A method is a member of a class. You use a method to ask an instance of a class to do something for you.

4. True. The statements are performed when the method is called. Used like this, a method lets you use a given sequence of statements from any part of your program simply by calling it.

5. False. A method that specifies a return type of **void** does not return a result to the caller.

6. False. A method can contain many return statements. If the method returns a result, each return statement must be followed by a result that's an expression of the correct type.

7. False. You've seen methods that don't accept any parameters.

8. False. The C# compiler is very picky about method calls. If the call doesn't exactly match the header definition (the signature) of the method, the compiler will produce an error.

9. False. When you work with test-driven development, you do the testing as you write the program. Often you write the tests before you write the code.

10. False. One of the many wonderful aspects of XNA Game Studio 2.0 is the way that you can set a breakpoint in your code even if it's running on an Xbox. When you run the program in debugging mode, the next time the program reaches the line, the program stops.

11. False. The **int** type holds a value that doesn't have a fractional part. This means that when you move a floating point value (which does have a fractional part) into an integer variable, the fractional part of the data will be lost. This is called narrowing. The C# compiler won't let a programmer unintentionally lose or damage data in this way, so it will refuse to allow such a transfer unless the programmer explicitly takes responsibility for the effect of the action by adding a cast.

12. True. The double precision type can hold all integer values, so there will be no loss of data when the move takes place. This is called widening.

13. True. It tells the compiler that although the actual data is in one type, for the purposes of the program, the data needs to be converted into an alternative type. This is the programmer's way of "taking responsibility" for the consequences of the action. When you move a floating point value into an integer location, you're destroying data in that the fractional part of the floating point value will be lost. The cast is the way that you tell the compiler that you know what you're doing, and the compiler then allows the conversion to take place.

14. False. Although casting does perform conversion between similar types (programmers can cast between integers, bytes, doubles, floating points, and the like), it cannot automatically convert any type to any other type. Only conversions that have been predefined are allowed.

Chapter 11: Pop Quiz Answers

1. False. You can use any image that you like in your games (subject to copyright laws, of course). The images must be in file formats that can be imported into the games, but you can create the images yourself.

2. False. The solution contains the project. A solution brings together a number of projects that are used to create a single application. When you create a new project, XNA Game Studio 2.0 will create a solution that contains it.

3. False. The Program.cs file is created for you when the project is created by XNA Game Studio 2.0.

4. True. The Program.cs source code starts the game running in that it creates an instance of your game class, but it doesn't contain the game program itself.

5. True. The compiler is told to search namespaces by `using` directives at the start of the program source file. When the compiler comes across the name of a resource it hasn't seen before, it will look in the namespaces to find the resource.

6. False. But this is really unfair. The method that starts the program is called `Main` (with an uppercase "M"). In C# this is important, because the case of letters in identifiers is significant.

7. False. Static means that the static item is always available. The static item doesn't need to be created by your programs, because it is automatically created when the program is loaded.

8. True. When program execution exits the block of code after the using statement, it means that the item created at the top of the `using` statement can now be removed and that any resources it uses can be reclaimed.

9. False. When a floating point value is converted into an integer, the fractional part is removed.

Chapter 12: Pop Quiz Answers

1. False. Cows are held in fields, but structures are not. A field is a member of a structure that holds data.

2. True. Whenever you have a number of related items, you should think about creating a structure to hold them.

3. False. Structures are managed by value. You can tell this because you don't have to use the `new` keyword to make a new structure variable. By default, the value in the structure is copied into a method call.

4. False. The `public` keyword is used to explicitly make members visible to code outside a class or structure. To restrict access to a member, you would use the `private` modifier.

5. False. An absolute value is always positive or zero.

6. True. In C#, all parameters are passed by value unless the programmer uses the **ref** modifier to generate a reference.

7. False. Oh yes you can. XNA Game Studio 2.0 lets you pause a program and add breakpoints even when it's running in an Xbox 360.

8. True. If you make a method static, that method is always around and not part of any object. This means that you can use **Abs** without needing to make an instance of the **Math** class.

9. False. Nothing in C# forces you to keep the name of a method once you've written some code. It was once difficult to change the name of a method because you needed to make sure that you changed all the places in which the method was used. Fortunately, XNA Game Studio 2.0 makes changing the name much easier (this process is called refactoring). You should consider refactoring whenever you notice that what a method does no longer fit its name.

Chapter 13: Pop Quiz Answers

1. False. A programmer can add a **return** key word anywhere in a method. In fact, a method can have as many **return** statements as you like, although the Great Programmer won't approve of this, because having too many ways that a method can return can make programs harder to understand.

2. False. The type of the variables is not usually changed, although the name used to identify a variable might be changed if you decide on a better name to use.

3. False. The Visual Studio Refactor menu can be used to change the name of a method in your program. The only provision is that you can't change the name of methods that are part of the system; for example, it's not possible to change the name of the **Update** method, because this is based on a method that's part of XNA.

4. False. A code region is a way of grouping together a number of items in your program source file. A single source code file can hold a large number of regions.

5. False. A code region just lumps together parts of your program. Certain Intellisense information is retrieved from specially formatted comments that programmers can place inside the code as they write it.

6. False. A state machine can have as many states as the application requires. The Great Programmer uses an enumerated type (**enum**) to keep track of the states that a state machine can occupy. The state machine that we created for the game had two states: the game was being played, and the title screen was being displayed. It would be easy to add a third state in which the high-score table is displayed.

Appendix B
Glossary

- **Algorithm** An algorithm is a description of the solution to a problem. You can think of it as a recipe if you like. It gives a sequence of steps to be followed and decisions to be taken. A good "getting wet avoidance" algorithm would be "If it is raining, take an umbrella."

- **Analog** A digital value changes in a set of discrete steps, whereas an analog value can have any value in a given range. If an analog value is a ramp, a digital one is a staircase. The thumbsticks on an Xbox gamepad are described as analog in that their position is represented by an output that can be one of a wide range of values. This is in contrast with the digital d-pad and buttons, which can be either on or off.

- **Arithmetic** The adjective "arithmetic" is applied to operators that perform some form of calculation on their operands and generate a numeric result. The * (multiply) operator can be used as an arithmetic operator to multiply values together.

- **Array** An array holds a large number of items in a single variable. A one-dimensional array holds a number of values in a single row. You use a *subscript* to indicate which box in the row you want to use. Consider the following, which creates an array to hold 10 integer high scores and sets all the elements to 0:

```
int [] scores = new int[10];
for (int i = 0; i < 10; i = i + 1)
{
    scores[i] = 0;
}
```

The `int[] scores` part tells the compiler that you want to create an array variable. You can think of this as a *reference* that can be made to refer to an array of integers. The array itself is created by `new int[10]`. When the program runs, a 10-element array will be created; if the value 10 is replaced by a different number, an array of that size will be made. Each item in the array is called an *element*. In the program, you identify which element you mean by putting its number in square brackets [ ] after the array name. This part is called the *subscript*. The size of an array can be set using an expression as well as a constant, allowing the program to create exactly the right-sized array for a given task.

Arrays can have more than one dimension; a two-dimensional array equates to a grid, with two subscripts used to specify the row and column of the desired element. A three-dimensional array equates to a pile of grids and requires three subscripts. The C# language can handle arrays with a very large number of dimensions, but it is unlikely that you'll ever need to go beyond three.

- **Aspect Ratio** This is the ratio of height to width of a display screen. The first TV sets had an aspect ratio of 3:2 (the screen is 3 units wide and 2 units high). Wide-screen displays have a ratio of 16:9 (the screen is 16 units wide and 9 units high). Games must be written to accommodate the possibility that they will be used with different display formats.

- **Assembly** An assembly is used by .NET to bring together program code and resources that the program might need. It is created when a project is built. There are two forms of assembly: programs that can be executed (which have the language extension .exe) and libraries (which have the language extension .dll). Only program assemblies have a `Main` method, which starts the program running.

- **Asset** An asset is any item of content that is used as part of a game. This includes sounds and images that the game requires as well as 3D models and any other game information. The XNA Framework provides a *Content Manager*, which manages the assets in a game project.

- **Assignment** There are two parts to an assignment: the thing you want to assign and the place you want to put it. For example, consider the following:

```
int first, second, third;
first = 1;
second = 2;
third = second + first;
```

The program declares three variables: `first`, `second`, and `third`. These are each of integer type. The last three statements are the ones that actually do the work. These are assignment statements. An assignment gives a value to a specified variable that must be of a compatible type. The value that is assigned is an expression. The equals sign in the middle is there mainly to confuse you; it does not mean equals in the numeric sense. I like to think of it as a gozzinta. Gozzintas take the result on the right-hand side of the assignment and drop it into the box on the left.

- **Bit** A bit is a single "binary digit." It is the smallest unit of data that a computer can hold and has two possible states: on (1) or off (0). Bits are combined together so that values larger than 1 can be represented. Each bit that you append doubles the number of possible values.

- **Block** A block is a number of statements that are enclosed in curly brackets. These are the characters{ and } and are also known as braces. Any block can contain any number of *local* variables, that is, variables that are local to that block.

```
{
    int localToThisBlock; // create a variable local to the block
    localToThisBlock = 99; // OK because the variable exists here
}
localToThisBlock = 100; // will cause compilation error
```

Blocks are used as the bodies of methods and in any situation where you want to lump a number of statements together so that they can be treated as a single entity, such as in an **if** condition or loop.

■ **Boolean**   Boolean arithmetic deals only with values which can be true or false. A variable of type **bool** can hold a value which is true or false. Sometimes that is all you need. An example of a **bool** variable could be one that holds the state of a network connection:

```
bool networkOK;
```

This variable can be set to indicate the state of the network. The results of conditions are boolean values and variables of type bool can be used directly in conditions.

```
if (networkOK) sendPlayerMove();
```

The preceding statement would call **sendPlayerMove** if **networkOK** was set to **true**.

■ **Bounds (of an array)**   The bounds of an array is the range of possible subscripts that can be used to access elements in the array. This ranges from 0 (the element at the base of the array) to (size-1), which is the element at the end of the array. If your program "goes outside the bounds of the array," that is, tries to access an element with a subscript that is not in the permitted range, then it will fail with an exception.

■ **Brace**   The curly bracket characters ({ and }) are sometimes called braces. This is perhaps a reference to the fact that they come in pairs; that is, every open bracket must be matched by a closed bracket. Braces are used to enclose statements and create *blocks*.

■ **Break**   The **break** keyword is used in looping constructions and **switch** statements to allow program execution to exit from the construct.

```
for (int i = 0; i < 10; i++)
{
   if (i == 5) break;
}
// get here when i reaches 5
```

The loop would terminate when the value of i reaches 5. The **break** causes execution to transfer to the statement immediately following the loop block. The **break** keyword is used in the **switch** construct to end the execution of the **switch** statement.

■ **Breakpoint**   Breakpoints are used when debugging programs. They are a way of finding out what a program is doing. Within XNA Game Studio 2.0, you can mark program statements with breakpoints. In debugging mode, a program will run until it reaches (or hits) the breakpoint, at which point it will pause and return control to you so that you can investigate the state of the program. You can then resume execution or step through statements. Note that you can set breakpoints while your program is running, even if it is running inside an Xbox.

■ **Byte**   A byte is the smallest unit of addressable storage in a computer. It is made up of 8 bits, meaning that it can represent any one of 256 possible values, from 0 to 255.

- **C#**   "The Programming Language of Champions," I reckon.

- **Call**   When you want to use a method, you call it. When a method is called, the sequence of execution switches to that method, starting at the first statement in its body. When the end of the method, or a **return** statement, is reached, the sequence of execution returns to the caller.

- **Cast**   A cast gives an additional instruction to the compiler to force it to convert a value in a particular way. You cast a value by putting the required type in brackets before the value. For example:

```
double d = 1.5;
int i = (int) d;
```

Because the double type has greater *range* and *precision* than an integer, the programmer must explicitly tell the compiler that the assignment is sensible. In the previous code, the message to the compiler is "I don't care that this assignment could cause the loss of information. I, as the writer of the program, will take the responsibility of making sure that the program works correctly."

- **Char**   The **char** type is used to hold a single character in a program. The character can be a letter, a digit, a punctuation character, or a nonprintable character, such as the newline character.

```
char ch = 'A';
```

Some characters have special "control" behaviors that are expressed using a sequence of characters that starts with a special escape character. Escape in this context means "escape from the normal humdrum conventions of just meaning what you are and let's do something special." The escape character is the backslash (\) character. Possible escape sequences are the following:

Character	Escape Sequence
\'	Single quote
\"	Double quote
\\	Backslash
\0	Null
\a	Alert
\b	Backspace
\f	Form feed
\n	New line
\r	Carriage return
\t	Horizontal tab
\v	Vertical tab

The effect of these escape sequences depends on the device you send them to. Some systems will make a beep when you send the alert character to them. Some clear the screen when you send the form feed character. You can use them as follows:

```
char beep = '\a';
```

Note that the "a" must be in lowercase. Within XNA, you can use the New Line control character '\n' in a string to cause the **DrawString** method to add a new line.

- **Class**   A class is a collection of behaviors (methods) and data (fields). Class instances are managed by *reference*. Declaring a variable of the type of the class will create a reference to an instance of that class. To make an instance of a class, you have to use the *new* keyword.

- **Comment**   Something you put into your program for the humans to read and the compiler to ignore. Comments can be given in two forms, depending on how much you want to say:

```
// This is a simple comment that just runs to the end of this line
/* This is a comment in which I'm going to try to express the
   creative forces that drove me to write this program which was
   forged in the smithy of my soul and for which all should be grateful.
*/
```

The first comment begins with the characters // and finishes at the end of the line. The second kind of comment begins with the /* characters and continues until the */ characters. Comments are a good thing; you can use them to provide useful information to someone trying to make sense of your program.

- **Compiler**   The compiler is the part of XNA Game Studio 2.0 that converts the C# program that you write into instructions to be executed on the target device. It ensures that the statements that you write have the correct C# syntax and that your code is broadly sensible. The compiler will produce compilation errors if it finds problems with your source code that prevent the compiler from being able to produce an output, such as a missing semicolon or mismatched brackets or braces. The compiler will also produce warnings if it detects something in the program that indicates you may have made a mistake, for example, a some variable is created but never used or that some part of the code would never be reached when the program runs.

- **Component**   A component is a piece of software that has a particular set of behaviors that are exposed in a particular way. It can be exchanged with another component that is configured the same way. An XNA Game class can be regarded as a component in that it has **Initialize, Draw,** and **Update** behaviors which can be used by other classes. The XNA Framework uses these behaviors when it runs your game. In this way, the XNA Framework can treat a game as a component that it is using. Components often expose their behaviors by means of an *interface*.

■ **Conditional Compilation**   This allows a programmer to "switch off" statements in the program so that the statements are compiled only if a given symbol is defined.

```
#if debug
// debug code goes here
#endif
```

The **debug** symbol is defined at the top of the program.

```
#define debug
```

If the debug symbol is not defined, the compiled program does not contain any of the statements controlled by it.

■ **Constructor**   A constructor is a method in a class or structure that gets control when a new instance of the class or structure is being created. Constructor methods often accept parameters so that an instance can be given values to set it up. The **Color** structure has a number of constructor methods that accept different numbers of parameters, depending on how the color is to be created. You used one constructor when you created the colors for the mood light.

```
Color background = new Color (redIntensity, greenIntensity, blueIntensity);
```

When you create your own classes or structures, you can give them constructors so that they can be initialized when they are created.

```
class Player
{
    public string Name;
    public int Score;
    public Player (string inName, int inScore)
    {
        Name = inName;
        Score = inScore;
    }
}
Player p = new Player("Rob", 100);
```

Once you declare a constructor for the **Player** class , the only way that an instance of the **Player** class can be created is by calling this constructor, which must initialize the **Name** and **Score** fields, typically based on values passed to the constructor.

A constructor method has the same name as the class or structure it is part of. Once you have added one or more constructor methods, programmers must call one of the constructors to create an instance.

■ **Content Manager**   The Content Manager is the component of XNA that manages all the assets used by a particular game. It includes the tools that prepare the content when a game project is being built and is also the component that makes the content available when the game is running. The Content Manager is component based so that it can be extended to handle new types of assets as required.

■ **Continue**   The **continue** keyword is used to cause the execution of a loop to return to the "top" of the loop and perform the update behavior.

```
for (int i = 0; i < 10; i++)
{
   if (i == 5) continue;
   // will never get here with i holding 5
}
```

In this example, the code after the conditional statement is not executed when **i** has the value 5 because the **continue** will have been performed, causing the execution to return to the top of the loop. Note that this behavior is not the same as the **break** keyword in that it does not cause the loop to be abandoned completely.

- **Control Characters**   Character variables normally represent letters, digits, or symbols that can be read from a keyboard or displayed on a screen. A control character is not visible but has some form of control effect—for example, adding a new line or returning the cursor to the start of a new line. A list of the control characters that can be represented in a C# program is given in the entry for *character* in this glossary.

- **Control Expression**   A control expression is used in a *switch* to select the case to be performed.

- **Creators Club**   See *XNA Creators Club.*

- **Debug**   Faults in programs are called bugs, perhaps a reference to an insect that was found trapped in a piece of computer hardware by Grace Hopper, one of the world's first programmers. The body of the insect was physically stopping the program from working, and she "debugged" the program by removing it. A bug is caused by a misunderstanding of the problem, a limitation in the algorithm that is intended to solve the problem, or a mistranslation when the algorithm is converted into program code. Programs are debugged by a mixture of skill, determination, and luck. You often have to add extra statements to find out what is going on in the program when it fails. You can also use *breakpoints* to stop a running program and investigate the state of the variables in it.

- **Declaration**   A declaration is a program statement that tells the compiler about a new variable or method in your program. The new item must be given an identifier and a type. If a method is being declared, the source code must also give the method signature (the type of the method and the identifiers and types of any parameters) as well as the method body.

```
int i; // declare an integer with the identifier i
int doAdd( int first, int second) // declare a method
{
    return first + second;
}
```

Variables can be *local* to a block or *members* of a class or structure. Local variables must be declared in a block before they can be used. Methods are *members* of a particular class or structure and are declared within it.

- **Directive**   A directive is a command in the source of a program that tells the compiler to do something. The **#define** directive tells the compiler that a symbol is being defined. The **using** directive tells the compiler to look in a particular *namespace* for objects.

- **Directory**   A directory is a place in a file store where you can store a file. It is sometimes called a *folder*. Directories can contain directories so that file storage can be arranged in a hierarchy. The path to a file identifies all the directories that must be traversed to get to that file. Each directory name is separated from the next by the backslash character, as in `c:\code\program\progfile.cs`.

- **Do – while**   The `do-while` construction allows a program to repeat a block of code until a controlling condition at the end becomes `false`. Note that the test is performed after the statement or block; that is, even if the test is bound to fail, the statement is performed once.

```
do
    statement or block
while (condition);
```

This form of loop can be used as an alternative to the `for` loop constructions. It is very useful in programs where you want to request something, check that it is okay, and then repeat if not. There is an alternative form where the condition is tested before the statement:

```
while (condition)
    statement or block
```

In this looping construction, the statement is not performed at all if the condition is false at the beginning of the `while` loop.

You don't have to use these constructions if you have no need to; it's simply provided for situations where a loop is required but there is no need for a counter as would be used in a `for` loop.

- **Element (of an array)**   An element is an individual item in an *array*. Each element is identified by its *subscript* value.

- **Enumerated Type**   An enumerated type is one for which you can set the range of values that it should have.

```
enum SeaState {
    EmptySea,
    Attacked,
    Battleship,
    Cruiser,
    Submarine
} ;
SeaState openSea;
openSea = SeaState.EmptySea;
```

The type `SeaState` could be used to hold the state of the sea in a battleship game. It has five possible values, which are created as shown. The variable `openSea` is of type `SeaState` and is set to `EmptySea` in the previous code.

- **Exception**   An exception is a way that a C# program can signal that something has gone wrong when it runs. The exception itself is an object that is created when the exception is "thrown" and can be "caught" by an exception handler. The C# language provides the `try-catch` construction, which can be used to deal with exceptions that might be thrown.

■ **Expression** An expression is a collection of *operands* and *operators* that can be evaluated to produce a result. You have seen numeric expressions, logical expressions, and text expressions.

```
int i = 0;
i = i + 1;                  // arithmetic expression adding 1 to i
bool iIsPositive;
iIsPositive = i > 0;   // logical expression
string IValue;
IValue = "Value of i is : " + i.ToString(); // text expression
```

■ **Field** A field is a member of a class or structure that stores data within an instance.

```
class Player
{
    public string Name;
    public int Score;
}
```

The **Player** class contains two fields: the **Name** of the player, which is a string, and the **Score** the player has reached, which is an integer. A program makes use of a field by giving the identifier of the instance, followed by a period (.), followed by the name of the field.

```
Player p = new Player();
p.Name = "rob";
```

The **Name** and **Score** fields can be accessed in this way because they have been made *public*. Fields can also be made *private*, in which case they are not visible to code outside the class or structure.

■ **File Extension** Files on a computer system have file names that are used to locate them. The file extension is information on the end of the file name. An extension is made up of a number of characters on the end of the name, given after a period (.) character. The Windows operating system uses the file extension to select the application to be used to open a particular file. "Program.cs" identifies a C# program file, while "Background.png" would identify a Portable Network Graphics (PNG) file.

■ **Folder** A folder is directly analogous to a *directory*.

■ **Framework** A framework is a set of software resources that programmers can fit together and extend to create solutions to problems. The .NET Framework provides a way that programs can run on a computer platform. It also provides a comprehensive set of resources that can be used to create general purpose applications. The XNA Framework provides resources for the creation of games.

■ **Fully Qualified Name** A fully qualified name is one that provides a complete path to the resource that is being identified. It identifies all the namespaces in the path to the resource with that name.

```
Microsoft.Xna.Framework.Graphics.Color background;
```

You can avoid having to use the fully qualified name of a resource by adding a *using* directive at the top of your program source. A set of using directives is inserted automatically into the Game1.cs file when XNA Game Studio 2.0 creates a new game project.

■ **Garbage Collector**   The garbage collector is a process that runs as part of a .NET application and searches for and removes resources that are no longer used.

■ **Generic Method**   A C# method is supplied with parameters for the method to act on. In a generic method, the parameters are not restricted to one particular type. Generic methods are used when the programmer wants to create a method to perform a particular action but wants the action to be performed on variables of different types. In XNA, the Content Manager provides a generic method called **Load**, which is supplied with the type of the item to be loaded. It can then perform the load action and deliver a result of the required type.

■ **Header (of a method)**   A C# method can be broken into two parts: the block of code, which is the body of the method and contains the statements that the method will perform, and the header, which indicates the type returned by the method, the identifier which is the name of the method, and the parameters that the method accepts.

```
int doAdd(int first, int second) // declare a method
{
   return first + second;
}
```

The header of the method doAdd is `int doAdd(int first, int second)`.

■ **Identifier**   An identifier is a name chosen by the programmer to identify something in a program. This includes the names of variables and the names of classes, structures, and methods. The C# compiler has rules concerning the construction of identifiers; they can contain letters (a–z or A–Z), digits (0–9), and the underscore (_) character. An identifier must not start with a digit. The case of the letters in an identifier is significant in that the identifiers **count** and **Count** could both be used in the same program to refer to different variables:

```
int count;
double Count; // legal C# - but the Great Programmer wouldn't approve
```

There is a convention in C# that *local* variables, *parameters*, and *private members* of a *class* or *structure* should have identifiers that start with a lowercase letter. Identifiers for classes and structures and *public* members of classes and structures should have identifiers that start with an uppercase letter.

■ **Instance**   Instances of objects are created as a program runs. If the object is manipulated by value, there is no need to use *new* to create an instance of it, although you can use new if you wish to call the *constructor* for that type.

- **Integer**   An integer is a value that has no fractional part. The C# language provides a number of integer types; the programmer should choose the type that provides the most appropriate range of values for the program being written.

- **Integrated Development Environment**   An Integrated Development Environment (IDE) combines an editor for creating the source code, a compiler, and a debugger in a single tool that can be used for development. XNA Game Studio 2.0 is based on the Microsoft Visual Studio IDE.

- **Intellisense**   Intellisense is the name given to the feature of XNA Game Studio 2.0 that provides context-sensitive help and suggestions to you as you write your program source. The system constantly monitors what you are typing and suggests appropriate items on the basis of what it sees.

- **Interface**   An interface defines a set of actions. The actions are defined in terms of a number of method definitions. A class that implements an interface must contain code for each of the methods defined in the interface.

```
interface ISinger
{
    void SingSong(int loudNess);
}

class OperaSinger : ISinger
{
    public void SingSong(int loudNess)
    {
    }
    public void SingAria(int loudness, int vibrato)
    {
    }
}
class PoliceMan : ISinger
{
    public void SingSong(int loudNess)
    {
    }
    public void MakeArrest ()
    {
    }
}
ISinger singer = new PoliceMan();
```

The interface **ISinger** contains a single method called **SingSong**, which is supplied with a parameter to indicate how loudly the song is to be sung. Both **OperaSinger** and **PoliceMan** implement the interface, meaning that either of them can be asked to sing (although you might get a better tune out of the **OperaSinger**). This means that you can regard **PoliceMan** and **OperaSinger** in terms of their singing ability, even though they are completely different classes. A reference to **ISinger** could be made to refer to either an `OperaSinger` or a `PoliceMan` interface and ask it to sing by calling the `SingSong` method. Viewing classes in terms of what they can do is a large part of component-based development.

- **Italics** Italic text is text that *leans to the right*, like the Leaning Tower of Pisa in Italy, when viewed from the correct direction.

- **Keyword** A keyword is a word that is part of the C# language. Keywords that you have seen include **for**, **if**, **new**, **class**, **struct**, **switch**, and **case**. Keywords have a particular meaning, and you cannot create an identifier that is the same as a keyword. The XNA Game Studio 2.0 editor will display keywords in bright blue.

- **Literal** A literal is something in a program that is literally just there. Examples of literals include values in expressions and strings:

```
width = width + 2;
playerName = "rob";
```

In the preceding statements, the literals are the value 2 and the value "rob."

- **Local** A *variable* that is local to a *block* is declared in the block and will be discarded when the execution of the program leaves that block. Local variables are used in the situation where you want a variable for a very short part of the program.

- **Localization** Localization is the name for the process of making a program work in a manner appropriate to a particular part of the world. It includes aspects such as the language used for the user interface, the character set, and how dates, times, and currency values are displayed.

- **Logical** Logical values can be either true or false. C# provides the **bool** type to hold logical values, comparison operators (for example, less than) that will compare values and produce logical results, and logical operators (for example, or) that allow logical values to be combined.

- **Machine Code** This is a generic term for low-level instructions that can be processed by a computer. This is in contrast with *source code*, which contains the program instructions that were written by the programmer and that contain a high-level, human-readable description of a solution to a problem. The *compiler* takes the high-level source code and converts this into a form that is eventually made into machine code for execution on a target device.

- **Member** A member of a class is declared within that class. It can either do something (if it is a method) or hold some data (if it is a variable). Methods are sometimes called behaviors. Data members are sometimes called fields.

- **Method** A method is a block of code preceded by a method *header*. The method has a particular identifier and may return a value. It may also accept one or more *parameters* to work on. Methods are used to break a large program up into a number of smaller units, each of which performs one part of the task. They are also used to allow the same piece of program to be used in lots of places in a large development. If a method is *public*, it can be called by code in other classes. A public method is how an object exposes its behaviors.

- **Modifier** A modifier is used to modify a declaration. It gives the compiler additional information about the thing that is being declared. Examples of modifiers are *public*, *private*, and *static*.

- **Namespace** A namespace is a way of categorizing related resources. Each resource provided by a framework must have a unique name. Putting all the names at the same level would result in confusion; for example, the name `Device` could have many possible meanings, as you might want to have audio devices, graphics devices, and so on. A namespace is a space where particular names have meaning. You could create a `Graphics` namespace and an `Audio` namespace, each of which could hold a `Device` resource.

```
namespace Graphics
{
   class Device
   {
   }
}

namespace Audio
{
   class Device
   {
   }
}
```

You would refer to them as `Graphics.Device` and `Audio.Device`. It is possible for a namespace to contain a namespace, allowing a hierarchy of names to be created. A particular source file can contain a number of different namespaces, and a namespace can be spread over several source files.

The XNA Framework is organized into a series of namespaces each of which holds a set of related resources. You can access them by *using* a particular namespace or by giving a *fully qualified name*.

- **Narrowing** Narrowing can occur when a variable of one type is assigned to another. C# provides a number of different data types that are used to hold values in programs. Each type has a particular *range* and *precision*. For example, the byte type can hold values in the range 0 to 255, whereas an integer can hold values in the range −2,147,483,648 to 2,147,483,647. Narrowing would occur if a program assigned a value from an integer variable into a byte. If the integer had a value greater than 255, the narrowing might result in the corruption of the value. The C# compiler will ask the programmer to use a *cast* to confirm that a narrowing operation is valid.

- **Null** The C# keyword `null` allows a program to express the fact that a reference points nowhere. Newly created reference variables are automatically set to refer to `null`, and it is possible to test this in your programs.

```
Player p;
if (p == null)
{
 // will get here because p is initially null
}
```

You can actually assign the value **null** to a reference to indicate that the reference is not set to refer anywhere.

- **Object**   An object is an instance of a given data *type*. Many types are provided by C# and XNA, and you can create your own types by declaring classes (**class**) and structures (**struct**).

- **Operand**   An operand is something that is worked on in an *expression* by an *operator*. Operands are either *literals, variables, or expressions*.

- **Operator**   An operator is used in an *expression* and identifies an operation to be performed on one or more *operands*. Arithmetic operators that you have seen include plus (+), minus (−) , multiply (*) and divide (/). Relational operators include less than (<), greater than (>), equals (= =) and not equals (!=). Logical operators that you have seen include logical AND (&&) and logical OR (||).

- **Overflow**   Overflow occurs when a program is running if the capacity of a *variable* is exceeded. Variables are declared as being of a particular *type*, and the programmer must be careful to use the type appropriately. For example, the **byte** type is able to hold values that range from 0 to 255. If a program put 255 into a **byte** variable and then added 1 to this variable, the result would cause the variable to overflow, as the **byte** type is not able to represent that value. While some forms of program error, such as exceeding the *array bounds*, will cause an *exception* to be thrown, this is not always the case with overflow.

- **Parameter**   A parameter is supplied by a *call* to a *method* to give the method something to work on. A parameter that is a value type is passed into the method by value. A parameter that is a reference type is passed into the method by the value of the reference rather than the value referred to. If you want to pass a value type by reference, you must mark the parameter as a reference type using the **ref** qualifier.

- **Pixel**   A pixel, or "picture element," gives the color of a single, small area of the display screen. The more pixels a screen contains, the higher the quality of the picture but the more memory the screen will use and the longer it will take to create an image.

- **Precision**   C# provides several types that can hold numbers with fractional parts, and these types have different precisions. The precision of a type determines how accurately that type can represent a particular value. Because computer storage is finite, the precision to which numbers are stored is limited. The float type can represent values to a precision of seven digits, whereas the double type provides 15 to 16 digits of precision.

- **Private**   A **private** member of a class is visible to code only in methods inside that class. It is conventional to make data members of a class private so that they cannot be changed by code outside the class. The programmer can then provide methods or C# properties to manage the values that can be assigned to the private members. The only reason for not making a data member **private** is to remove the performance hit of using a method to access the data.

- **Program** A program is a description of a solution to a problem. The program sets out the steps to be taken and decisions to be made and that will ultimately be performed by computer hardware of some sort.

- **Programming Language** A programming language is a special form of language that has a simple and unambiguous syntax and grammar. Programming languages are designed so that programs written in them can easily be converted into forms that can be executed by computer hardware.

- **Project** A project is a collection of program files and other resources that can be brought together to produce a single assembly that can be deployed as part of a solution to a problem. XNA Game Studio 2.0 will manage projects and also bring a number of projects together to create a single solution.

- **Property** Properties are extremely useful and make your code a lot cleaner. Essentially, you can have code like the following:

```
x.Width = 99;
```

This looks like an assignment to a member of a class, but it can be much more than that and can result in additional code running. The **Width** property could be managed like this:

```
class ThingWithWidth {
   private int widthValue;
   public int Width
   {
     get
     {
        return widthValue;
     }
     set
     {
        widthValue = value;
     }
   }
}
```

When a program performs the assignment to the property, the **set** portion runs. The keyword **value** is set to the value of the incoming property. This code performs a simple assignment, but you could validate the value and throw an exception if you don't like it. I've decoupled the names of the property value from the value of the property (one convention is to put the word **value** on the end of the name of the internal value). Of course, you don't actually have to have a value inside the class; you could calculate a result rather than return a member.

When it comes to setting the value, you can get code to run when you change the value of your property. This makes creating state machines easy. Furthermore, you don't have to implement both a **get** and a **set** behavior; you can have just one so that you can create write-only (or read-only) properties. You can have lots of getters for the same property; perhaps you would like to read the speed in kilometers per hour as well as miles per hour.

The only downside is that you must be aware that substantial amounts of code can run when you perform innocent-looking assignments.

- **Public**   A `public` member of a class is visible to methods outside the class. It is conventional to make the method members of a class `public` so that they can be used by code in other classes. A `public` method is how a class provides services to other classes.

- **Range**   The range of a given type sets out the largest and smallest values that can be held in a variable of that type. Each C# type has a particular range, and one of the tasks for a programmer is to select a type with a range that is appropriate for the data they wish to store.

- **Reference**   A reference is a bit like a tag that can be attached to an instance of a class. The reference has a particular name. C# uses a reference to find its way to an instance of the class and use its methods and data.

```
class Player
{
    public string Name;
    public int Score;
}
Player p = new Player();
p.Score = 100;
```

The variable **p** is a reference variable that can refer to instances of the class **Player**. It is set to refer to a new **Player** instance. The reference is then used to access the **Score** field inside the instance referred to by **p**.

One reference can be assigned to another. If you do this, the result is that there are now two references that refer to a single object in memory. In C#, references are *typesafe* in that a reference to one particular object, such as a **Texture2D**, would not be allowed to refer to any other type of texture. This means that when the reference is followed to an object, the actions are performed with that object will always be appropriate.

- **Signature**   A given C# method has a particular signature that allows it to be uniquely identified in a program. The signature is the name of the method and the type and order of the parameters to that method:

`void Silly(int a, int b)`—has the signature of the name `Silly` and two `int` parameters.

`void Silly(float a, int b)`—has the signature of the name `Silly` and an `float` parameter followed by an integer parameter. This means that the code

`Silly(1, 2);`

would call the first method, whereas

`Silly(1.0f, 2);`

would call the second.

Note that in C# the return type of the method has no effect on the signature.

- **Software Development Kit**   A Software Development Kit (SDK) is a collection of tools and library resources that can be used to create software on a particular platform.

- **Solution**   XNA Game Studio 2.0 brings together one or more *project* files to produce a single solution. The same project file can be used in more than one solution, which allows libraries of code to be created and reused. Within a solution, one of the projects is designated the "start-up" project and will be the one that will run when the system produced by the solution is started.

- **Source Code**   This is the text written by programmers. It is stored in plain text on the development computer and converted by a compiler into the machine code that actually performs the program instructions on the target machine.

- **State**   At any given instant a running program is in a particular state. Many game programs contain variables that explicitly manage the state of items in the game. It is often the case that an *enumerated* type is created to represent a particular state.

- **Statement**   A statement is a single action that a program performs. Statements in C# programs are separated by the semicolon (;) character.

- **Static**   In the context of C#, the keyword **static** makes a member of a class part of a class rather than part of an instance of the class. This means that you don't need to create an instance of a class to make use of a static member. It also means that static members are accessed by means of the name of their class rather than a reference to an instance. Static members are useful for creating class members that are to be shared with all the instances, such as currency conversion rates for all the accounts in a bank.

- **String**   The **string** data type lets programs work with strings of text. The string is held as a one-dimensional array of characters. Strings can be used with the + operator, which cause them to be concatenated together. String literals are given in the program enclosed in double quotes. A string literal can contain control characters; see the item on *char* for details of these.

```
string firstname = "Rob";
string surname = "Miles";
string fullname = firstname + " " + surname
```

- **Structure**   A structure is a collection of data items. It is managed by value, not by reference, and **struct** contents are copied on assignment.

```
struct Particle
{
   public int X;
   public int Y;
}
```

```
Particle position;
position.X = 99;
position.Y = 00;
Particle[] Smoke = new Particle[1000];
```

The `Particle` structure simply holds the `X` and `Y` positions of a particle. Because it is a `struct`, I can declare a variable of type `Particle`, and an instance is created automatically. The `Smoke` array, which contains 1,000 particles, is also created automatically. There is no need to use **new** to create any `Particle` instance.

Structures are also passed by value into methods. Structures are useful for holding a simple set of related data in a single unit. They are not as flexible as objects (which are managed by reference), but they can be more efficient to use because accessing structure items does not require a reference to be followed in the same way as for an object. An array of `struct` values is stored in a single block of memory, which contains a row of the items. An array of items managed by reference (for example, instances of a class) is stored as an array of references, with each element in the array able to refer to one instance.

■ **Subscript**   This is a value that is used to identify the element in an array. It must be an integer value. Subscripts in C# always start at 0 (this identifies the initial element of the array) and extend up to the size of the array minus 1. This means that if you create a four-element array, you get hold of elements in the array by subscript values of 0, 1, 2, or 3. The best way to regard a subscript is the distance down the array you are going to move to get the element that you want. This means that the first element in the array must have a subscript value of 0.

■ **Switch**   The `switch` construction allows a program to select one option from a number of them based on a *control expression*. Switches are often used to select particular behavior based on the value of an enumerated type.

```
switch (player.PlayerState)
{
  case PellPlayerState.NotPlaying:
    doNotPlaying(player);
    break;
  case PellPlayerState.SelectingFirstCard:
    doSelectingFirstCard(player);
    break;
  case PellPlayerState.SelectingSecondCard:
    doSelectingSecondCard(player);
    break;
  case PellPlayerState.ShowingPair:
    doShowingPair(player);
    break;
  default:
    doShowError();
    break;
}
```

The `switch` construction uses the control expression to decide which option to perform. It executes the case that matches the value of the control expression. The purpose of the

break statement after the call of the relevant method is to stop the program from running on and performing the code that follows it. In the same way as you break out of a loop, when the break is reached, the switch is finished and the program continues running at the statement after the **switch**.

Another useful feature is the **default** option. This gives the **switch** somewhere to go if the control expression doesn't match any of the cases available.

- **This**   The keyword **this** means "a reference to the current instance." Its use is implied within methods in classes.

```
class Player
{
    public string Name;
    public int Score;

    public void IncreaseScore ()
    {
        this.Score = this.Score + 1;
    }
}
```

It would be possible to write **Score** rather than **this.Score** in the **IncreaseScore** method, as the compiler will insert **this.** automatically if required.

The **this** reference can also be used to pass an instance as a parameter in a call to another method:

```
DisplayScore(this);
```

The **DisplayScore** method accepts a reference to a **Player** as a parameter. It can be called from a method in the **Player** class to display the score of that player instance.

- **Type**   In C#, all data items have a particular type associated with them. Some types are "built in" to the C# language. These types, such as **int**, **float**, and **bool**, are available to all programs written in the language. Other types can be added from libraries, such as **DateTime**. Finally, you can create your own types to hold a collection of data and behaviors that are specific to the problem at hand.

The C# compiler will ensure that whenever variables of different types are used together, there is no potential for error or loss of data. For example, an attempt to move a value from a variable of floating point type into an integer will result in the compiler generating an error unless programmers use a *cast* to indicate that they are aware of the issue, and in this context the action is valid. Type checking is performed at compile time (this is called static type checking) and also when the program runs. This means that even if the programmer uses a cast to force one thing to be used as another, at run time any inappropriate mixing of types would be rejected. This extra stage makes C# programs much safer, but the extra runtime type checking does slow the program down.

- **Using**   The word **using** can serve as either a compiler directive or a keyword in a program.

C# provides the **using** directive:

```
using Audio;
```

The **using** directive must appear at the start of a source file. It identifies a namespace that is to be used to resolve the names of classes in that file. If the **Audio** namespace contains a class called **Device**, I could add a **using** directive to my program so that I can create instances of **Device** without having to add **Audio** to the name.

I can still use other **Device** classes, such as **Graphics.Device**, but I will need to give its fully qualified name. You can add multiple **using** directives at the start of a source file; when you create a new project, you will often find that a number of them have been added automatically. If there is a name clash (for example, you use two namespaces, both of which contain a class called **Audio**), the compiler will require you to use the fully qualified name for that particular class. It can also be sensible to use the fully qualified name in circumstances where you want a reader of the program source to easily identify where a class is defined.

C# also provides the **using** keyword, which lets you state precisely where in a program a variable is being used.

```
using (PellMellGame game = new PellMellGame())
{
    game.Run();
}
```

The **using** keyword introduces the declaration of a variable to be used in the block that follows the **using** statement. When the block is complete, the variable is no longer required and can be removed by the runtime environment. Without the **using** statement, the Garbage Collector would have to deduce that there were no remaining references to the variable **game** in the preceding code.

- **Value Type**   A value type holds a simple value. Value types are passed as values into method calls, and their values are copied on assignment; that is, **x** = **y** causes the value in **y** to be copied into **x**. Subsequent changes to the value in **x** will not affect the value of **y**. Note that this is in contrast to reference types, where the result of the assignment would make **x** and **y** refer to the same instance.

- **Variable**   A variable holds a value that is being used by a program. A given variable has a unique identifier and is declared as having a particular type. Variables can be *local* to a block, or they can be members of a class.

- **Void**   A programmer who wants to create a method that does not return a value can tell the compiler this by making the type of the method **void**. A **void** method is one that performs a task but does not return a value.

- **While**   The **while** keyword is used in looping constructions, which are described in the *Do – while* entry in this glossary.

- **Widening**   Widening is the reverse of *narrowing*. When a value is widened, it is moved from a type with a narrower range and precision into one that has a wider range, such as from the **byte** type (with a range of 0 to 255) into an **integer** type (with a range of 2,147,483,648 to 2,147,483,647). The compiler is quite happy to produce code that will perform this conversion since there is no chance of data being lost.

- **Workspace**   A workspace is analogous to an XNA Game Studio 2.0 solution in that it contains programming resources and projects that are used to create a solution.

- **Xbox Live**   Xbox Live is a networking solution for Xbox 360 and PC games. Gamers pay an annual subscription that gives them an identity on the Xbox Live network and allows them to engage in network play using Xbox games. They can also download game demos and other content that is then stored on the hard disk of their Xbox 360. An Xbox Live account is required if you wish obtain an XNA Creators Club membership.

- **XNA**   The best game development environment in the world. Bar none.

- **XNA Creators Club**   If you want to run your XNA programs on an Xbox 360, you must be a member of the XNA Creators Club. Members of the club pay a membership fee (currently $99 per year), and their Xbox Live account is extended to include XNA game development. XNA Creators Club membership also gives you access to extra sample programs and the XNA Creators Club forums. You can find out more at *http://creators.xna.com*. If you want to create and run your XNA programs on a Windows PC, you don't have to be a member of the XNA Creators Club.

Index

Rob Miles

I wrote my first computer game on the original Commodore PET in Microsoft Basic, having learned to program some time before that at school, where I began by writing my first programs on cards using a hand punch, posting them off to a distant mainframe and getting a message back two weeks later that I'd omitted a semicolon. A good many years have gone by since then. I'm still omitting semicolons, but the turnaround has improved quite a bit. I've been at the University of Hull in the United Kingdom for over 25 years now, moving from the Computer Center to Electronic Engineering to Computer Science, where I now work. In that time, I've

also had a hand in quite a few industrial projects, and it is a matter of great personal pride to be the man who wrote the software that puts the date stamps on Budweiser beer cans, among many other products. I've also been known to turn out bad verse, the highlight of this being a whole page of poetry for the British *Independent* newspaper. I'm a Microsoft Most Valuable Professional (MVP) for embedded devices, and I live happily in East Yorkshire with number one wife Mary (she calls me "husband zero"). Number one children David and Jenny return from their studies every now and then so that we can play happy families properly.

Additional Resources for C# Developers

Published and Forthcoming Titles from Microsoft Press

Microsoft® Visual C#® 2005 Express Edition: Build a Program Now!
Patrice Pelland • ISBN 0-7356-2229-9

In this lively, eye-opening, and hands-on book, all you need is a computer and the desire to learn how to program with Visual C# 2005 Express Edition. Featuring a full working edition of the software, this fun and highly visual guide walks you through a complete programming project—a desktop weather-reporting application—from start to finish. You'll get an unintimidating introduction to the Microsoft Visual Studio® development environment and learn how to put the lightweight, easy-to-use tools in Visual C# Express to work right away—creating, compiling, testing, and delivering your first, ready-to-use program. You'll get expert tips, coaching, and visual examples at each step of the way, along with pointers to additional learning resources.

Microsoft Visual C# 2005 *Step by Step*
John Sharp • ISBN 0-7356-2129-2

Visual C#, a feature of Visual Studio 2005, is a modern programming language designed to deliver a productive environment for creating business frameworks and reusable object-oriented components. Now you can teach yourself essential techniques with Visual C#—and start building components and Microsoft Windows®–based applications—one step at a time. With *Step by Step*, you work at your own pace through hands-on, learn-by-doing exercises. Whether you're a beginning programmer or new to this particular language, you'll learn how, when, and why to use specific features of Visual C# 2005. Each chapter puts you to work, building your knowledge of core capabilities and guiding you as you create your first C#-based applications for Windows, data management, and the Web.

Programming Microsoft Visual C# 2005 Framework Reference
Francesco Balena • ISBN 0-7356-2182-9

Complementing *Programming Microsoft Visual C# 2005 Core Reference*, this book covers a wide range of additional topics and information critical to Visual C# developers, including Windows Forms, working with Microsoft ADO.NET 2.0 and Microsoft ASP.NET 2.0, Web services, security, remoting, and much more. Packed with sample code and real-world examples, this book will help developers move from understanding to mastery.

Programming Microsoft Visual C# 2005
Core Reference
Donis Marshall • ISBN 0-7356-2181-0

Get the in-depth reference and pragmatic, real-world insights you need to exploit the enhanced language features and core capabilities in Visual C# 2005. Programming expert Donis Marshall deftly builds your proficiency with classes, structs, and other fundamentals, and advances your expertise with more advanced topics such as debugging, threading, and memory management. Combining incisive reference with hands-on coding examples and best practices, this *Core Reference* focuses on mastering the C# skills you need to build innovative solutions for smart clients and the Web.

CLR via C#, Second Edition
Jeffrey Richter • ISBN 0-7356-2163-2

In this new edition of Jeffrey Richter's popular book, you get focused, pragmatic guidance on how to exploit the common language runtime (CLR) functionality in Microsoft .NET Framework 2.0 for applications of all types—from Web Forms, Windows Forms, and Web services to solutions for Microsoft SQL Server™, Microsoft code names "Avalon" and "Indigo," consoles, Microsoft Windows NT® Service, and more. Targeted to advanced developers and software designers, this book takes you under the covers of .NET for an in-depth understanding of its structure, functions, and operational components, demonstrating the most practical ways to apply this knowledge to your own development efforts. You'll master fundamental design tenets for .NET and get hands-on insights for creating high-performance applications more easily and efficiently. The book features extensive code examples in Visual C# 2005.

Programming Microsoft Windows Forms
Charles Petzold • ISBN 0-7356-2153-5

CLR via C++
Jeffrey Richter with Stanley B. Lippman
ISBN 0-7356-2248-5

Programming Microsoft Web Forms
Douglas J. Reilly • ISBN 0-7356-2179-9

Debugging, Tuning, and Testing Microsoft .NET 2.0 Applications
John Robbins • ISBN 0-7356-2202-7

For more information about Microsoft Press® books and other learning products,
visit: **www.microsoft.com/books** *and* **www.microsoft.com/learning**

Additional Resources for Web Developers

Published and Forthcoming Titles from Microsoft Press

Microsoft® Visual Web Developer™ 2005 Express Edition: Build a Web Site Now!
Jim Buyens • ISBN 0-7356-2212-4

With this lively, eye-opening, and hands-on book, all you need is a computer and the desire to learn how to create Web pages now using Visual Web Developer Express Edition! Featuring a full working edition of the software, this fun and highly visual guide walks you through a complete Web page project from set-up to launch. You'll get an introduction to the Microsoft Visual Studio® environment and learn how to put the light-weight, easy-to-use tools in Visual Web Developer Express to work right away—building your first, dynamic Web pages with Microsoft ASP.NET 2.0. You'll get expert tips, coaching, and visual examples at each step of the way, along with pointers to additional learning resources.

Microsoft ASP.NET 2.0 Programming
Step by Step
George Shepherd • ISBN 0-7356-2201-9

With dramatic improvements in performance, productivity, and security features, Visual Studio 2005 and ASP.NET 2.0 deliver a simplified, high-performance, and powerful Web development experience. ASP.NET 2.0 features a new set of controls and infrastructure that simplify Web-based data access and include functionality that facilitates code reuse, visual consistency, and aesthetic appeal. Now you can teach yourself the essentials of working with ASP.NET 2.0 in the Visual Studio environment—one step at a time. With *Step by Step*, you work at your own pace through hands-on, learn-by-doing exercises. Whether you're a beginning programmer or new to this version of the technology, you'll understand the core capabilities and fundamental techniques for ASP.NET 2.0. Each chapter puts you to work, showing you how, when, and why to use specific features of the ASP.NET 2.0 rapid application development environment and guiding you as you create actual components and working applications for the Web, including advanced features such as personalization.

Programming Microsoft ASP.NET 2.0
Core Reference
Dino Esposito • ISBN 0-7356-2176-4

Delve into the core topics for ASP.NET 2.0 programming, mastering the essential skills and capabilities needed to build high-performance Web applications successfully. Well-known ASP.NET author Dino Esposito deftly builds your expertise with Web forms, Visual Studio, core controls, master pages, data access, data binding, state management, security services, and other must-know topics—combining definitive reference with practical, hands-on programming instruction. Packed with expert guidance and pragmatic examples, this *Core Reference* delivers the key resources that you need to develop professional-level Web programming skills.

Programming Microsoft ASP.NET 2.0
Applications: *Advanced Topics*
Dino Esposito • ISBN 0-7356-2177-2

Master advanced topics in ASP.NET 2.0 programming—gaining the essential insights and in-depth understanding that you need to build sophisticated, highly functional Web applications successfully. Topics include Web forms, Visual Studio 2005, core controls, master pages, data access, data binding, state management, and security considerations. Developers often discover that the more they use ASP.NET, the more they need to know. With expert guidance from ASP.NET authority Dino Esposito, you get the in-depth, comprehensive information that leads to full mastery of the technology.

Programming Microsoft Windows® Forms
Charles Petzold • ISBN 0-7356-2153-5

Programming Microsoft Web Forms
Douglas J. Reilly • ISBN 0-7356-2179-9

CLR via C++
Jeffrey Richter with Stanley B. Lippman
ISBN 0-7356-2248-5

Debugging, Tuning, and Testing Microsoft .NET 2.0 Applications
John Robbins • ISBN 0-7356-2202-7

CLR via C#, Second Edition
Jeffrey Richter • ISBN 0-7356-2163-2

For more information about Microsoft Press® books and other learning products,
visit: **www.microsoft.com/books** *and* **www.microsoft.com/learning**